Ronnie Wallace

The Authorized Version

Ronnie Wallace
The Authorized Version

ROBIN RHODERICK-JONES

Quiller Press
London

For Sophie
and
For Lucinda who died far too young

First published 1992 by
Quiller Press Limited
46 Lillie Road
London SW6 1TN

ISBN 1 870948 83 1

Produced by Hugh Tempest-Radford *Book Producers*
Printed in Great Britain by
St Edmundsbury Press

Contents

The illustrations appear in a section between pages 90 and 91.

Acknowledgements

I thank first all those historians and writers whose works I have read over the years and from whom I have gleaned my knowledge of the history of foxhunting, and Anthony Hart, the Secretary of the Masters of Foxhounds Association, who made available to me the details of the early days of that body.

Next I thank Vivian Wallace for his recollections of the childhood of his brother and the very many others who also gave so freely and patiently of their time during my researches. In this context I thank particularly Michael Clayton, the Editor of *Horse and Hound*, for his help and encouragement.

I thank *The Field* magazine for permission to reproduce the account of a day with the Cotswold in 1951.

Finally I am deeply grateful for the wholehearted way in which Ronnie and Rosie Wallace entered into the spirit of this enterprise and for the splendid and generous hospitality that they showed to me over the two years of its gestation.

Robin Rhoderick-Jones

CHAPTER 1

The Sporting Legacy

GOLFERS and sailors are beginners; even fishermen can barely compete. When it comes to discussing their sport in all its arcane intricacies and comparing their experiences, triumphs, disasters and delicious scandals, the devotees of foxhunting lead the field by a distance. In the clear dawns of autumn during the endless waits as young hounds are taught the skills of the game by their elders and by the patient huntsman; at the numbingly cold meets of winter where mounted and foot followers alike sip gratefully at the port and the whisky thoughtfully provided for them by their hosts for the day; in pubs, clubs and private houses up and down not only the United Kingdom but in Ireland, America and even further afield, the uninitiated, hovering on the edge of conversational circles, will be puzzled to hear the frequent references to God.

Soubriquets are often hard to bear. However amusing, apt or even affectionate, they are invariably born out of a teasing maliciousness – the verbal equivalent of a lampooning cartoon – designed to disconcert the subject as well as encapsulate neatly a personal foible. Members of the Royal Family, the leaders of our great political parties, newspaper proprietors and many more whose stars ride high in public awareness have borne the burden with varying degrees of equanimity. Ronnie Wallace, on whom the foxhunting faithful have bestowed this particularly exalted epithet, dislikes it with a passion not far removed from hatred; but as Chairman of the Masters of Foxhounds Association for over twenty years and leader of the sometimes acrimonious and often political fight against those who would wish to see his sport abolished, he has become the guardian of a tradition evolved during many centuries of British history. If not a god he is certainly the oracle.

* * *

The origins of hunting in these islands lie in Anglo-Saxon and

1

Norman times but then it was not the fox but the deer that men loved to chase. Saxon game laws were first formalized by the Dane, Canute II, who, having failed to bend the waves to his will, turned his attention to more biddable targets and ruled that although every man was to be entitled to hunt over his own land, no-one was to trespass on the King's hunting wherever he wished to preserve it for his own exclusive use.

William of Normandy, who landed some 50 years later, had hunted deer all his life and was quick to pursue energetically a policy of afforestation on his newly acquired kingdom. Afforestation to William meant something very different from that of the Forestry Commission of today. To William it meant simply that once he had declared a tract of land to be a 'forest', only he could own it and only he could hunt over it. The authors of the Anglo-Saxon Chronicle were aggrieved:

> A hard man was the King . . .
> He was sunk in greed
> And utterly given up to avarice.
> He set up vast deer preserves and imposed laws . . .
> Whoever slew a hart or hind
> Was to be blinded.
> He forbade the killing of boars
> Even as the killing of harts.
> For he loved the stags as dearly
> As though he had been their father.
> Hare also he decreed should go unmolested.
> The rich complained and the poor lamented,
> But he was too relentless to care though all might hate him.

The 'forbidding' and the 'unmolesting' were not, of course, decreed in any spirit of conservation, except in the very narrowest sense of that word – the deer and the boar in the Royal Forests were to be hunted only by the King and the few to whom he granted much sought after licences. Noblemen whose lands marched with the King's were at particular risk when their hounds ran out of effective control. Retribution was harsh: foresters finding a dead deer and able to identify the offenders, brought them before courts that imposed sentences ranging from fines on whole villages to blinding and castration. If a serf was found guilty he was executed. Resentment ran deep and smouldered on until Magna Carta provided relief, at least for the nobility. Poachers were still treated with little mercy but the Forest Laws, as a major source of grievance between the King and his knights, were largely removed. For those with no land on which to hunt – not for sport but for food – the problems remained. Meat, not the chase and its attendant ceremonial and ritual, was their concern and the securing of it often involved either pursuing animals to which they had no right, or going after animals on land to which they had no lawful access.

Deer remained the preferred quarry – and the only one worth the full panoply of the hunt – throughout the Middle Ages and the Tudors. But, in the seventeenth century, two slowly emerging developments led to its irreversible decline. The first was the rapid improvement in firearms: poaching became easier and the deer, as the largest of targets among British mammals, suffered most. The second, and perhaps the more decisive, was the clearing of forests and deer parks to make way for pasture and arable. For a time the hunting of carted deer held some attraction for those loath to give up their traditional sport, but it proved a poor substitute for the real thing – especially as it was often necessary to ensure that the carted animal was preserved unharmed and returned to its van so as to be available again on another day. Only in the West Country did deer remain plentiful enough to be hunted in the old ways, although carting retained a tenacious hold in pockets of England until well into the twentieth century – the comedian Tom Walls ran a pack in Sussex in the 1920s and the Mid-Kent continued even later.

The real answer to this unsatisfactory state of affairs was to find an alternative quarry and this proved not to be a problem for the squirearchy, who were anyway apt to chase anything that moved, and who were quicker to adapt than the great aristocrats of the day. The countryside was plentiful with hares and foxes, and of these the former came to be regarded as the supreme test of hunting skills. The fox continued to be seen by nearly everyone as the most cunning of vermin – a stinking creature which had to be hunted down on foot, and with a price on its head. Whole villages assembled, armed with sticks and stones, as foxes were dug out, killed and carried back in triumph to be exchanged for a parish payment.

Such, then, was the general way of things in Tudor and Stuart times, but there were exceptions. In Derbyshire and in Yorkshire, as early as the late sixteenth century, they had discovered the delights of hunting foxes above ground and were busy breeding and entering hounds solely for that purpose. Sir Thomas Cockaine of Derbyshire even wrote a short work of reference on the subject and claimed to have killed a fox after a run of fourteen miles. It is supposed that he was on a horse at the time but generally the early sport was a dismounted affair.

In the second half of the seventeenth century, this still embryo and certainly unfashionable activity, acquired a royal and ducal glamour. The 2nd Duke of Buckingham, having been retired forcibly from the Court of Charles II for seducing Lady Shrewsbury and then shooting her unfortunate husband, fled to Yorkshire where he spent his time hunting foxes, until he caught a chill watching one being dug out by night, and died in 1687, mourned only by those who had come to admire him for his expertise in the chase. In the south, the Duke of Monmouth had joined Lord Grey in Sussex to hunt with the Charlton (later the Goodwood), and James II wore a red coat while out with his Tory friends. Hunting the fox had suddenly become the thing, and by 1700 a large minority had forsaken deerhunting on the one hand and harriers on the other.

The sport, though, was a staid affair when compared with the madcap scurry it later became. Nicholas Coxe's description in his 'Gentlemen's Recreation' of 1694 is little different from Cockaine's a hundred years before:

> To this purpose you must draw with your hounds about groves, thickets and bushes near villages, for a fox will lurk in such places to prey on pigs and poultrey. But it will be necessary to stop up his earths the night before you intend to hunt. At first, cast off your sure finders; as the drag mends so add more as you dare trust them. Let the hounds kill the fox themselves. Foxhunting is very pleasant for by reason of his strong scent he maketh an excellent cry.

The accent appeared to be on staying power, both mounted and dismounted. The vainglorious Sir Roger de Coverley records a fifteen-hour chase during which two horses died whilst covering half-a-dozen counties and losing over half his hounds. He and others like him bred hounds for cry rather than pace, and horses jumped hedges off their hocks – anything attempted at a canter or faster would have resulted in serious and indelicate injury on the high pommels of the age. It was not until the 1750s that obstacles began to be taken at speed.

Until the Stuarts, both horses and horsemanship were rough and ready affairs. Successive attempts to improve the quality of the English warhorse had foundered because of the inbreeding of hybrid with hybrid, with unpredictable results. Elizabeth, towards the end of her reign, had learnt the need to keep careful records in the royal stud but the lesson had not filtered down widely among her subjects. It was not until the fashion for racing that soundness, speed, stamina and courage were clearly revealed as guides to the selection of breeding stock, and a hundred years and more before Captain Byerley's Turk and the Godophin Arab laid the foundations of the English thoroughbred. By 1800, English horses were the best in the world and the vast army of half- and three-quarter-breds were proving the perfect hunting instruments.

It was in Derbyshire that the first Golden Age of foxhunting dawned. Hugo Meynell, a squire's son brought up on the accepted practice of getting up at four in the morning and hunting the fox before it had digested its nightly meal and incapable of covering much distance at any speed, noticed that if hunted in full daylight the fox would run. He began to breed hounds for this purpose and, in 1753, he moved to Leicestershire and established himself at Quorn Hall in the village of Quorndon.

Meynell raised the sport to heights to which it had never before aspired. He invented the winter season and to Quorn Hall flocked men of fashion and of letters. Not all agreed with his methods – particularly the time of his meets. The old guard of squires and yeoman farmers liked their early morning hunting at a leisurely pace which left them sufficiently fresh and free to enjoy a good long afternoon's drinking.

Hugo Meynell was master of the Quorn for 47 years; rich, well-mannered and considerate far ahead of his time, he ran his country on the basis of almost contractual consent. He negotiated with arrogant, aristocratic land-owners and prickly, truculent graziers with equal and happy facility. His personality, his science, his hounds and his grassland brought sportsmen to the Midlands in droves – by 1758 there were 300 horses stabled at Grantham alone – and he saw the rise of Melton and Market Harborough as wintering places for the fancy. He had his acolytes, too: young squires with their own packs. William Childe of Kinlet in Shropshire and Cecil Forester of Willey uprooted themselves to hunt with Meynell. Not everybody appreciated his primary concern for hounds and the space he liked to allow them; Childe developed the 'Leicestershire Style' of galloping and jumping right up to hounds, a practice which although appealing much to the younger bloods and the London thrusters, caused Meynell a great deal of anguish.

At the start of the nineteenth century the change from hare and deer to fox was widespread and by 1830 the primacy of the great Midland packs was complete. Life at Melton revolved round horses and heavy drinking; the all-male society was a continuation of Library at Eton and Rooms in Christ Church. The Marquis of Waterford painted the town red and exclusive clubs sprung up almost overnight; Meltonians hunted to ride – the very antithesis of Meynell and of Peter Beckford the other notable theorist of the day and author in 1779 of *Thoughts on Foxhunting*.

Outside Leicestershire, the world was divided into smart packs emulating the pace-setters in pageantry, quality horses and cavalry dash and those, sickened by the excesses of the exclusive set, who were determined to return to the leisurely days of old-fashioned but skilful woodland hunting. Of the former, the Duke of Beaufort's, the Brocklesby, and the Duke of Cleveland's (a vast country in Yorkshire) were perhaps pre-eminent, but other rich masters were quick to imitate them. Thomas Assheton Smith, an All-England cricketer and the best and bravest of riders across country, took the Quorn in 1806 at the age of thirty, never having hunted hounds before, stayed ten years and then moved to the Burton in Lincolnshire, preferring the knowledgeable farmers he found there to the Melton thrusters. The inheritor of the Dinorwic slate quarries in North Wales, he was immensely rich and after another ten years sold his hounds and moved again, this time to Hampshire, where for a time he hunted a scratch pack much to the delight of the local gentry. When his father died in 1828 he rebuilt the classical Tedworth House and added kennels of heroic dimensions. He then set about creating an open country by cleaning up huge areas of woodland with such single minded zeal that the sleepy little town of Andover set up a timber industry rivalling any in England. In 1840 he was invited, with his hounds, back to the Quorn where two thousand horsemen came to the meet to pay tribute to the man acknowledged as the greatest huntsman in England.

At the age of 66 Assheton Smith was hunting hounds four days a week – he had recently bought the Duke of Grafton's pack and engaged his huntsman George Carter who hunted the other two days – and giving hunt breakfasts consisting largely of barons of beef and interminable venison pasties. He had become an MP of the high Tory persuasion and when he wasn't hunting or dashing off to London to vote, he created steam yachts to such good effect that the Admiralty took up one of his designs for a gunboat. He hunted until he was 80, by which time he was suffering frequent falls, not because his horsemanship had failed him but because his courage had not. In 1858 he died, leaving his hounds to the country, which owns them still.

Masters such as Assheton Smith, Squire Osbaldeston (who succeeded Smith at the Quorn), Tom Smith of the Craven and 'Handsome Jack' Musters of the Pytchley were almost mythical figures, certainly larger than life, and left subsequent generations with visions of a golden age when horses were faster, hounds keener and foxes as brave as lions.

At about the time that Thomas Assheton Smith was completing his kennels at Tedworth House and congratulating his architect on their classical beauty, another architect – who had bred six sons and four daughters since the time that he had left the west of Scotland to find commissions south of the border – contemplated a very different vista. What he saw was not a triumph of Portland stone but a vision of the future – a future for his sons, who clearly had no taste for their father's profession and, regrettably, showed no obvious inclination for finding acceptable alternatives. Having given the problem a great deal of thought, he decided to send them into the world with just a little money and all his profoundest good wishes. His instructions were nothing if not concise: they were to make their fortunes.

They sailed to India and to Africa: strange and exciting places, one virtually run by the all-powerful East India Company and the other a continent for pioneers pushing north and east from the Cape Colony. George Wallace, the youngest of the brothers, went to India and was soon hard at work extracting teak with elephants and helping to meet the almost insatiable Victorian demand for furniture fashioned from exotic woods. All the boys prospered and their varying enterprises complemented each other to such an extent that it seemed only sensible, in both family and business terms, to amalgamate them into one company of merchantmen. The name they chose was as much to the point as their father's orders all those years before. Wallace Brothers became a force in the City of London.

George Wallace fulfilled his father's hopes in a way which would have gratified the old man immensely if he had lived long enough to savour their fruition. This youngest and most prodigal of the sons made enough money by middle-age to retire comfortably to Eardiston near Tenbury Wells in North Worcestershire, where he bought a modest estate and devoted the rest of his life to his family and to growing hops – then unheard of in the county.

He had found time to have seven children, four of them girls who never married but who eventually – primogenitureship not being a Wallace custom – inherited Eardiston. The three boys were brought up in the notably patriarchal way of those times and, in their turn, were invited to make a mark for themselves. The financial imperatives were not quite so severe for this generation but nevertheless the eldest son, Park, and the youngest, Lewis, followed their father's footsteps to India. Tragically, Park failed to return having disappeared in circumstances still not satisfactorily explained. Meanwhile George, the middle son, joined the Essex Regiment and then, tiring of soldiering, went to try his hand at farming in British Columbia.

Lewis Wallace had not been in India long when he was summoned home to become a working director of Wallace Brothers. The shares in the company had been widely scattered among the numerous progeny of the Wallace family, few of whom were concerned enough to take an active interest, and Lewis became the de facto head of the organisation. He lived in London, in Buckingham Gate, had a house in Surrey on Hayes Common, and later bought Hawford, not far from Worcester. He took enthusiastically to foxhunting and often hacked from Hayes to meets of the Old Surrey. So keen was he that he was asked to take on the mastership, declining regretfully because of the demands made on his time by the disparate strands of the family firm. Like his father he had three sons: Eden, Geoffrey and finally Henley, whom the family called Bill and who lived his adult life as something of a recluse.

Eden, the eldest, was born in 1893 and was educated at Uppingham, where he saw Lord Lonsdale hunt the Cottesmore, and Brasenose College, Oxford, where he was able to indulge his inherited taste for foxhunting, travelling on the special trains then widely available for days with the Warwickshire, the Bicester and, notably, the Heythrop where Charles Sturman, the huntsman, was the last of his kind to wear the heavy plush coat, a knee-length covering with a half-inch nap which could weigh four stone when wet – an attribute which persuaded even the Duke of Beaufort to abandon it for his staff in 1904.

Uppingham was a great success but later in life Eden was to regret openly, but with no hint of bitterness, that he had not been sent to Eton and so acquire the close circle of influential friends so often characteristic of that school. He attributed this lack of foresight to his mother who had, he claimed, been led to her decision by sinister stories of the goings-on there, related to her with relish by some of her more gossipy women friends.

Shortly before the First World War Eden joined the 5th Dragoon Guards intending to make his life in the regular army. After the outbreak his regiment was drafted to France where he was wounded in action. As it turned out he was the lucky one for Geoffrey, who had enlisted in the Worcestershire Regiment with a platoon of men drawn largely from Eardiston, was killed in Flanders.

Eden was evacuated from the front and transferred to a rest and recuperation hospital at Maresfield in Sussex. There he met an attractive nurse doing war work with the Voluntary Aid Detachment and fell in love.

Cecily Lindsay Hogg was 20 and lived with her parents at Rotherfield Hall near Crowborough. Her father, Lindsay, had briefly been the Member of Parliament for Eastbourne until his party had required him to resign this safe seat in favour of a heavier political weight. For this unselfishness (and for his services to light-horse breeding) he was awarded a baronetcy and, at the same time, added a second Lindsay to his name. Sir Lindsay Lindsay Hogg, whose family had once owned Shanghai Racecourse, had two passions in life – coaching and his terriers. He was a famous and much respected whip, being Vice President of the Coaching Club when Lord Lonsdale was at its head, and he was inordinately proud of his working dogs, buying them from a breeder in Ilfracombe who claimed that they were descended from those of Parson Jack Russell. Whatever their strain they were in constant demand after the ladies retired from the Sunday luncheon table, when Sir Lindsay would lead the gentlemen into the quarry behind his house to watch them work.

Captain Eden Wallace and Cecily Lindsay Hogg married in 1918 and rented Dewlands Manor close to Rotherfield, in which they were to live for the next four years. Their happiness in each other's company, which was to last throughout their lives, was clouded briefly by the fact that the 5th Dragoon Guards were under orders to sail for Egypt. Cecily, who was pregnant, felt that she could not possibly accompany her husband to such an uncongenial climate and neither did she wish for them to be parted. Eden solved this little difficulty by transferring to the Cinque Ports Battalion of the Royal Sussex Regiment – a convenient arrangement which allowed him to work largely from home.

As the War had approached it had become clear that foxhunting could no longer sustain the claim that Trollope, with some exaggeration even then, had made for it in the 1860s – that it was *the* national sport. The decline of rural England and the increasing urbanization, coupled with the growing popularity of shooting, racing, cricket and football, had diminished its primacy among the public school set. Foxhunting could never be part of the classless world of spectator sport and the demands it made upon the time and purses of its practitioners had begun to make their mark; nevertheless it remained a major force in the countryside.

Cubhunting was about to begin on 4 August 1914 when the long awaited call to arms was sounded. The hunting countries emptied as the sons of landowners, tenants, farmers and tradesmen alike enlisted for France or joined the Yeomanry. They did so in the same euphoric spirit that they had taken to the hunting field and within ten days of the declaration, 15,000 hunters were ready for departure. The editor of *Baily's Hunting Directory* wrote: 'They shall do and they shall dare, as becomes their blood and their breeding.'

The hunting fields were practically deserted and boys of twelve whipped-in to those masters that remained; all lawn meets (those by invitation to private houses) were cancelled and no-one wore scarlet. In London the Masters of Foxhounds Association met, chaired by the Duke of Beaufort, to decide how hunting should be carried on. The agreement reached was that hunts should not be allowed to die but that activity should be restricted to one or two days a week and that hounds too should be reduced in number. But foxes must still be killed to keep faith with the farmers. The farmers themselves rallied to the cause – wire was taken down and damage claims waived. Women came to the fore, both as labour in kennels and stables and as masters in their own right. A notable example was Mrs Inge of the Atherstone, immortalised by Siegfried Sassoon in his *Memoirs of a Foxhunting Man* as Mrs Oakfield of Thurrow Park: . . . 'a lady who made friends wherever she went . . . her quickness to hounds was a revelation to me.'

From the Front, men sent subscriptions to bolster finances; many knew that they would never hunt again. The cavalry and yeomanry regiments had gone to war believing that they would charge the enemy and chase him back to Germany but by 1916 most had become mounted infantry – a euphemistic term for those engaged in trench warfare just like any other foot-soldier. *Baily's* gave them their obituaries, the grand and the humble alike: 'Colonel Lord Manners – a great hunting man with all the Manners charm; Private Ginger Jack – well known to everyone in the Oakley country as a terrier-man and a really good chap at his work; Trooper Matthew Cleminson, one of the gallant band of hunting farmers in the York and Ainsty country,' and so on and so on – hundred upon hundred, thousand upon thousand.

When it finally ended at the Armistice, foxhunting had just begun its new season. In a few weeks the fields began to fill again and those who came back were keen to forget. There was a determination to resume a life as near to that left behind four years earlier as could be possible. But left behind too – in the mud and shambles of the battlefields – were the remains of the 450,000 horses that had served in France and Flanders – nearly half of them hunters. Only the officers' chargers were shipped home, the War Office considering the expense too great for the rest. It would take some time for the packs to regain their hound numbers but many years to resolve the shortage of quality horses.

Into this aftermath of war – on 23 July 1919 – Ronald Eden Wallace was born.

CHAPTER 2

The Young Entry

HE arrived at tea-time, weighing in at 7½ pounds and it is recorded that his hair was straight and dark – a feature that, despite the curls which briefly emerged when he was eight months old, has characterised his appearance ever since. He was, it would seem, an equable child, giving neither his parents nor the usual quick turn-over of nurses, a moment's trouble. Cecily, who had inherited her father's love for both dogs and horses, saw to it that her small son became quickly accustomed to both. Indeed, so keen and proficient was she at her hunting with the Eridge that she might well have taken on a mastership after the war had not marriage and childbirth taken precedence.

The Victorian prejudice against women in the hunting field had largely disappeared by this time. During the nineteenth century it seemed to have been forgotten that both Queen Elizabeth and Queen Anne had hunted and that around 1800 Lady Salisbury had run her own pack of dwarf hounds. The complaints had come from both men and women with those of the latter focussing frostily on the appearance of several dashing ladies of slightly less than impeccable breeding and a decided paucity of sexual morals. Lady Stamford, the wife of the Master of the Quorn (1856–63), tried hard to persuade her husband to ban a number of high-class tarts, including the most notorious of them all, Catherine Walters, but without success; the bloods of Leicestershire were too keen to continue the chase in other spheres well into the night and determined enough to defy their women-folk who continued to object most strongly even after Lady Yarborough, a brilliant and enthusiastic horsewoman, began to hunt regularly with the Brock-lesby in 1859. The more serious of the male-inspired worries were concerned with what happened if a lady fell off her horse. Even mounting in the stable-yard was a pretty indecorous affair – given the prevailing moral standards – which required a groom to avert his eyes. Respectable men quailed at the thought of clasping bruised ladies to their manly bosoms in public and positively dreaded the thought of assisting the fallen to vault back onto their horses. The invention of the side-saddle around 1850 eased this delicate matter somewhat although the safety skirt which accompanied the innovation was designed to rip off in a fall and soon became known as the 'fig-leaf'; it was not until the 1890s that the advent of the apron put the seal on respectability. Breeches were advocated by a few of the bolder spirits but dark hints about painful injuries and sexual excitements were enough to deter the majority until well after the war. In 1905 Lord Annaly at the Pytchley refused to award the white hunt collar to ladies riding astride.

Motherhood had put pay to any mastership aspirations entertained by Cecily and she remained content to hunt (side-saddle naturally) with the Eridge in the congenial company of her husband. There is little doubt that their shared and knowledgeable interest began to influence their son at a very early age.

Ron (his parents used the diminutive always) was quick to talk and slow to learn to walk – not taking his first steps until 14 months, a few weeks after he had thrilled his parents by taking second prize at the local baby show. In April 1921, he was joined by a brother, Vivian, born at Dewlands and considerably bigger – appearing at a hefty 9 pounds. Within five weeks of this happy event, the family were spending an extended month's holiday at Hastings, an entirely agreeable event for Ron who had quite taken to the sea on his first acquaintance with it at Eastbourne the previous summer. The boys were also taken to Hawford that year to be inspected by their Wallace grandparents, an expedition often repeated but which Cecily came to dislike intensely. She was alarmed by her mother-in-law who tended to play the authoritarian Victorian matriarch with little time or inclination for pleasantries.

As the boys grew they became close friends and constant companions, there being few children of their own age or station within a convenient distance. In 1922 the family moved to Leylands, a Rotherfield farmhouse, and Eden retired from the army to become a justice of the peace and secretary of the hunt, in whose activities he and Cecily were very much embroiled. Sir Lindsay Lindsay Hogg died in that same year and shortly afterwards the Hall was sold – some of the land being retained to be managed by Eden.

Although hunting was now a major part of their lives, neither Ron nor Vivian have any clear recollection of ever being taught to ride through any sort of formal instruction. The family groom, who had been a military rough-rider, seems to have passed on his expertise without them being much aware of it, and doubtless their parents corrected them when out hunting on a leading rein.

From those earliest days it was evident that Ron was not really interested in horses for their own sake – hardly even liking them. To him they were a conveyance, a means of getting out to the hunting field and as near hounds as he and whoever was leading him, could manage. The Eridge, at that time, was under the mastership of Lord Henry Nevill (later Marquis of Abergavenny), who was particularly kind and considerate to children; he encouraged their presence, making them feel not only welcome but at home. He was killed in 1938, breaking his neck in a fall caused by wire. Ron's very first day's hunting was at Bayham Abbey, the home of a Nevill cousin where, led by his mother, the occurrence that impressed him most was her production of toasted sandwiches for lunch and he wondered when he, too, would be allowed to carry some instead of the breaded variety with which he had been provided. Soon he began to practise at Leylands what he had seen in the field. At first with only his imagination to conjure up both hounds and quarry and later with a collection of terriers, he hunted endlessly round the garden and over the estate with Vivian loyally whipping-in.

In 1926, the boys were sent to kindergarten in Crowborough, a journey of some three miles, undertaken daily in a taxi. Ron, as observant then as all his life, would press his nose against the glass panel that divided the driver from his young charges, in an effort to see better the world ahead – a habit that was to leave him with a scar, when the taxi one morning was forced to stop abruptly to avoid an accident.

Holidays were spent either with the Eridge at home or in taking a house near Minehead from which the whole family would hunt on Exmoor. There were stays too at the Anchor, a sporting hotel at Porlock Weir, and one never to be forgotten journey to Scotland pulling a caravan, with another car manned by a manservant going ahead to erect a tent – a long cherished dream of Cecily's which could not have been an unqualified success as it was never to be repeated. Each summer there was a pilgrimage to Hawford where, despite their mother's unease, the boys loved the marvellous hothouse with its peaches and its grapes, and where they strained to hear the curses as Arthur Jones, the master of the Worcestershire, retrieved his hounds from beneath the breakfast-room windows when cubhunting. Alas the windows were always slammed shut by a scandalized parlour-maid, on grandmother Wallace's instructions, before the full flow of Mr Jones's invective could be relished by his young and eager audience. Grandmother was a powerful lady who led her family to church in a donkey cart each Sunday, and Ron incurred her wrath when he managed to avoid this sacrosanct ritual to play cricket with the butler – an interlude which the unfortunate servant found harder to forget than his partner in crime.

Eden's family led a self-contained life of a pattern which has now virtually vanished to become a part of social history. There was little radio and no television. Motor-car travel was a great adventure and still not lightly undertaken. Family pursuits were paramount – the hunting, the holidays, the games at home. Social obligations were important too: to the estate, the village, the County and to the extended family, with whom regular visits were exchanged. Eden would take his sons to Hove to watch Sussex play cricket and there they would marvel at the skills of Maurice Tate. Even more exciting were the expeditions with Ron's eccentric great-uncle George who, back from Canada, had managed to serve in the war at a pretty advanced age, and now lived at Upton-on-Severn. George's chief source of pleasure was watching Worcestershire play cricket and he was in the habit of dragging an embarrassed small grand-nephew in a straight line across the ground when he wanted a cup of tea, thereby causing a temporary halt to the play – an unimaginable proceeding now but tolerated without rancour in the less frenetic atmosphere of the day.

1928 was a very important year in Ron's life. First he broke his ankle and spent a fortnight in bed at his grand-parents' house in London, where, to keep him amused, his mother gave him a hunting horn which he learnt to blow, not without causing the household some anguish. Up and about again at Leylands, he used it on his bobbery pack to good effect – once the terriers had recovered from their initial puzzled surprise.

In the same year he went away to school, to St Peter's at Seaford, where he was later followed by Vivian. As preparatory schools of the 1920s went, St Peter's was probably more civilized than most, despite the ritual cold baths. Certainly it harnessed the intelligence and the ability to concentrate what were to be Ron's intellectual hall-marks during his hunting career, and masters and pupils alike were impressed by the natural cricketing talent shown by both brothers.

But of all that happened in that year, it is arguable that nothing was to have as great an influence on later events as the arrival at the Eridge of Will Freeman to be its huntsman. A brother of the legendary Frank, who was then still at the Pytchley, Will was a hound man and a dedicated slayer of foxes. Although a great woodland huntsman, he was perhaps not quite single-minded enough to be one of the very best, for he was passionately keen on racing and not above announcing to Lord Nevill that prospects for the rest of the afternoon were so poor that they would all do well to go home: a harmless conceit contrived to allow him to read the racing results in the early evening paper. 'There's no 'opes, me Lord, no 'opes,' he would say, and the phrase became something of a standing joke among those in the know. Despite this weakness he had shown great sport at the Zetland and the Old Surrey and Burstow, as well as the Eridge, and had an unremitting respect for the proprieties: when presented with a bagged fox by an influential master of the Old Surrey he sniffed and said, 'We don't hunt them things.'

It had not been until the latter half of the nineteenth century that professional huntsmen rose from the ranks of trusted servants to become respected members of a profession. Their skills earned them universal approbation and their names are still redolent of the Golden Age: Will Dale of the Brocklesby and the Duke of Beauforts, the Leedhams of the Meynell, Arthur Thatcher of the Cottesmore and the Fernie, Charles Payne, Will Goodall and Frank Freeman all of the Pytchley, Frank Gillard of the Belvoir who served two Dukes of Rutland and turned the Belvoir kennels into something of a national institution (his hounds, it was said, gleamed like thoroughbred horses) and, perhaps above all, Tom Firr of the Quorn. Both Firr and Frank Freeman were undoubtedly the greatest of their respective times; both have strong claims to have been the greatest ever but few people, if any, saw them both at their best for Tom gave up the horn six years before Frank began his career. A parting shot in the once perennial argument regarding their relative merits was delivered by an old foxhunter who knew both men well: 'I don't know who was the better, but I tell you who I had the most fun with and that was dear old Arthur Thatcher!'

Both Firr and Freeman were from hunting families – traditionally the right background for the best of the professionals. Tom was born at the Essex Hunt kennels in Epping Forest where his father was the kennelman and Frank was a huntsman's son who married a huntsman's daughter. By the end of his service in 1931, after which he came regularly to stay with his brother, Freeman had come to look upon himself more as the guardian of his pack than as any form of servant, however privileged. An autocrat and not always liked by the farmers, to whom he was not over-polite, he was the complete professional, killing 512 foxes in his first two years at the Pytchley.

Will Freeman and Eden Wallace, as huntsman and secretary, had frequent dealings, often carried out in the kitchen at Leylands over tea and cake – often something a little stronger. Cecily, too, spent many hours talking with them of breeding and of hound-work generally, and all of this the young Ron listened to and absorbed. The theory was supplemented by the practical – in the school holidays he would spend hours at the hunt kennels and in summer he went on hound exercise. When Frank Freeman put in an appearance, young Wallace would listen to the great men talking at breakfast and hear their different philosophies. From then on there was never to be any real doubt as to how he wanted to spend the rest of his life – for one thing real huntsmen didn't have to go home early!

Shortly before Christmas, Eden gave his elder son a hardbacked exercise book. This was to be kept as a hunting diary – the first of the unique volumes which today record for us the facts, the musings and the sometimes trenchant comments of Wallace the venerer. He was not yet nine-and-a-half years old when the first entry was made:

December 22nd
Eridge Foxhounds, Crowborough Station.

Rode Maggie. First time off leading-rein. Found in Scallon Wood and ran through the gipsy camp to Redbridge Farm; then through Pipings Wood to Grey Birchetts where the fox was lost.
Found again in Grove Wood, ran to Smallbury Hill and then back to Little Buxted Wood to the railway where the fox was lost. Came home at two o'clock.

The writing is neat and the facts precise; the spelling is faultless and the geographical record of the activities of fox and hounds would still, today, be the envy of the most experienced and accurate of hunting correspondents. It is a model for the thousands of the more mature and expansive entries it precedes; from a small boy, it and its companions from the early days are astonishing.

There is one further characteristic which it shares with practically all the others: there is no mention of horses or fences or going – the young Wallace only rides to hunt. An exception though occurs in the account for Christmas Day 1928:

> . . . Had my first jump today.

He hunted Maggie during both Christmas and Easter holidays and then, on the last day of the season, she broke down. A week later she was dead, but the diary entry is severely unemotional:

> Maggie, bay mare, 13 hands, aged, was destroyed on 18th April 1929.

Those who saw the family out during the first season that the boys were off the leading-rein remember Eden (always known as Captain Wallace), large and jolly on a bang-tailed horse, apparently slow across the country, but somehow always there at the end; Cecily, elegant in her habit and always going well, invariably closely shadowed by Vivian, and Ron, accompanied by the stud-groom, taking his own line so as to see hounds from the best of vantage points. He was making his own decisions in the field and he was still not ten years old.

Hunting was not confined to foxes. The Bolebroke Beagles, whose master was Percy Mann, had their country astride the Sussex-Kent border, taking in the Eridge, West Kent, Old Surrey and Burstow and the Ashford Valley foxhunting countries. Percy was a brewer and owned his hounds, having bought, in 1925, the Basted Beagles, who had previously hunted the country. The Manns were fanatical about their sporting activities – three of Percy's sons became masters of foxhounds (Jock of the VWH, Douglas of the South and West Wilts and Alistair of the South Oxfordshire) and the family all hunted on grey horses. Percy was something of a tribune for beagling and persuaded the impressionable young Wallace that the fox was all very well but nothing could compare with the hare for wiliness in the chase. In January 1929 there were two outings with the Bolebroke, apparently because a hard frost had temporarily curtailed the activities of the Eridge; both are written up in painstaking and adult detail which belie the youth of the author.

That August, the family went on the now familiar holiday to Exmoor and Ron had his first taste of a form of hunting which was to become very important to him, going out with the Culmstock Otterhounds on the aptly named River Otter at Honiton. It was a hot, frustrating day with little water and the last straw, having vanned the hounds to Ottery St Mary in search of better sport, was to find that the banks were being repaired. The disappointment is evident in the curt and unenthusiastic diary entry ending: '. . . so we came home.'

School holidays in 1929–30 were spent hunting with the Eridge, supplemented by occasional outings with the Bolebroke Beagles. Ron was also busy extending the activities and scope of his bobbery pack by adding 5 or 6 couple of beagles and at least one retriever to his terriers; as always Vivian was made to whip-in, but not without some protest – he would often linger at blackberry bushes in preference to attending to his duties, pretending not to hear the infuriated instructions of his brother. The pack tried to hunt hares but because they were in short supply at Rotherfield, rabbits were the more usual quarry although Henry Nevill twice asked him to hunt the Eridge foxes on cold and frosty days, making every effort to see that the small master was not too disappointed, at least in the finding. Will Freeman, when he could spare a moment, would come and tutor the aspiring huntsman and the experience of those times was to prove valuable thereafter. Especially important were the lessons concerned with the handling and treatment of hounds: the developing of a special relationship between huntsman and pack: 'Always go and pay your hounds the compliment of fetching them,' was a maxim Freeman repeatedly drummed into his young charge.

Eden Wallace was determined that his sons would enjoy the advantages he felt had been denied to him by his parents' decision not to send him to Eton. Soon after the birth of his eldest son (a third boy, Lindsay was born in 1932), he had arranged for Ron to be placed on the acceptance list for Blakiston's house, but his plans had received a setback when the housemaster was appointed head of Lancing and his list split up. Ron was then relegated to what was known as a 'chance' vacancy – to be taken up should a gap appear in some other house. One occurred in the summer half of 1932 in Assheton's and Eden was told he could have it if his son could come straightaway. Ron could hardly have been better placed. Richard Assheton was a kind and understanding man who was determined that every boy in his charge should be encouraged to exploit to the full what talents he seemed to possess.

At Eton, Ron became known as Ronnie and found that he was expected to work harder than he had been used to at St Peter's where he had been able to coast academically and still be near the top of his form. One of his contemporaries, Kit Barclay who was in his year and class throughout their time at Eton, remembers him as a very bright and intelligent boy who, had he applied himself, could have been a serious scholar but whose interest in the Beagles took such precedence over all else that his true place in the academic pecking order was never realised.

During his first year, Ronnie in common with all new boys, was not allowed to beagle – the Field Game had to be learnt and his proficiency at cricket had given him the reputation as something of a games player. Although a small boy – a late developer not built to compete on level terms in the rough and tumble – he was of a competitive nature and enjoyed the challenges, both sporting and intellectual, with which his new environment presented him. He liked (and was good at) English, history and Latin, but something of a reluctant attender at maths and the sciences. Assheton, who taught science, was disappointed at this apparent character deficiency but set out to discover exactly what made young Wallace tick. He found the task straightforward – all this somewhat extraordinary, rather serious small boy wanted out of life was to hunt hounds. He was clearly single-minded to a degree so unusual for his age as to be outside his tutor's experience but Assheton was wise and no doubt secretly harboured the thought that if not obviously thwarted in his ambition, Ronnie might well grow out of his obsession. And there were more pragmatic considerations: a contented boy presented no problems and, besides, house-tutoring was a competitive business, measured in part by the number of trophies amassed each year, and the silver horn of the master of the Eton College Hunt was a much sought-after prize among them. Whatever his reasoning, Richard Assheton arrived at the right conclusion – from the start he encouraged Ronnie in his hunting activities.

The Eton College Hunt was formed in 1867 by amalgamation of the College Hunt, a pack of beagles whose country was roughly east of Slough Road, and the Oppidan Beagles who hunted to the west. Both packs had been founded some ten years earlier and there had been frequent attempts to merge them – usually thwarted by the Collegers, whose country was significantly the better. The first master of the joint pack was W. C. Calvert, an Oppidan, who gave up drag hunting to concentrate solely on the hare.

In 1932 it was a small country, largely Eton owned, lying mainly between the school and Taplow to the north-west. There was some arable, a fair amount of grass and a great deal of market garden; already urbanization had had its destructive effect and some parts, notably north of Slough, were detached. The whole was dominated by the river on the one hand and the railway, recently electrified, on the other. Small and restricted as the country was, it gave Etonians and local inhabitants the opportunity for plenty of sport and it continued to provide a training ground for aspiring masters of foxhounds – a facility eagerly exploited by many since the war.

Ronnie's first sight of the beagles was on 8 November, during only his second half and presumably thanks to the indulgence of his housemaster. The day is forever inscribed on his memory, not so much for the quality of the sport but because the huntsman got into the river still wearing his stock wound tightly round his neck, and nearly drowned as the tie shrunk during the immersion. The master and huntsman in 1932 was the Honourable F. H. P. C. Wood (Peter Wood), a son of Lord Halifax who was later to become Foreign Secretary. Wood was professional in the way he went about his duties and Ronnie, already apt to be critical of any aspect of hunting which smacked of lax organization, was impressed.

He was impressed too by the kennels, at which he spent most Sunday afternoons picking the brains of Bill Perkins the kennel-huntsman and learning the names of the twenty-odd couple of hounds then kept. Bill Perkins was a wonderfully hard-working man of the old school: so short in the leg that he found it difficult to keep up with the more athletic masters, he had won a Military Medal whilst serving with the Light Infantry – a regiment he had joined in the mistaken belief that it would suit short men better. He had been second whipper-in to many high class establishments (the Old Berks, the Garth and the Brocklesby) before the war and had come to Eton in 1926, at the age of 35, from the Wilton. He kept the kennels and the hounds in immaculate condition, knew the art of control and was an interested and skillful breeder. He was also a vivid and enthusiastic raconteur who kept his young audiences enthralled with blood-curdling and improbable tales of life in the trenches. As with Will Freeman, Ronnie was lucky in this new influence in his hunting career.

Having established his own priorities, he settled down quickly into a routine which centered round the beagles at school and the Eridge at home. Vivian came to Eton in 1934 and, rather to his relief, was placed in a different house where he was able to pursue his own interests; he was developing into a fine cricketer and eventually played for the Eleven. All seemed set fair for both boys when they were shaken by the news that the family would have to leave Leylands.

Wallace Brothers had suffered badly in the stock market slump at the turn of the decade and with a reduced income, Eden and Cecily decided that the remainder of the Rotherfield estate would have to be sold. Cecily had, since Lindsay's birth, given up hunting almost entirely, but was keen that her family, and perhaps especially her eldest son, should have the maximum opportunity to enjoy a variety of sport. They were undecided as to where precisely they would prefer to live but had so loved their holidays at Porlock Weir that they determined to rent a property there until they found a more permanent establishment. They alighted on Chargot, a remote and romantic house on the Brendon Hills, owned by the Malet family who had crossed with the Conqueror and whose Norman leopard crest adorned the furniture with which the house was stuffed. There was no telephone and no electricity but there were stables, of course, and deep, mysterious trout pools. There was also a shallow lily-pond from which Vivian, lying face down, was one day retrieved. Sadly there was little room for the familiar family possessions which had to be put in store, Leylands being left empty until the intended sale was complete.

Ronnie's hunting experience was now widened considerably: days with the Devon and Somerset Staghounds, the Exmoor, the Minehead Harriers, the West Somerset and the Culmstock Otterhounds were added to his repertoire. As his knowledge grew he became more critical in his account of a day's sport, both on holiday and at Eton:

> 10 November 1934
> Farley Hill Beagles, Wellington Hotel, Crowthorne.
>
> ... They were quite a smart little pack, though one or two were rather on the coarse side, but their performance was not impressive. They had little drive about them and were inclined to babble.

(This rather dismissive comment may not have been unrelated to the fact that the Farley Hill Beagles were in a state of almost constant dispute with the ECH over the boundaries of their respective countries and were to provide a test of both his organizational and diplomatic talents when he became master.)

21 December 1934
Minehead Harriers, Periton (foxhunting)

... The hounds seem a workmanlike lot and are handicapped
by a dreadful country. Mr Hosegood, the huntsman, has no
experience and his shouting may be most unprofessional, but
he does his best and trys [sic] really hard.

and

Boxing Day 1934
Devon and Somerset Staghounds, Cloutsham.

These hounds are very fast and good to look at and not entirely
mute as I was told. Of course when scent is literally breast-high
in places then they are. They get rather scattered owing to the
number of deer and the rough going. Their discipline is very
rigid and they work surprisingly well under it.

It is usually the hounds that are the focus of attention: their
ability, their looks and their relationship with the huntsman. But
the performance of the latter, too, is subject to penetrating and,
occasionally, even complimentary scrutiny:

14 January 1935
Quarme Harriers, Hillhead Cross

Being a Pony Club meet, Mr Allen who hunts the Dulverton
twice a week, gave some exceedingly bad hints. ... The pack
is workmanlike and very level. I liked them very much when
I saw them in kennel; they are nearly all white and small.
Rabbits they are not above, but they stick well to their hare.

7 March 1935
Christ Church Beagles, The Burning Bush.

These hounds go at a great pace on the grass but their hound
work is poor. The Hon P. Wood leaves them too long at it as
he always did and never pushed them on. His casts are
effective though unorthodox.

20 April 1935
West Somerset Foxhounds, Leighland.

These hounds are respectable looking and above all even. In
hunting they are excellent. Perhaps flashy on a bad scent, but
they hunt with great drive and cry and practically hunt
themselves. Today's performance speaks for itself. The pace is
just right for the country. Charlie [Back] is a wonderful
huntsman.

These accounts, written in an adult script by a boy of fifteen, bring out several facets of the young Wallace's character – an astonishing maturity, a seriousness of purpose and a facility for getting straight to the point. There is, perhaps, a touch of priggishness about them, as there was about some of his verbal comments on the conduct of a day's sport, but they were easily forgiven by his contemporaries because of the respect already being generated for him by his dedication and growing authority.

In the spring of 1934 the mastership of the ECH had passed to Charles Clerke-Brown, a popular boy and fine athlete, who did much to widen the appeal of beagling at the school, and in 1935 to Desmond Hamilton-Russell, son of Lord Boyne. Both young men were killed in the war, as was Hamilton-Russell's knowledgeable whipper-in, Gerald Heathcoat Amory. All three were ambitious to be masters of foxhounds and were much admired by Ronnie; had they lived, the post-war hunting scene would have been illuminated brightly by their presence.

In the late summer of 1935, Eden found a suitable establishment at Bishop's Cleeve near Cheltenham, Leylands being finally sold and the family furniture reunited with its owners. Cleeve Grange was a Victorian gothic house, reputedly haunted, with a let farm in which Eden interested himself. They were to stay there for three happy years in relatively easy reach of both grandmothers (now living in London) and with a variety of readily available hunting. The Captain and his two eldest sons were soon cubhunting with both the North Cotswold and the Cotswold, whose country then incorporated the Vale which ran down to the Severn at Tewkesbury. In November Eden was able to attend the historic meet at Nether Swell which celebrated 100 years of the Heythrop, an occasion graced by the Duke of Beaufort accompanied by his bitch pack.

The master of the Cotswold was Cyril Heber Percy, late of the Welsh Guards, who became a close and influential family friend. Ronnie, though, was not uncritical:

19 August 1935
Cotswold Foxhounds, Ullenwood

. . . The first morning the bitches had not killed. Mr Heber Percy does not know when hounds have marked. They were not a bit keen at the earth.

This, about a man who became a distinguished master of the Cottesmore after the war, was decidedly bumptious but the young critic was right; Heber Percy, despite his fine qualities – he gave much encouragement to the young and was a conscientious and thorough stopper of earths (sometimes on his way to a meet) – had less than perfect control over his hounds, tending to fuss at them. Ronnie was reminded again of the wisdom imparted to him by Will Freeman, the need to develop a special relationship between huntsman and hounds – the 'invisible thread' on which much of his later success was based.

Otterhunting now began to play a significant part in Ronnie's life: the Wye Valley, the Bucks and, most importantly, the Hawkstone under Lord Coventry, a pack which was to figure largely in the years ahead. There were many days that summer when he cubhunted until mid-morning and then went out with a pack of otterhounds, travelling by bicycle and train or begging lifts from family friends and a long-suffering father. Altogether between December 1928 (when the first diary opens) and December 1935, Ronnie hunted on 354 days with 26 different packs, one day in every seven for seven years, made up of:

    13 days with Staghounds.
   188 „   „ Foxhounds (including 84 days cubhunting).
     4 „   „ Harriers.
   134 „   „ Beagles.
    15 „   „ Otterhounds.

In 28 hunting days between 13 August and 18 September 1935 he hunted 32 times with 7 packs – dedication indeed.

In February 1936, Desmond Hamilton-Russell, for whom Ronnie had already carried an unofficial whip on several occasions, appointed him second whipper-in of the ECH. At the end of that half he became their master and huntsman.

CHAPTER 3

Master of the Eton College Hunt

NOT everyone was pleased. The mastership carried with it a number of privileges and by passing it on to a sixteen-year-old, Hamilton-Russell had caused something of a stir. No-one doubted that Wallace was the best man for the job, but the deep-seated intricacies of Eton 'form' were such that some sensibilities were bound to be outraged. The house governing body – the house prefects, known as the Library – were particularly unhappy. It had become the automatic right of a new master to join them and they considered Ronnie too junior. Much the same applied to the members of the Eton Society, or Pop, who anticipated with some misgivings the arrival among them after Christmas 1936 (another custom) of a young upstart.

Richard Assheton, noting these reservations, made it clear that Wallace would not be promoted over the heads of others, but ruled that if he behaved himself in an unconceited manner and ran the Beagles well, then there would be no obstacle to his election to Pop. In that way the school's hard won traditions were bent to accommodate this unusual young man.

The new master faced three principle problems: a serious lack of money in the hunt account, a country which was already becoming too small for comfort and the state of the hounds: few bitches had been put to (kennel vernacular for mating), because Hamilton-Russell had wanted to hunt them until the end of the season, and there was an unfortunate outbreak of distemper which had to be dealt with. In addition, Ronnie was far from satisfied that he had inherited as level a pack as he would wish.

He tackled his problems with characteristic energy and organisational flair beginning at his first official engagement, the puppy show at the end of March. Already a stickler for social niceties, he began by following the approved pattern of events by making a pretty speech thanking Desmond for his year and presenting him with a silver horn. He went on to thank the judges (one of whom was Lord Knutsford, an MFH whose son Julian Holland-Hibbert was later to be one of his whippers-in), the puppy walkers, the farmers and land-owners and (typically) their employees as well as Perkins; he then spent the rest of the afternoon trying, unsuccessfully, to sell off his unwanted hounds.

The problems associated with the pack were perhaps the easiest to solve. The distemper cleared up without undue carnage, and during the summer half he was able to dispose of all his surplus – and make a little money. Extending the country was more difficult, but, by assiduously visiting all the land-owners and farmers during the summer half, he managed to hang on to, and even add a little to the list of places where his hounds would be made welcome. Slightly concerned about an apparent lack of hares in that part of the country nearest Eton, he obtained fifteen from Major Harry Birkbeck (a Norfolk landowner who hunted his own beagles) and released them in the late spring – an investment that was to pay off handsomely. He next set about securing hunting further afield by going to see incumbent MFHs, and gained a foothold in some country beyond Reading as well as permission to hunt bits of the Chilterns and further land near Marlow. Finally he wrote to Vivian's godfather, Sir George Courthope, then MP for Rye and director of the Southern Railway, to ask him to use his influence to fence the track against beagles – an initiative nonetheless commendable in its failure.

The finances of the ECH were distinctly groggy. The treasurer, Bertie Herbert, was a beak – a member of the teaching staff – who made it clear to Ronnie that unless there was a rapid and substantial improvement in income, this would be the last year that the hunt could be sustained. Not in the least daunted, the master made a plan, recorded laconically in the diary: 'I hope to increase it [the income] by:

1. Sale of Draft
2. More subscribers; to be obtained by canvassing.
3. A Hunt Ball; Lady MacAndrew has said she will organize one.

The disposal of his unwanted hounds had already raised £50 and the active recruiting of subscribers was a success from the moment he put his mind to it. By persuading one or two Eton nobs, notably the Captain of Boats, that beagling could be fun and getting him and his influential friends to appear in the hope that they would then subscribe, he increased the number of paying customers from around 40 to above 150 during his mastership. Herein lie the seeds of a philosophy which was to become very important to him later in life – that of arranging 'a seal of approval' for hunting by persuading people distinguished in public life to appear in the field. In these early days, however, there is much evidence that the important factor in popularizing the sport was the new master's burgeoning reputation for organization and his single-minded pursuit of excellence. The truth no doubt lies somewhere in-between, but the result was that the ECH regained an even financial keel.

Many Saturdays in the Summer Half of 1936 were spent at beagle puppy shows: the New College and Magdalen, the Christ Church, and the Old Berkeley, where at the invitation of Captain John Hill, a keen supporter of the Eton Beagles, he judged for the first time. There was also the Aldershot Hound Show which then rivalled Peterborough and Ronnie went to them all, criticizing the entries and the speeches with equal facility. At the Aldershot Show there was a minor confrontation between the master and his kennel-huntsman, Bill Perkins, who was among those who doubted that a sixteen-year-old could manage the mastership. He had been a little scathing of Ronnie's efforts to prepare and then show the hounds but was not left in doubt for very long:

'Look here,' said the boy, 'you are the expert but I am the master.'

'Quite right, sir,' said Perkins. The air was cleared.

An ECH doghound came close to winning his class that day, spoiling his chances by sulking. Wallace, in his diary report, was disdainful of the winners: 'I cannot say I was particularly taken by the champion hounds, Christ Church Marksman and Mildred and Peter Wood was too busy chasing young ladies to see his hounds win!' Wood, unaware of these strictures, achieved an unwitting revenge when he captained a Christ Church Beagles cricket side which beat the ECH Eleven by 3 wickets that same summer. They remained, as always, good friends.

Hound exercise now began to play a large part in the daily routine, and the Wallace mind started to develop and practise the theory which has formed the basis of his hound training ever since. In his own words, written at the time:

> In the early summer I walked out the old hounds in the playing fields and the young hounds were walked out in hand on couples. Later, on half-holidays, I went out for about 3 hours with a young hound coupled to an old 'un; on whole schoolday evenings I took the Aldershot Show ones for an

hour or so on a bicycle. This all served to start breaking them in and showing them things.

We started hound exercise immediately after Aldershot (4 July), for 3 mornings a week. At first I was able to get back for early school as we only did 2 hours, but later when we were going longer, I had no early school due to School Cert. By the end, Perkins was going out for 5 hours. The young hounds were never let off their couples until a fortnight before hunting began. This was done when they had already been out for a couple of hours. I am sure that this is the best way; they are more or less broken before they are let loose, and thus the risk of them making a bad breakaway (which they will never forget) is minimised. The hounds were as fit as could be and looking very well when they started hunting.

The place that they started hunting was Cleeve, having been transported there by Eden Wallace in a hired two-horse trailer. This most supportive of fathers had also fashioned kennels out of two loose-boxes in his stables, fenced off a grass yard and provided a boiler as well as arranging accommodation for Perkins. The Wallaces were thrilled to have the hounds at home and had set about arranging several meets during the remainder of the holidays.

Lord Coventry at Croome Court was host on more than one occasion, coming to the rescue when meets had to be rearranged because of the late harvest, and others were held as far afield as Newnham Bridge in Worcestershire. They were all carefully chronicled by the master and distilled by him for the *Horse and Hound* under the by-line 'Hillsman'. In all the ECH hunted 14 times in under a month and Ronnie pronounced himself well satisfied. As always, both personally and in the sporting press, he thanked punctiliously all those who had helped him in any way. He had taken the opportunity to put into practice his own philosophy, drawn in part from his observations of others: the quiet control of Will Freeman, no noise, no fuss and only the merest touch of the horn when it was absolutely necessary to impart a truly important message and the equally simple and effective hound management of Bill Perkins who had taught him it was possible to take his pack down the main street of Slough without a whipper-in, and who had emphasized the importance of breeding. To these lessons he had added his own deductions drawn from recognizing the faults of others. Above all he now had the confidence to follow his own instincts, even when it was in

conflict with the received wisdom of the day. He was ready for his
opening meet.

Seventeen couples of hounds met at Willowbrook on the day
after the return from Cleeve. Preparations had been so hectic that
Perkins was not able to come out but a large and curious crowd of
Etonians had assembled to see the new master in action. They did
not have to wait long. A brace of rather unenterprising hares
succumbed after hunts of about half-an-hour each and then a third
was accounted for after a slightly better performance. The real
excitement began when hounds found a fox in a sewage bed. What
followed gave the day a most unusual flavour and not a little
public interest. Charlie sped away towards Dorney before being
turned into Eton Wick village. Here he elected to take refuge in
Mrs Amelia Harris's cottage in Bell Lane, jumping into her kitchen
copper. The locals gathered round as a very out-of-breath master
puffed up to sort the situation out, only to be accosted by an
agitated Mrs Harris: 'Hey, Mister,' she said, 'there's a great big
rabbit thing in my kitchen. He's broken a lamp.' Asked whether
she was sure it was a rabbit, she was adamant: 'Course it's a rabbit;
great brown thing with a bushy tail. Can't you get it out?' The
master considered the problem quickly, and scooping up the
hound Miner he introduced him into the copper to join the
incumbent; there was a brief scuffle and Miner retired hurt.
Outside, chaos reigned; the locals were yelling enthusiastically for
the fox's blood, some pointing out to anyone who would listen
that it had taken many hens from near-by runs during the last few
weeks and had even had turkeys from a farm at Dorney. Hounds,
hitherto so steady after a summer of the Wallace treatment, caught
the general air of hysteria and were milling about in Mrs Harris's
garden. The first whipper-in heroically managed to dislodge the
fox, but not without suffering injury through being struck on the
hand several times by an over-eager follower trying to incapacitate
the quarry. Eventually it was killed in the flower-bed.

The event made spectacular (and sometimes inaccurate) headlines
in the national newspapers: 'Fox killed in Washhouse' reported one;
'Fox Chased into Scullery' said the *Daily Telegraph*; 'Eton College
Beagles Kill Fox in Washhouse' screamed a third. The tone of
the articles which followed was generally approving, although
anti-hunting groups made much of the matter, comparing the
behaviour of Master Wallace and his cronies unfavourably with
that of hooligans baiting a cat. As a high profile start to his career,
Ronnie could hardly have done better.

In his account of the day he expresses himself well satisfied: three hares, a fox and not inconsiderable sport, all on a warm day with little scent. He was not entirely satisfied, however, with the performance of all his whips. One of them, he reported resignedly, even wanted to go home early.

The conduct of hunt officials was always a matter for reflective scrutiny at the end of a day, and credit as well as criticism was carefully recorded. There were many instances during that half's mastership when recalcitrant whippers-in were accorded generous praise as well as marked disapproval. In choosing those that were to follow, a number of aspirants were given a whip to carry with a view to assessing their suitability. Many failed spectacularly despite being close friends; Wallace's ability to distinguish between friendship and loyalty on the one hand and talent and competency on the other is clear from his records and is further evidence of his mature handling of a hierarchical society in which many of those who served him in the ECH were his seniors in the school.

Despite this slight personality clash the 1936 season had started so well that renewed interest was kindled to a degree that had not been seen for many years. Ronnie was lucky to the extent that the opening meet was not the only one to contain an added ingredient which stirred the imagination. During the second day for example, when another three hares were killed, hounds and their master (the latter not forgetting to remove his hunting tie), took to the River Thames, swimming in pursuit of their quarry; the field requisitioned boats to see the fun and were amply rewarded when the hare was finally dispatched on an island.

In his efforts to persuade people to hunt, Wallace carefully avoided courting popularity. At the time the Beagles had acquired something of a reputation for attracting boys who saw the activity as a haven from less agreeable chores, or indeed as providing the perfect cover for snatching a quick drag at a cigarette whilst out of view of potential sources of retribution. Ronnie was determined to stamp out that sort of behaviour: subscribing to and following the ECH was to become a respectable occupation, deserving the full attention of those who came out. It was not to be seen as a refuge for the faintly disreputable. To help bring this about he appointed the first ever field-master at Eton, whose role was to be a mixture of the traditional and that of a policeman preventing petty crime. There is no doubt that subtle Etonian pressure had been exerted to bring something of the sort about but it was much to Ronnie's credit that he read the signs correctly. The choice of Gavin Astor was diplomatically brilliant and illustrates sharply the talent for manipulating affairs to general advantage that Wallace has since developed to a high degree. Astor was a senior boy and a member of Pop, not much given to beagling, but trusted by College authorities and pupils alike. At the end of his time he wrote a charming letter (in reply to one from Ronnie thanking him for all he had done), in which he expressed how much he had enjoyed his duties and deprecating his performance of them – typically understating their critical importance in the context of ECH affairs at the time.

At the end of that first eventful half the master took written stock of his achievements: hounds had performed well in largely poor scenting conditions; attractive sport had been shown (there were only two poor days out of thirty-five) and there had been such an increase in subscribers that the account showed a profit of £80, the first time that it had been in credit for many years; he was cautiously satisfied as he looked forward to the Christmas holidays.

The day after the College broke up Perkins and the hounds travelled to Cleeve. The little kennelman much enjoyed his absences from home and often recalled the exploits of the masters' families with whom he stayed – the more noble the family, the more embroidered the stories. He could hardly ever have come to a place where the organization surpassed that of Eden Wallace, who had not only arranged the meets, the transport and the accommodation, but also the finer points that spell success – down even to Perkins's daily supply of beer. Such attention to detail, a feature of Eden's secretaryship of the Eridge, rubbed off on Ronnie who, to this day, puts sound organization top of the list of the requirements for successful mastership.

During the holiday they hunted on eighteen days, mostly local to Cleeve, and hounds continued to show remarkable sport helped by a succession of make-shift whippers-in including two young Etonians, Jonathan Blow and John Hamilton Stubber, who later made their own, more permanent, marks on ECH affairs. Ronnie found time to produce very full accounts of his activities for the hunting press, over his now familiar 'Hillsman' by-line, which were notable for both their accuracy and an uncharacteristic confession that he had enjoyed such a good Christmas Day that hounds were late at the Boxing Day meet. As in the autumn hunting was by no means confined to Gloucestershire; just before

going back to school hounds were taken to Eardiston to be
entertained by the aunts and draw the hop fields before ending the
holidays at Cleeve Grange where Ronnie, summing up, wrote:

> So now we go back to Eton after a marvellous five weeks in
> an ideal beagling country. Hounds were out on 18 occasions
> and killed 8½ brace; they stuck it well, hunting 4 long days a
> week in very heavy going. A perfect visit.

The 1937 Lent half saw R. E. Wallace firmly established in the
Eton Society, the only representative of his house in that collection
of demi-gods. The probationary period set for him by Richard
Assheton was over. Now feeling more secure, he set about
reorganizing his hunt officials, appointing Mike de Chair, a year
his junior, to carry the first whip with Robert Windsor-Clive,
Jonathan Blow and Philip Pardoe as his assistants; Gavin Astor
continued to marshal the field.

The hunt's popularity grew in a startling fashion. It was not
unusual to see fields of 120 and there were plenty of hares to
provide exciting and varied sport. It had become apparent that
Ronnie was already a master in the art of venery such as had
seldom, if ever, been seen at Eton. He seemed to think like a
hound, but with perfect anticipation of his quarry. When hounds
were drawing, and they drew thoroughly for him, he would be
seen suddenly to change direction, give a flick of his whip and
away would go a hare that they had at first drawn over. He never
appeared to be in a hurry but travelled with a sort of triple gait
reminiscent of an American saddle-horse, and he stayed forever.
He was evangelistic in his enthusiasm. Contemporaries remember
well how he held forth at the kennels and on the beagle bus that
the only form of hunting worth doing was that carried out on foot,
in pursuit of either hare or otter. Other variations were much
inferior, largely because the horse was such an infernal nuisance.
There is little reason to believe that, as far as the horse is
concerned, he has ever substantially changed his mind, although
of course recognizing unreservedly the importance to a huntsman
of a first-class horse as an essential aid in producing the best of
sport.

Contemporaries also recall his use of expletives, scattered like
confetti when he was displeased by a dozing whipper-in or an
encroaching follower. Gilbert Dunning, who hunted the ECH in
1912 and had closely followed its fortunes from his home at
Holyport, giving much assistance to Ronnie and his predecessors,

observed that, 'Wallace had the appearance of a cherub and the language of a Billingsgate fish-porter.'

These manifestations of a growing confidence were complemented by the fact that the new team, having been cajoled by the master, was fully turned out in ECH livery: dark brown velvet coat with brass hunt buttons, white breeches, black stockings and velvet cap. Perkins, too, had a new uniform, thanks to the unfailing generosity of Eden Wallace, and this new smartness enhanced further the rising status of the Beagles.

In the field Ronnie began to be more critical of both his own and his pack's performances, drawing sharp distinctions between hound-work and the number of hares killed when evaluating a day:

> Tuesday February 2nd
> Cannoncourt Farm
>
> A whole holiday and there was an enormous field of over 130; Perkins said that it was the largest he had ever seen with these hounds.
> The day cannot be described in any detail but the field pronounced it a very good one. Looking back I do not call it a real corker. However it served its purpose for an Etonian likes to see some hares killed. We got hold of 3 brace and had a series of short hunts with two excursions into the bottom below the railway. I suppose sport was ideal for the occasion.

This is, by any standards, a pretty unenthusiastic account of a successful day's work but barely a week later, hunting from Oakwells Manor where hounds killed half the number of hares, he was lyrical in his description of the sport he showed:

> I prophesied a great day and I was not wrong. . . . Found in the field opposite (the meet) and quickly gathered pace as they hunted across the arables past Lowbrook Farm. Once off these they fairly raced along the grass field and over the market garden beyond. Next across the aerodrome (White Waltham); they bore slightly left-handed into Shottesbrooke Park and thence towards Knowl Hill. They crossed and re-crossed the main line without mishap and sped on to Waltham St Lawrence. They left the village on the left and pointed for Stanlake Park with all of us toiling behind. Short of the coverts they turned at last and killed their hare near the level-crossing. It was 45 minutes without a check; about 8 miles as they ran and a 4½ mile point. There can never have

been a better hunt . . . found in some cabbages near Heywood
Farm. They hunted all through Cox Green to the main
line but mercifully turned back along the new houses to
Lowbrook Farm for Haywood Farm where they bowled her
over. 30 minutes. Found again on Ockwells big arable and ran
first towards Cannon Hill. Eventually they turned back
past the find and killed again by the banks of the brook
after another 30 minutes. We then went on to a new view
and hunted through the swamp and away across Heywood
Farm. Gathering pace they went faster than ever across the
aerodrome and on past Shottesbrook. With everyone beat
and a possibility of hounds disappearing into the night, I
borrowed a bicycle and succeeded in stopping them. They
had made a 3 mile point.
The best day of the season – I've never seen a better.

His growing knowledge and the steady development of the
Wallace instinct were matched by an almost awesome maturity
in one still only seventeen. An example of his now confident
authority occurred during a day when he and his first whip
paused to arrest a poacher and his lurcher and marched them both
to the farmer on whose land they were hunting (and the poacher
was poaching). There was a spectacular row ending with the
farmer calling the police. There seems though to have been an
absence of the arrogance so often and easily assumed by those
who find their adult feet early in life; far more evident was the
talent for diplomacy, already remarked on and given further scope
when reprimanded sharply in a formal letter from three Eton
'Beaks' who objected to the fact that hounds had run through their
gardens at Willowbrook (the scene of many an ECH meet) and
demanding that there should not be a recurrence. Ronnie's reply,
sadly no longer in existence, was so charming and apologetic that
not only was wrath turned aside but no further complaints ensued
despite the fact that the trespass was repeated several times when
hounds were in hot pursuit.

The statistics for the 1936–7 season make startling reading when
compared with previous ECH records. The Beagles hunted on 93
days, over twice the number achieved in most years and considerably more than even the fanatical Peter Wood had been able
to arrange three years earlier. During the year they had accounted
for 58 brace of hares (and Mrs Harris's fox) – almost 20 brace more
than had ever been killed before. Everyone: master, whips, kennelman and the swelling number of Etonian subscribers were more

than well pleased. Even the headmaster, Claude Elliot, who had only just been persuaded to keep the Beagles on against the better judgement and firm recommendation of his predecessor, was now satisfied that the ECH was not only well run and financially sound, but a positive force for good in the school.

At the end of the Lent Half, the by now well oiled organization suffered a setback when the puppy show had to be cancelled because of an outbreak of distemper. As a result an informal affair was arranged in July to take its place. Among the judges was Peter Wood, who had developed very definite ideas on breeding and whose book *Thoughts on Beagling* was later to cause some controversy in the columns of *Horse and Hound*. In so far as it was relevant to proceedings at the substitute show, the argument was about size: Wood's view being that the ideal hound should stand at about 15½ inches in order to cope better with all types of country, whereas the opposition to this move towards a 'miniature foxhound' would have it that there was little point in increasing the length of leg and therefore the speed, as then the pack would often outstrip the field. Wood had started to put his evolutionary theories into practice when master of the ECH and continued to do so at the Christ Church Beagles whose master he became in 1935. Ronnie, an admirer of Wood's inclined to his mentor's line without quite going all the way – the Wallace taste for compromise as well as a healthy common-sense led him to favour a type which was neither so racy as a miniature foxhound nor so small and stuffy as the traditional 14-inch beagle. Whatever the relative merits of the arguments, judges had already started to favour the slightly more long-legged variety and at the Aldershot Show that summer, the awards seemed to go in the main to bigger hounds, with the ECH's Vagabond winning the unentered class ahead of the champions at the prestigious Peterborough Show – a triumph not without irony as the latter had been bred by Wood.

The losses from distemper were remarkably few and the kennels were able to move to Cleeve for the holidays, having started hound exercise at Eton at the end of June. By Mid-August the pack was hard and fit and an early harvest allowed them to begin hunting on the 20th; Eden Wallace again having unobtrusively smoothed the way for a busy and trouble-free month. The meets were all arranged for around 6 a.m. so as to maximize the scent before the sun warmed up both the air and the ground, and this routine enabled Ronnie to hunt later in the day with the Hawkstone Otterhounds, a procedure enacted regularly and which entailed much travel, sometimes by train or by begging a lift with friends, but more often driven by his understanding and supportive father. The Hawkstone ranged widely over Worcestershire, Shropshire and the Welsh Marches and right into Wales itself. It was not unusual for the Wallace family to finish four hours beagling at 10 a.m. and then drive to, say, Builth Wells to pursue an otter.

In all there were nineteen days beagling and as many outings with the Hawkstone to be fitted into the summer; Eden and Vivian, with sometimes Cecily and Lindsay (now aged 5), were kept busy trailing in Ronnie's enthusiastic wake. Despite the hot, dry start and a subsequent plethora of thick fog, the sport shown by the ECH was again good and the young entry performed well, much to the pleasure of Bill Perkins who had worked hard through the period of distemper to produce them in good order.

Back at Eton in September things went smoothly, with de Chair and Blow carrying the principle whips, joined by Julian Holland-Hibbert and Mark Mainwaring. Holland-Hibbert was the son of Viscount (Thurston) Knutsford, then master of the VWH, a family friend who had often stayed at Leylands when judging at horse shows in Sussex. He had been master of the Trinity Foot Beagles at Cambridge and had become a much valued adviser to Ronnie. There is no doubt that he was as powerful an influence on young Wallace's thinking in breeding and hound matters as Eden was in the mechanics of organizing and operating a hunting country.

Gavin Astor's place as field-master was taken by Francis Collin, an unusual member of Pop in that he was hopeless at games and could not therefore wear any of the distinguishing headgear which marked out the corinthians from whom the membership of the Eton Society was generally drawn. Collin believes strongly that Ronnie took pity on this lack of distinction, awarding him a whip and the field-master's appointment to compensate. Whatever the reason, it was another wise decision, for Collin despite his lack of sporting prowess, was a boy much admired for his intelligence and wit, being immensely popular with his peers and the beaks alike – projecting, as Astor had, the sort of image of the ECH that Wallace wished to convey.

A matter of some discussion between Eden Wallace and Richard Assheton as Ronnie entered his last school year, was the question of his future. Given his single-minded devotion to hunting at a time when to be a master of hounds still carried considerable social weight, there seemed little point in planning a more conventional career for him, either in the City or elsewhere. It was therefore decided that he should go up to Christ Church College Oxford, more widely known then as 'The House' – a path trodden by most Etonians with university pretentions but modest academic ability, mainly because of Christ Church's close (and often closed) links with the school. There would, for a boy of Ronnie's ability, be little problem in satisfying the entrance examiners, provided that he did a modicum of work. How that work was fitted in to his hunting calendar, it now seems difficult to see, but somehow it was achieved by concentrated cramming in the period immediately preceding the examination. Christ Church would enable him to go on hunting for almost as many days as he chose and there was already talk of war which made longer term planning a matter for almost idle speculation.

The 1937 season started well although the weather remained almost intolerably hot. A greater number of hares than usual took to the river and the hunt staff found themselves swimming a great deal more often than they would have chosen, while the Field enjoyed the requisitioning of punts from which to stay in touch with the sport. There were many of the by now almost expected incidents to lighten the serious business of the day: Mainwaring, fleeing from the master's wrath after he had inadvertently turned a hare, was chased by a determined bull and arrived back at his first tormentor's side only inches in front of the enraged animal as he reached the fence. On another day, never to be forgotten by either Perkins or the unfortunate fellow members of the houses of the hunt staff, a hare elected to run through the sewage works and all concerned, hare, hounds, master and whips, emerged coated with sludge and giving off the same unmistakable smell. Ronnie was amused to be accosted on his way back to kennels with the hounds, by a curious cottager who wanted to know: 'Ow, what with them being the same colour an' all, you tell 'em apart, Guv'nor?'

An outbreak of foot-and-mouth disease at Latimer in November would, under most masters, have curtailed activities for a while, but Wallace's foresight in having extended his country, and the energetic way in which he persuaded masters of foxhounds to allow him to bring the ECH to hunt their countries meant that not a day was missed. On one such occasion they made the long journey to Petworth in the Eton Boat Club van, the usual form of hound transport to faraway meets, at the invitation of Lord Leconfield, an eccentric peer, and the Storrington Foot Beagles. They had an exciting start to the day, finding a hare, several foxes and number-less rabbits in a kale field. They got their hare and then withdrew, much to the indignation of his Lordship who would clearly have preferred them to kill everything in sight. He was mollified (and volubly impressed) when, later, they found a hare in an allotment plot the drawing of which he had declared to be a waste of time. It is of Lord Leconfield that the story is told of him hearing what he took to be an unmistakable holloa when hunting his hounds in 1943. Gathering up the pack he set off in the general direction of the noise only to find a football match in progress. Having discovered his error he was furious: 'Haven't you people got anything better to do?' he bawled, rising in his stirrups. 'Don't you know there's a bloody war on!'

At the end of the half came the long awaited hunt ball. It was organized by Lady Warrender and several other Society hostesses, most of whom had sons at Eton, and was to take the form of a Pay Party (that is a subscription dance) at the Savoy. Nearly 250 people paid two guineas each and the event hit both the social and the popular press, particularly as the Duke and Duchess of Kent had promised to look in. Not all the comment was favourable:

> It seems to me, and it is looking the same to an increasing number of people, judging by current conversation, that so long as there are better causes for which to work, if the gilded youth of Eton cannot afford to maintain its beagles out of its own pocket it ought not, with such a winning confidence ask us to do so. Is life at Eton now so hard?

So wrote one correspondent sniffily. Another was even more critical:

> There are charity balls for Dockland Settlements, for old horses, for the children of blind ex-servicemen, for baby clinics in Shoreditch, for the welfare of tubercular char-ladies and for many another deserving cause. The best that has come my way is the forthcoming charity ball – tickets at two guineas a nob – in aid of that beautiful, Samaritan, almost St Francis-of-Assisi institution, the Eton College Beagles. I sincerely hope that all readers will cough up their forty-two bobs to help the dismal little pauper children to have an occasional afternoon in the fresh air with those sweet little hares.

This sort of adverse publicity, probably not seen by most of the prospective patrons, had little effect on the success of the evening – there was a handsome profit of £504 2s 6d, enough to secure the future of the Beagles for some years to come. The party's balance sheet makes astonishing reading: the hire of the Savoy Ballroom plus refreshments cost £186 and the Band (Ambrose, the most fashionable of the day) only £40. Ronnie, who at about this time had discovered that girls were not necessarily to be deprecated as unwelcome distractions from the main purpose of life, enjoyed the night enormously, but only as an interlude – he hunted his hounds both on the day of the dance and on the morning after.

In the Christmas holidays at Cleeve, the relentless pursuit of hares continued. Meets had been arranged as far afield as Shropshire and Hereford and Eden was again kept busy driving the hound van. There was no let up in the pace. They were out for eighteen out of a possible twenty-four hunting days with never a blank, and killed 15 brace bringing the tally for the season to 50. By mid January 1938, even Ronnie was moved to write: 'A good day but we were rather jaded by all the hunting lately.' Among those who held meets were Lords Coventry, Knutsford and Boyne, themselves masters of hounds and all of them interested, perhaps fascinated, by the extraordinary talent for the sport shown by this dedicated young man.

Back at Eton once again he found that he had reached the social pinnacle by being elected chairman of Pop, but his obligations to the Society and the pressure of work began to tell – not so much on the number of days on which the Beagles went out (they hunted three and four days a week), but on the detail of the entries in the diaries. There was, too, on Ronnie's part, a certain impending gloom as he faced up to the fact that this was his last half as master and perhaps Thurston Knutsford's wise advice to him was forefront in his mind: 'You must savour this,' he had been told when he took on the ECH, 'for you will never have such a trouble-free mastership again.'

His last appearance as master of the beagles he loved, was fittingly a bye-day with only Bill Perkins as company. There was no pressure from an eager field and he was able to enjoy himself in the company of the little kennelman and his hounds with a relish that was evident.

The season ended in a welter of statistical records: they had hunted for 104 days and accounted for 75 brace and three foxes, figures which have never been approached let alone surpassed. He had made his mark on the hunting world in a way in which even he could hardly have imagined when, as a small serious boy, he had cajoled his younger brother into whipping-in to the bobbery pack at Leylands.

William de Geyer, a slightly odd figure, who haunted the beagle world of the thirties, following packs throughout England, wrote him a flowery valediction: 'There is no pack in England which can compare with the ECH during your mastership.'

But the final and characteristically terse words in this chapter must be written by Ronnie himself as he closed his diary:

> I leave the best pack of beagles there will ever be, an adequate and varied country, increased support and sound finance to Mike de Chair. Good luck to him.

CHAPTER 4

Christ Church and the War

AMONGST the boys who had carried the horn of the Eton College Hunt in the 1930s were those of whom it can be said with certainty that they had the talent and the ambition to develop into masters of foxhounds to rank with the best in England had they lived into the second half of the century. Sadly, with the exception of Gerald Gundry (at the Duke of Beaufort's), Charles Wood (at the Middleton) and Ronnie Wallace, the war depleted their number terribly: Peter Wood, Charles Clerke-Brown, Desmond Hamilton-Russell, Gerald Heathcoat Amory and Mike de Chair were killed and Julian Holland-Hibbert was so badly injured that he was confined thereafter to a wheelchair.

All had established reputations that far exceeded the bounds of Eton, but none, except Peter Wood, had enough time left to them to hunt their own foxhounds for even the briefest of periods. Comparisons therefore cannot be fairly made, except to say that by 1939 it was already clear that although each possessed the qualities necessary to succeed in his chosen profession, none was better equipped than Wallace who, by that time, had become the unchallenged *prima inter pares* of his generation.

There appear to be five factors which set him apart from his peers. First was the single-minded determination to show good sport; hunting came first and last in his young life and there were no other interests either to engage him or dilute his will to succeed. Second was a highly developed sympathy for traditionally high standards, tempered by a talent for diplomacy. Everyone with whom he dealt, hunt staff, land-owners, farmers, subscribers and followers alike, knew exactly what was required of them and were charmed into providing it. Third was a flair for organization, partly inherited and partly learnt from his father. Under his mastership the ECH had been directed clearly at a set of well defined objectives (an extended country, a level and fit pack and sound finances), which were then achieved by careful and far-sighted administration. Next was his close relationship with his hounds, the 'invisible thread', which for example allowed him to walk them through the streets of Slough under perfect control without the assistance of whippers-in, or pick up a scattered pack and redirect them on to a line with a quiet word or the most economical and unfussy use of his horn. And finally and perhaps most striking, was his uncanny instinct. He seemed to think as his quarry would think. Time and time again contemporaries remark on this ability to know precisely where a hare would be found and where it would then run – an almost perfect anticipation which accounted in no small measure for his record number of kills.

Wallace left Eton at the end of the summer half of 1938 poised to consolidate his considerable reputation but aware of the irksome fact that he had no mastership to progress to – a state of affairs which he was anxious to ameliorate as soon as possible.

The family was on the move again. The lease on Cleeve Grange had come to an end and Eden and Cecily decided that they would like to settle in the familiar country not far from Tenbury in which they had so many friends. Accordingly they took the Lodge at Ludlow, a short-term arrangement which was to last barely a year and which was followed by another lease, this time of the near-by Ashford Manor, before they bought Whitton Paddocks, a comfort-able family house some five miles south-west of Ludlow and, most significantly, only two miles from the Caynham kennels of the Ludlow Foxhounds.

That summer, the Earl of Coventry asked Eden Wallace if, from the following January, he would take on the joint-mastership of the Hawkstone Otterhounds with Philip Stanier, the hunt's secretary and treasurer. Coventry, who, as Lord Deerhurst, had hunted the Carmarthenshire Foxhounds, was an enthusiastic and knowledge-able breeder of hounds from whom Ronnie had learnt a great deal, and he had also been unfailingly generous to the ECH during school holidays, holding several meets at Croome and prevailing on his neighbours to do likewise. Seeing that war was inevitable, he made this early provision for the future of his Otterhounds, possibly even planning to take them back in due course, but it was not to be for he was killed at Dunkirk. Eden, egged on by his eldest son, who recognized in this proposal an opportunity to hunt the hounds himself, agreed and arranged for the hounds to be ken-nelled at the Lodge from where they later moved to Caynham.

When Ronnie and Vivian were small the Wallace family had not been much exposed to otterhunting having been out only once in Sussex and that on a day when nothing happened at all except that

Eden was accosted by a lady who had clearly alleviated her boredom with a lengthily liquid lunch and insisted on selling him a vast number of unwanted raffle tickets. Eden, whose views on the proprieties of life excluded drunken women, had mentally written off the sport as being both dull and attracting the 'wrong sort of person'. Apart from occasional sorties into Devon and the Welsh borders, it was not until after the move to Cleeve and his acquaintance with Coventry had ripened into friendship, that he took to it enthusiastically, constantly chauffeuring his family from Gloucestershire into Wales and Shropshire in the summer having, as we have seen, often already completed either a morning's hound exercise or several hours beagling with his son.

The Hawkstone had once hunted over most of Wales and the Marches until gradually other packs came into being and the country was broken up to be shared by the Wye Valley, the Border Counties and the Pembroke and Carmarthenshire. It still retained a considerable country including the Wye above Hereford, the Usk above Crickhowell, the Teifi, the Irfon, the Cothy, the Lugg and the Arrow, and in north Shropshire the Tern, the Roden and the Meese. It was too big to be hunted from the kennels on a daily basis and each summer would turn itself into a travelling circus, moving, for example, to Llandysul, for three weeks to hunt the Teifi. The practice of setting up otterhunting camps had been started by Billy Wardell, the master of the Hawkstone at the turn of the century, whose habit it was to have tents erected for a fortnight at Builth Wells from which he would range far up and down the Wye. This proved for a few years to be particularly popular with the young until Victorian mamas, eventually realizing the implications for their unprotected daughters, took fright and withdrew their permission, effectively turning the proceedings into single sex affairs – not nearly so much fun.

Ronnie spent the summer of 1938 whipping-in for both the Hawkstone and the Wye Valley Otterhounds. The latter were hunted by Ray Thompson who was also master of the Ross Harriers and who was an able performer with otterhounds, well capable of giving his eager pupil a thorough grounding in an art about which Ronnie felt he still had much to learn. Thompson, who was a member of a prominent Burton-on-Trent brewing family, was a hard-drinking yet charming and immaculately mannered man who impressed Ronnie mightily by his quiet and sparing use of voice and horn – the latter carried in a leather case slung high across his chest.

In October Wallace went up to Oxford to read history. The University in general and Christ Church in particular had so many Etonians that it was rather like returning to school and from the beginning Ronnie felt at home. He moved into rooms in College and began the course of general studies which it was then the practice to complete in an undergraduate's first year before specializing thereafter. Oxford was buzzing with the excitement of political events at home and abroad and few believed that they would be able to complete their studies without some kind of military interruption. Ronnie relished his new found freedom; under the guidance of slightly older companions he discovered the delights of the dining clubs, notably the Grid-Iron, the pleasures of drinking late-night decanters of port and the charms of girl friends. His dark good looks together with his burning devotion to a sport about which he was already an authority, gave him an aura of power which belied his years and made him attractive company for a wide variety of women.

Although not interested in politics, he was by upbringing and inclination a natural Conservative and as such campaigned vigorously for Quintin Hogg in the much publicized 'appeasement' bye-election that winter – so vigorously that he was arrested for disorderly behaviour. He had little idea of the import of the pro- and anti-Churchill factions which then divided the Tory Party, feeling merely that the Conservative candidate, whatever his views on Chamberlain and Munich, deserved Wallace support.

Social and political distractions, new and exciting as they may have been, were not allowed to interfere in any substantive way with the main business of the term which was to get to grips with the beagling scene. The university had two packs, the New College and Magdalen and the Christ Church. The New College, founded in 1896, had been partnered variously with Magdalen, Balliol and Trinity over the years, whilst the Christ Church pack, formed in 1874 from an establishment which had alternated between beagles and harriers, had managed to preserve its independence. Its master was Gerald Heathcoat Amory who had been first whipper-in to Desmond Hamilton-Russell at Eton and who had now become one of Ronnie's closest and most influential friends, being mainly responsible for floating his protégé on the social scene. The Heathcoat Amorys were an extensive and well-connected Devon family who were active in hunting circles in the south-west. Two Amorys had the joint mastership of the Tiverton Foxhounds in 1938 – the latest of an unbroken line of Amory masters stretching back to 1892. Derri (later to become Sir Derek and Chancellor of the Exchequer, the younger of the pair) had his business in Tiverton and much diverted the work-force by riding to his office in full hunting kit, doing a couple of hours at his desk, and then calling for his horse to be brought to the factory gate before hacking on to the meet.

The Christ Church Beagles were kept at Garsington and looked after by Walter Clinkard, a kennel-huntsman who had followed his father into the appointment. Clinkard and his wife were prolific breeders of children whose practice it was to ask the master of the year to stand as godfather. There appeared to be as many children as masters, although when Ronnie assumed the job the following year, it was with some relief that he noticed that Mrs Clinkard had decided to give herself a well earned rest. Gerald Amory and Clinkard had a good understanding, much along the lines of the Wallace-Perkins partnership at Eton, and of this Ronnie much approved. He had already firmed up his ideas on how such a relationship should be conducted and like all such intimacies, fraught with unspoken nuances, it is difficult to define the essential ingredients in a few words. Perhaps they can best be encapsulated in a postcard once sent to the master of the New College pack by its kennel-huntsman, Joe Webb:

> Meet me at the station at 6.45 am. Do not be late. Your obedient servant, Joe Webb.

Ronnie also generally approved of the way in which Heathcoat Amory hunted his hounds and was pleased to be appointed both first whipper-in and secretary, but he was not entirely uncritical of the master believing, accurately, that Gerald was not devoted to the sport in quite the same way as himself. He summed up that first year at Oxford thus:

> During the season 1938–39, I did secretary to Gerald H-A who really is very keen, although not entirely mad about hunting hounds. There could have been no-one nicer to help. We had a good season until Christmas and some outstanding hunts including a 3-mile point from Waterperry Common to kill at Castle Hill, and also from Kingsey to Ford and back, catching the hare near the main road. Not so good after Christmas. Caught 21 brace. We had a mounted meet on Dartmoor and I fell off! I found the hounds rather wild after Eton, which lost them some hares; several babblers and a noisy kennel-huntsman – though an excellent kennelman.

He was allowed to hunt hounds himself only once, towards the end of March 1939, when they went by invitation to Eton. Several old friends were out, including Perkins and the Dunnings and he had a very satisfactory day ending by getting a difficult hare in chancy circumstances. Perkins drily observed that the Wallace luck still held and Ronnie himself learnt enough from the experience to conclude that, 'Judging by the hounds reaction to the horn and voice, they could become a really good pack.'

Meanwhile the Hawkstone had made their move from Croome to Ludlow and a new establishment had been appointed in January 1939. Jack Stallard had come from the Courtenay Tracey Otterhounds to be kennel-huntsman and first whipper-in whilst a boy of fifteen, Henry Bundy, son of the Wye Valley huntsman, was the second whip. There was a Curtis horse-box as a hound van and even a driver – Eden Wallace had determined to do the job properly and the 25 couple started hound exercise shortly after assembling in their new home.

The plan was that Pip Stanier would hunt hounds alternately with Ronnie and for some time this was the case. Between them they took the Hawkstone out for thirty-three days, accounting for as many otters, despite the heavy rains that spring and summer which made many of the favourite rivers unhuntable for much of the time.

On 1 May Ronnie had become the master of the Christ Church Beagles and because of his Hawkstone responsibilities it would have been undoubtedly more convenient for him to have taken the pack home for the summer, both to exercise the hounds and introduce the new entry. In fact they stayed at Garsington, partly because of the lack of space at Caynham and partly due to the influence of several attractive young ladies living within easy reach of Oxford. Notable among them were Sonia Matthews who had often driven him up and down to Shropshire before he had a driving licence and Olivia Page whom he had met at a Commemoration Ball in May. With Olivia Ronnie fell in love and to their often tempestuous affair he brought all the enthusiasm and wholeheartedness which, hitherto, he had reserved solely for his hunting, recording in the diaries not only her presence at meets, but also her occasional absences. So devoted were they that they became engaged briefly, a development not viewed with much approval by either family on grounds of both age and because of Ronnie's uncertain military future. The constant travelling which this relationship and his hunting duties entailed was made easier by the fact that he had acquired a motor-car, a capacious Vauxhall, which commuted regularly between Oxford and Ludlow filled with his friends. Eden, much to his relief was at last relieved of his long-standing duties as a chauffeur.

In August 1939 Ronnie ceased to hunt the Hawkstone so that the season at Oxford could be given his full attention. The air was heavy with talk of imminent war and the Declaration on 3 September caused little surprise. Most undergraduates of military age, including Wallace, volunteered for the armed services, despite the gloomy outcome of the celebrated debate of six years earlier when the Oxford Union voted not to fight for King and Country. For many the call came unexpectedly early and the colleges emptied, but for Ronnie the wait was to be a lengthy one and he set about finding a suitable regiment. The Welsh Guards (through Cyril Heber-Percy) and his father's regiment were possibilities but he favoured the Shropshire Yeomanry and found himself up for interview before a Board consisting of the Treasurer of Christ Church, the Bishop of Oxford and an undistinguished military gentleman who asked him only if he could ride. The results of that interview were never to be made known for in common with millions of others his plans for a military future suddenly became subject to the passing of the Conscription Act; he would have to await his turn.

Whilst his fate was being decided he returned his attention to beagling, in which there had been a week's pause after the outbreak of war. There seemed little point in resuming his academic studies and, although still officially an undergraduate, he ceased going to lectures and tutorials. The reputation of the Christ Church stood high – they had won a disproportionate share of the prizes at the Peterborough Hound Show that summer – and he was determined to hunt as often as possible, at least until his call-up. There were difficulties: reduced support as the older undergraduate subscribers moved into uniform together with the beginnings of food and petrol rationing led to the New College and Magdalen pack disbanding for the duration and there was a clear danger that the Christ Church would have to follow suit. Ronnie was determined that whatever the problems he would keep going, particularly as New College had generously invited him to hunt its country which lay roughly within the Heythrop and the Old Berks foxhunting countries. This new acquisition, added to the South Oxfordshire and part of the Bicester countries over which the Christ Church traditionally hunted, presented a formidable task if he was to cover it all properly. He not only did so, but also found time to hunt with the Old Berks having bought three horses, one of which he kept with Townley Filgate, the vet at Faringdon.

The Old Berks had a professional huntsman, Oliver Moss, who had served in the First World War as batman to Bill Brown the master of the Portman. Brown had been in the Royal Flying Corps and Moss had caught the flying bug to such an extent that his field was frequently to be found lingering near Brize Norton or other major airfields, often to the detriment of the day's sport. He later joined the RAF and eventually became a test-pilot for the Gloucester Aircraft Company, being among the first to fly a Meteor Jet in which he was to lose his life – a unique second career for a professional huntsman.

Aircraft spotting not being entirely to Ronnie's taste, he managed to widen his experience still further by hunting with the Bicester (at whose kennels he kept another horse), where he was able to compare the methods of an amateur, Bobby Field-Marsham, who had been taught by Sir Peter Farquhar the most respected of all the great pre-war masters, and Clarence Johnson, a professional steeped in foxhunting, who had married Arthur Thatcher's daughter and who in many ways emulated his father-in-law. Wallace found the two schools of practice illuminating: Field-Marsham, who hunted hounds two days a week, encouraged them to cast widely and never seemed to be in a hurry; Johnson, on the other hand, exercised a strict discipline over both hounds and his whippers-in, progressing intently and at some speed from every check in search of his fox, leaving the whips to gather up the pack and put it once again on the line clearly marked for them by the wily and immensely experienced huntsman. Whilst admiring the knowledge and anticipation of Johnson, something akin to his own deft instinct, Ronnie found it impossible to approve of his general methods which he thought too strict and unsympathetic to both staff and hounds.

The Christ Church season came to a premature end in early March 1940 when the master caught jaundice. Despite his illness he was anxious to hunt one final day he had planned for the benefit of his mother and father. Walter Clinkard had flu and Ronnie hunted hounds alone. There was little scent and he soon had to give in, spending the rest of the day sitting in the sun with Betty Field-Marsham, Bobby's sister who was stone deaf, discussing the vagaries of life in a rather one-sided manner. The next day he handed over to Roly Beech, the most senior among a succession of whippers-in who had included Mike de Chair and Vivian Wallace (now also at Christ Church). It was a disappointing end and he felt it keenly:

> I have now got jaundice and cannot hunt again. It really was a season of good sport. So many outstanding hunts. I am very sorry not to be carrying on; they are getting such a good pack of hounds and far better than I thought last year that they ever could be.

He returned home to Ashford Manor from where Eden Wallace had been called-up some months before and was now Captain Wallace again, wearing the green trousers of the 5th Royal Inniskilling Dragoon Guards. Eden was too old for active military service and had become the Quartering Commandant at Shrewsbury, an appointment which allowed him to live at home fairly regularly but not often enough to continue with the sort of conscientious mastership which he felt the Hawkstone deserved. Pip Stanier tried to continue alone but patently needed help and on 1 January 1940, Ronnie was appointed deputy master and huntsman. Abandoning Oxford completely when he fell ill, he now confined himself to the Otterhounds. Money was very short and petrol rationing meant that the thirsty old Curtis van had to be used so sparingly that Ronnie often took hounds to meets in his car – as many as seven couple at a time and usually with human cargo as well. It was a hot summer and the temperature in the Vauxhall sometimes reached the unbearable.

This interlude with the Hawkstone proved to be brief for, on Wednesday 12 June on the Usk at Sennybridge, Ronnie had his last day with them for some time; his papers had at last arrived and he was under orders to report to Tidworth, as Trooper Wallace, to join the Royal Armoured Corps Training Regiment.

By now the question of a regiment had been resolved; the Shropshire Yeomanry idea was dropped when Ronnie was approached by Alan Apsley and invited to join the Royal Gloucestershire Hussars. Lord Apsley had served throughout the 1914–18 war and had won both the DSO and the MC with the regiment that he now commanded. He flew a private aeroplane of great antiquity and uncertain serviceability (it seemed to be held together largely by string), and continued to do so even after war was declared, much to the alarm of the Royal Observer Corps who found it difficult to identify from any of their recognition manuals.

The Royal Gloucestershire Hussars had existed as a regiment in one form or another since 1834 and were first commanded in that year by the Marquis of Worcester, later to become the Duke of Beaufort. The Beauforts have retained their close links with the regiment to the present day, successive Dukes either serving in or becoming honorary Colonels of the Regiment, thus making it an attractive military home for foxhunting men. Between the world wars it had been reduced to approximately squadron strength and had been equipped with armoured cars. In 1938, recruiting started in earnest and in the following year, shortly before the outbreak of war, its strength was such that it had been split into two regiments, 1st and 2nd RGH. 1st RGH was mobilized in September 1939 and had become a part of the defence system of the south-west of England, ready to counter the expected German invasion.

By the time Trooper Wallace was engaged in his basic training on Salisbury Plain, Mark Roddick, a regular 10th Hussar, had taken over command of 1st RGH and came down to Tidworth to interview potential officers. He clearly approved of what he saw for Ronnie was finally accepted into the regiment and, in September, moved to Sandhurst for officer training.

The Royal Military Academy, hitherto a more general school for officer cadets, had been transformed into a sausage-machine engaged in turning out officers for the Cavalry and the Brigade of Guards. There was thus no shortage of kindred spirits to encourage Officer Cadet Wallace in his efforts to organize some extra-curricular hunting. There was some suggestion that he might hunt a local Surrey pack but this was forgotten when Sir Newton Rycroft, master of the Dummer Beagles, suggested that Ronnie might like to have this little pack, kennelling them at the Academy in accommodation vacated the year before when Sandhurst's own pack was disbanded. He set about securing hounds from the ECH, Christ Church and elsewhere to supplement the Dummer pack and, within a fortnight was hunting on Wednesday and Saturday afternoons, as and when his military duties permitted.

There was no professional staff so that the administration had to be carried out by Ronnie and his friends in between parades much to the gently sarcastic amusement of Jack Cox who had been kennel-huntsman to the resident pack and who was now working as a full-time military storeman. During extended manoeuvres the hounds were sent to Caynham to be looked after by the Ludlow huntsman, George Knight, who also looked after the Hawkstone hounds as well as his own reduced pack. To this crowded and relatively expensive enterprise Ronnie contributed what little cash he could afford.

The opening meet of Mr Wallace's Beagles, as his scratch pack was now known, was held in front of the famous steps of Old College and was much enlivened by an air-raid siren. The adjutant, a Grenadier who disapproved strongly of any activity not directly connected with marching up and down, ordered them all to take cover in the shelters but was fortuitously counter-manded by a sympathetic 11th Hussar officer, Bertie Bingley, who advised them instead to move off sharpish to the first draw. Bertie Bingley continued to help Ronnie in every way he could, and in particular by persuading the Motor Transport Officer to release some petrol to carry hounds to meets on the grounds that hunting was character building. He was also required to give many assurances that the precious fluid would not be used to carry the huntsman to social engagements.

Social engagements were once more high on the list of Ronnie's priorities (although not permitted to interfere materially with hunt-ing any more than were military activities as far as was possible), for he was in love again. Jean Thornton was 18, red-headed and a twin. She and her sister Peggy were the adopted daughters of Spencer Thornton, an Ascot stockbroker who was, astonishingly in the light of present-day adoption rules, a bachelor. Jean and Ronnie met when, on his way during the summer to hunt the Hawkstone at Croome Court, he realized that he had forgotten his horn. Finding himself near the house of a friend whom he knew to be likely to have one (the friend's name was Williams-Wynn), he knocked on the door, intending to ask if he might borrow it. The friend was out but the twins, who were staying, not only found a horn but asked if they could come along for the day. Ronnie was smitten and in the next few months they were constant companions, as far as was possible given Ronnie's training commitments and the difficulties of petrol rationing. By the end of the year they were engaged, and Jean was often out with the Beagles. In March 1941 they were married at St Paul's, Knightsbridge. The honeymoon was spent partly at the Metropole Hotel in Minehead and partly at the White Horse at Exford from which hotels they hunted with the West Somerset, the Exmoor and the Devon and Somerset Staghounds. Jean had not done much hunting up to this point in her young life, but she rode well and was catching up fast!

At the time of his marriage Ronnie had been commissioned for two months and had gone to join his regiment at Warminster, sending his hounds once again to the long-suffering George Knight together with what little he could afford by way of keep.

There can have been few regiments to rival the officers of the Royal Gloucestershire Hussars in sporting pedigree: most seemed to be either masters of hounds or peers of the realm; some were both. Vivian Wallace, who had joined the Welsh Guards, was to say later in life that he had seen nothing like it. Lord (Robin) Leigh, himself a hunting man, was commanding B Squadron to which Ronnie was posted and the squadron was manned almost exclusively by countrymen drawn from around Cirencester, among whom the new troop leader felt immediately at home.

The regiment was engaged in playing a vital role in the national defence system which, since Dunkirk, was geared to resisting the expected invasion. It was equipped with bren-gun carriers armed with anti-tank weapons and its area of expected operations was the whole of the south-west of England. It later became one of the original members of 6th Armoured Division until shortly before the division left for North Africa when, because of a change in the order of battle, the RGH was left behind and became a training regiment based in East Anglia. From there most of its officers and men served as reinforcements in other, more operational units, including the 2nd RGH who were in the 8th Army. After the eventual defeat of Germany, 1st RGH was equipped with tanks and warned for duty with the forces then being assembled for the projected invasion of Japan.

In Warminster the regiment was quartered around the town in traditional Yeomanry fashion with the officers mess in a requisitioned private house, the soldiers billeted on civilian families and the bren-gun carriers lined up in car-parks. Robin Leigh was amused but unsurprised when Wallace's first request was to ask whether he could bring his hounds. But the winter of 1941 was hard; there was deep snow and the ground was frozen and this, together with the imminence of a large-scale manoeuvre, led to a firm refusal.

Despite his military duties, his wedding and the weather, Ronnie had still managed to hunt his pack for 29 days during the season and now, with spring approaching, he turned his attention both to the Hawkstone and to finding kennels and a country for Mr Wallace's Beagles near the regiment's forthcoming base at Newmarket where Jean, an inveterate home-maker and determined to follow the drum, had found a cottage not too far away at Mundford.

The Hawkstone was down to 6½ couple, all that could be afforded, and Ronnie decided to supplement their numbers by entering a number of the Ludlow foxhounds whom he knew to be adaptable enough to swim strongly and able to mark an otter. The committee, determined to keep things going and still steered by Eden and Pip Stanier, planned to hunt for fifteen days during the season, ranging as far afield as the severely limited petrol allowance permitted. In the event they managed nearly twice that number, the pack being hunted for 18 by Ronnie and 8 by Stanier. In July Ronnie was bitten in the leg by a hound which apparently mistook that appendage for an otter, an incident which incapacitated him for a fortnight and was unfortunately written up in *Horse and Hound* and read avidly by his brother officers, the most senior of which were heard to wonder with some asperity 'why the boy was not at duty'. Despite this setback he was more enthusiastic than ever about the sport:

> It has been a marvellous season. . . . We have 11½ couples well entered and I have not seen such a pack of otterhounds myself. Pray we can hunt properly next year and we will astonish the otter hunters. It *is* a good sport and I must stick to it whatever the foxhunters say.

This, on the face of it rather curious last phrase, requires some explanation. Otterhunting ranked rather low in the pecking order of the sporting fraternity. There were several reasons for this: many of the snootier fox- and deerhunting people looked down socially on some of the wider spectrum of otterhunting followers. Others hardly regarded it as a sport at all – summing it up as 'Love and Lunch', an allusion to the supposed promiscuity it promoted during halcyon summer days spent on river banks. Finally it had little of the solid farming support enjoyed by its winter rivals; otters were little trouble to farmers, who often had no fishing rights over the rivers which ran through their land. Ronnie was unimpressed by these criticisms. Socially, although very aware of the class structure and his and everybody else's places in it, he had discovered that a shared interest was what really mattered to him – backgrounds and accents were irrelevant when compared with a common enthusiasm. For this approach to life he owed much to his parents. Neither Eden nor Cecily Wallace were snobs in the pejorative sense of that word, and had brought their sons up to treat everyone with even-handed and friendly courtesy whilst being mindful of the social obligations which their rank and breeding demanded of them. Eden, in particular had very high standards of behaviour which led him, for instance and despite his own military background, into gently suggesting to his sons that they might not wish to join a regular cavalry regiment because of the hard riding and even harder swearing he had encountered whilst umpiring military polo matches in Sussex between the wars.

In one important regard, though, Ronnie differed from his parents. He had found an all-pervading passion in life which transcended both his natural good manners and any consideration of what others thought of him. Hunting came first second and last, and even his talent for artful diplomacy was exercised from a very early age in the advancement of that passion. Those set under him – soldiers during the war and hunt staff before and since – were never in any doubt if they failed in the duties laid down for them. Nevertheless plain speaking was not expected to be his prerogative alone – it is clear that it was (and is) encouraged from his staff when a point needs to be made. Wallace has never made the mistake of thinking he knows it all. Despite the sobriquet by which he was eventually to become known, this god, at least in his own estimation, is not omniscient.

In September 1941 seven couple of Mr Wallace's Beagles were taken from Ludlow to Bottisham, near Newmarket where John Towler, the master of the Cambridgeshire Harriers, had his kennels. Amongst them was little Active, now in her sixth season, having moved with Ronnie from Eton (where she refused to hunt for anyone else when Ronnie left) to Christ Church, and having also had two seasons with the Hawkstone – a hard-worked hound indeed. To supplement this small pack the master obtained a draft of four couple from Harry Birkbeck, who had taken a close interest in Wallace's activities at Eton where Birkbeck's son was a near contemporary. In addition to Harry himself, who lived near King's Lynn, several other Norfolk notables were helpful in providing land over which to hunt, including Maurice Barclay who made available some of the Trinity Foot Beagles country. Michael Dill, an ex-master of the TFB and Mike de Chair who was stationed near by, whipped-in; it was very like old times.

In his efforts to carve out a country, Ronnie had appealed for help to Roger Parker, the master of the Cambridgeshire Foxhounds, who had been in Eden's regiment during the First War. This resulted in a telephone call from Parker's son who asked if he could come out with the Beagles on the following day when they were to meet at the quaintly named Twenty-pence Bridge. So began Ronnie's close association with Charles Parker, who was to become a countryside legend in his own time. We have already seen that Wallace had developed not only a special, almost unique relationship with hounds but that he also seemed to have an instinct for anticipating the moves of his quarry. Parker, too, had this facility and in particular was to acquire an almost mystical affinity with foxes. He had been at Eton briefly as a very junior boy when Ronnie was master of the ECH and had then gone on to Gordonstoun. At the time of this meeting he was studying agriculture at Cambridge whilst awaiting his call-up.

On the day of the meet at Twenty-pence Bridge, Ronnie was engaged in drawing a hedgerow, a manoeuvre which Parker found so extraordinarily inept that he made his views plain to the remainder of the field. Almost as he spoke a hare broke out of the hedge and hounds were away. Charles was silent as he began to feel that Wallace perhaps knew what he was about after all, and from that moment on he became a devoted adherent, following Ronnie throughout his subsequent career. So faithful was he, and keen to hunt with his new friend, that in a few months he was breaking out of Sandhurst so regularly that the authorities invited him to leave on a permanent basis; as a result he was obliged to join his father's old regiment as a trooper. This he was pleased to do, as the regiment was in the same Division as the RGH and also based in Norfolk.

Charles Parker was not a military success. Even as a trooper he became something of an albatross round his Commanding Officer's neck – so much so that there was a suggestion, fervently favoured by Charles, that he should transfer into the RGH and join Ronnie's Reconnaissance Troop, already a home for most of the regimental desperados. Neither Colonel Roddick nor Lieutenant Wallace were much inclined to fall in with this plan, feeling not unreasonably that they had enough problems already, and the situation was resolved to everyone's entire satisfaction when Parker overturned a bren-gun carrier whilst on exercise (an almost impossible thing to do) and was invalided out of the Army as a result of his injuries (which were relatively slight) and with ulcers. He was, however, quick to recover and found himself a job on a nearby farm from which he was able to conduct his hunting and naturalist activities with fewer obstacles than had been placed in his way by the military.

The regiment's stay on Newmarket racecourse was brief. During

November it moved to West Tofts on the Stanford Training Area and Ronnie was obliged to move the hounds. As luck would have it Dick Taylor, later to become master of the Suffolk, lived at Ashley and generously offered suitable kennels.

Transport was a constant problem. Military vehicles were not available although there was a small petrol allowance for private cars and vans when they were used for hunting purposes, an illuminating commentary on official attitudes to field sports at that time. The Vauxhall was in daily use travelling the 25 miles between West Tofts and Ashley and then crammed with both hounds and people from the kennels to the meets. Taylor, with access to fuel for his farm, often helped out, taking considerable liberties with the strict wartime regulations by so doing.

Ronnie was particularly taken by the Birkbeck country east of King's Lynn, but the round trip to the grass marshes running down to the Wash severely taxed his administrative arrangements. He considered the trouble well worth the effort:

> A good country this; practically all rushy, rough fields and the right number of hares.

Travel problems not withstanding, the Wallace determination to overcome all difficulties in pursuit of his sport led him to accept an invitation to hunt his hounds in the Christ Church country after Christmas and he arranged to kennel them at Eton. From there, after two entirely agreeable days, he returned to West Tofts for two further days before driving to Ludlow where, in hard frost and on his feet, he hunted a mixed pack of the Ludlow Foxhounds, the Otterhounds and his beagles in search of local foxes. Returning to Norfolk for the remainder of the season, he finished proceedings in April by having to go at otters in the streams around Thetford. It had been another first-class year during which he had somehow managed to hunt on 62 days, and it was now time to activate the Otterhounds again.

The Hawkstone committee was short of both money and resources and had decided to try and hunt as often as possible but without going to the expense of hiring transport. The Vauxhall was again put to good use – one diary entry records it as containing seven couple of hounds, four terriers, George Knight, Jean and Ronnie for the ten-mile trip from Caynham to Leintwardine. Often hounds, which once more included Active, were either walked to meets or accompanied by Ronnie and a whipper-in on bicycles, a proceeding which so enraged a donkey in Ludlow that it charged through the pack and its minders, scattering them and severely frightening the more nervous. Charles Parker had managed to get leave to coincide with a week that Ronnie had also secured in April and was allowed, later in the summer, to carry a whip.

The Hawkstone was able to hunt for only 17 days in 1942, an average of about three days a month and a reflection not only of its stretched finances but also of its master's increased military commitments. There was, though, one extraordinary day in August. Ronnie, Jean, Charles Parker and half-a-dozen others had returned with the hounds by train from Pontrilas on the River Monmow some ten miles south-west of Hereford where they had been based for two days, in order to follow up reports that four otters had been seen in the Teme at Ashford, a mere mile or so from the kennels. They met at 10.30 in pouring rain and with a small field. After a slow start hounds hunted non-stop and it seems probable that all four otters were found in turn, though none were caught. The star was a little bitch which shot out from under a sycamore tree at about five in the afternoon. Over land, across an island and in and out of pools and shallow waters she led them for five hours before they gave her best in the darkness. In poor scenting conditions hounds stuck well to their task and Ronnie was pleased:

> We had to leave a very game and clever little otter. It was an outstanding five hours and a good end to a capital week.

The 1942–3 beagle season opened with a bye-day from the Caynham kennels which began, characteristically, after a morning's cub-hunting with the foxhounds. It was the only day in Shropshire because during the summer the RGH had moved to Ogbourne St George near Marlborough and duty called. Jean had again been busy looking for houses and had found lodgings for them in the village, close to the camp. From there she undertook to look after hounds during Ronnie's increased absences on duty. Helen Stibbard was a sporting and indulgent landlady, making only mild protests from time to time about the noxious smells issuing forth from behind the closed doors of her kitchen when Jean was preparing the feeds. She did, however, draw a firm line when she discovered a dead donkey being dismembered to fit into her stewing pans.

The pack was accommodated in some otherwise disused huts within the regimental lines and little Active was again among those pressed into service, but on the day of the opening meet she was found to be paralysed and had to be sent home to Ludlow to recover. In November she died, much mourned by Ronnie and all who had had the delight of watching her eagerly hunt so many different prey over the years.

The chalk Downs around Marlborough are open and steep and there is little in the way of natural obstacles to provide cover for hares or impede the progress of hounds; they are in short, extremely hard work for a huntsman on foot. By early November, Ronnie was noting ruefully:

> . . . They ran very fast yet I was able to see them driving on. I fancy a horse is very nearly a necessity here.

The followers were mainly fit young men drawn from the RGH and its sister regiments in the Brigade stationed at Ogbourne, notably the Northamptonshire Yeomanry whose ranks, as the name suggests, were not short of hunting adherents. Among them was George Gillson, a most respected professional who had made his name with the Warwickshire in the four years preceding the war. One day, in Ronnie's absence on a manoeuvre, he took the hounds out whilst mounted on a borrowed pony, wearing jack boots (without spurs), a pair of immaculate white breeches, battle-dress blouse and a beret but with all the superior air of one on a thoroughbred hunter, dressed in his red coat and leading some 22½ couple of Warwickshire bitches!

Observing this vignette was Major, the Lord Ashton of Hyde, Headquarter Squadron Leader of the Royal Gloucestershire Hussars and master of the Heythrop. Ashton hunted with the Heythrop as often as he was able to during the first, relatively quiet year of war, driving up to the meets in his Rolls-Royce. One morning, near Stow-on-the-Wold, the regimental adjutant happened to be motoring through when he observed his lordship stepping out of the car and preparing to mount his horse. The field was riveted to see the adjutant saluting their master and then saying, quite firmly: 'You will be back for the parade at 1800 hours, won't you, Master?'

By January 1943 the pace of military events had quickened. There was talk already of a Second Front to relieve the pressure on Soviet Russia and the intensity of training was such that it was no longer practical to keep the hounds at Ogbourne. They returned to Ludlow where Ronnie was able to snatch the odd day with both them and the Foxhounds, recording that on 14 January he had the best day with beagles that he had ever experienced. Hounds had met in Dean Park at Tenbury on a bright, warm morning with a holding scent. After finding several hares which they chivvied round the Park for an hour or so, they suddenly wheeled and went away out into the country. For well over two hours they clung to their task, swimming first the little River Ledwyche and then the Teme which was in spate. Hounds and huntsman were swept over a hundred yards downstream before emerging on the far bank where they again picked up the line, eventually killing the hare after a point of 5¼ miles – more, of course, as they ran (and swam).

Nineteen days were snatched with the Hawkstone during the summer including a week at Brecon. George Knight took the hounds by train to the Brecon Farmers kennels, Ronnie and Jean (now pregnant) following by car and putting up at the Castle Hotel. They hunted five days on the Usk, the Honddu and the Irfon (from Builth Wells) and 'had as good a week as I could have wished for'. It was clearly going to take a great deal more than a few sniffy remarks from dedicated but blinkered foxhunters to wean Ronnie away from his otterhounds.

As summer turned to autumn, an article appeared in the *Sunday Times* discussing the future of hunting, with particular reference to up and coming huntsmen and masters of hounds. That a national newspaper should concern itself with such matters seems extraordinary today, but is a reflection of the general interest which foxhunting then generated. The piece was written under the bye-line 'Dalesman', a pseudonym adopted by C. N. (Bay) de Courcy-Parry, a correspondent who also wrote regularly for *Horse and Hound*. Some of his observations bear reproduction, if only for the prophetic nature of the first and the perceptive observation of the remainder:

> . . . Amongst these young men is that remarkable sportsman and athlete, Ronald Eden Wallace, whose father is Master of the Ludlow and who himself is Master of the Hawkstone Otterhounds and his own pack of beagles. That he will hunt a pack of foxhounds is a certainty and that he will be brilliant in the doing of it is only in keeping with his keenness and thoroughness in all his hunting pursuits.
>
> . . . As a runner (when Master of the ECH) he outran the fleetest and when his hounds needed him he was invariably there to help them, quietly and unobtrusively.
>
> . . . No other interest ever took him from hunting, not even his marriage. . . .

Wallace's is the only name singled out in this otherwise general article and is a measure of the high regard in which he was already held by those who commented knowingly and professionally on the hunting scene.

Ronnie enjoyed the widening fame that this pleasant publicity brought with it although he had to endure the good-natured ribbing with which his brother officers chided him. The regiment was again at West Tofts and still engaged in the never-ending training cycle which, if they only knew it, was now producing the manpower to crew the armoured spearhead which was to land in Normandy, a brief eight months later. By this time, after four years of a war in which his lot had been to play a pretty pacific role, he had begun to search for ways in which he might play a more active role. The 2nd RGH, fighting in the Western Desert, had suffered such severe casualties that after the retreat to El Alamein, the Regiment was never reformed to fight as an entity. That avenue then was closed to those who chafed at the military bit in England. Most, Ronnie included, believed that there would be an invasion in the not too distant future and that their chance would come then.

Meanwhile there was hunting to be done. As usual Mr Wallace's Beagles acquitted themselves well, their master often taking to the field mounted on a succession of borrowed horses, a new departure which foreshadowed the future. Another new experience, undertaken at Dick Taylor's request, was the using of his hounds as beaters on a Sunday in December when Taylor wished to shoot pheasants off a kale field. Hounds behaved beautifully and the birds flew well; everyone was pleased, with the exception of Lord Milford who owned the adjoining coverts and who was slow to appreciate the attractions of shooting and hunting on the Sabbath.

As 1943 drew to a close Ronnie's name again appeared in print. This time it was by way of a signature to a letter he wrote to *Horse and Hound* in which, in robust fashion, he rebuked a correspondent who had earlier complained gloomily, and in verse, about the future of hunting:

> I do not agree with the spirit of the rhyme in your issue of November 19.
> All these letters which bemoan the future of hunting and harp on the 'good old days' are not encouraging to those who are keeping all forms of hunting going. It is necessary that everyone who has enjoyed hunting in the past and is able to spare a little time now should help to ensure the future.

Dalesman, who understands these matters, says that he has never found barbed-wire a hindrance to hounds in catching their foxes and I have not noticed that the increase of plough has been a hindrance to our hounds either.

There may be reasons (money not being the least of them) for expecting that the sight of two hundred people charging across country, dressed and horsed in the height of fashion, is a thing of the past. Nevertheless, in most countries today there is a small pack of well cared for working hounds and an enormous element of support from the farmers (far stronger than there is from pre-war subscribers).

If we can add to that help, there is good reason to hope for sport at least equal to that enjoyed in the past.

It is the case with foxhunting as it is with life that there will always be those who bewail the passing of time and who maintain that what is past is necessarily best. It is refreshing to note that the Wallace clarion call to look to the future is just as apposite today as when it was written.

1944 dawned full of promise. In February Jean gave birth to a son, David. The christening photographs portrayed a happy family group of proud mother and father and smiling god-parents. Among them was Jean's twin, Peggy, and her husband Michael Stewart; Vivian (in the uniform of the Welsh Guards) was there and, in the background, a brother officer of Ronnie's called Major Russell Perkins. There were those who wondered in passing how Perkins had become quite so close to the family; they were soon to find out.

Hand in hand with the happiness at the birth of his son was the sadness of having to disperse Mr Wallace's Beagles. Against all the odds he had hunted them for a full three years, but military pressures and a new development at home made it impossible for him to carry on. The best of them went to the Newcastle and District pack where their blood figures still in the pedigrees of those hounds.

The Ludlow Foxhounds were looking for a new master. Jimmy Delmege, who had hunted them before the war, had always been expected to return, but had written to the committee from his regiment in Italy that he would not be doing so when hostilities ceased. They turned to Ronnie who, with the full support and encouragement of his father, accepted the post on a guarantee of £300 a year from the committee and under certain other conditions, including the continued keep of the Hawkstone Hounds.

He also made it clear that as his military future was uncertain he could not promise to hunt the hounds regularly until the war ended but that George Knight would do so in his absence.

Having satisfactorily arranged his hunting future he now took up the reins of his military career in earnest. In his search for active service he had sought the advice of Mark Mainwaring, an Old Etonian friend who had whipped-in for him in 1937. Mark had joined an organization called Phantom and was engaged in special training at a secret establishment in, of all unlikely places, Richmond Park. Ronnie, attracted by what seemed to be some challenging aspects of this unusual set-up, volunteered and was accepted.

Phantom was a code-name for the British General Headquarters Liaison Regiment, Royal Armoured Corps whose role, after the invasion of France, was to be to gather information on activity in the forward areas and beyond and report direct to the General Officer commanding the Army. The qualities required of its officers and soldiers were similar to those demanded of the Special Air Service of the day with particular emphasis being placed on above average intelligence and communication skills. Despite its name the regiment's personnel were drawn widely from the army as a whole and included a large contingent from the Royal Corps of Signals.

D-day found Ronnie under training in Richmond Park, characteristically noting rather wistfully that the many foxes in the park were allowed to go about their business unmolested by all save the occasional V-1 rocket. Shortly after the completion of his training he was sent to General Omar Bradley's 12th Army Group Tactical Headquarters, the formation that broke through the Siegfried Line in October and was to bear the brunt of the German Ardennes offensive in the Battle of the Bulge later that year. The Phantom teams were composed of a mixture of reconnaissance officers and communicators and Wallace was kept excitingly busy keeping the Army Group Commander informed of the position at the front, whilst also updating the local commanders on the intelligence picture as presented by the higher formations.

He remained with the Americans until the war ended, escaping once to England on an aircraft sent by Bradley to collect a special birthday cake for one of his staff – a break which, it hardly needs recording, was utilized in renewing his acquaintance with the Ludlow Foxhounds.

After hostilities ceased the Phantom teams were gathered

together in the British sector of Germany to await redeployment, possibly to join the projected invasion of Japan. We have seen that this fate also awaited the RGH who, in Wallace's absence, had been re-equipped with tanks and were under orders to sail for the Far East. It was at this stage that Ronnie developed a duodenal ulcer and was flown out of Germany to a military hospital in Leeds, arriving there in July 1945.

He found the forced inactivity of hospital life suited him not at all and, feeling far from ill, persuaded the authorities to send him home for rest and recuperation. Whitton Paddocks certainly provided recuperation but very little rest, either physical or emotional. There were the hounds, both otter and fox to look to, for the former were still just in being and the latter were about to start cubhunting. The real upset was that Jean, who had spent most of Ronnie's time away with her father in Ascot, announced her intention of leaving her husband and wanting a divorce. Her declared wish was to marry Russell Perkins and take David with her. Perkins was an older man whom Ronnie had counted among his friends in the Regiment; he was able to give Jean the attention she now craved and which she found a more attractive proposition than Ronnie's frequent absences in pursuit of his sport. The long days hunting and looking after the various countries in which the beagles had hunted and her husband's military duties which also took him away from her, were not so taxing when she, in her initial keenness shared her man's obsession, but had now become less bearable with the added tie of a baby to look after. Ronnie had failed to appreciate the strains that his life must have caused and was shaken to the core, particularly at the loss of David. His parting with Jean was a good deal less than amicable and as things turned out he was to be deprived of his son's company for the rest of the boy's life. Russell Perkins, with Jean's full approval, felt that it would be in the best interests of all concerned if David was brought up as his own and Ronnie was deprived of access to him. It may well have been that a powerful incentive in reaching this harsh decision was that Perkins, a confirmed bachelor until this affair and uncertain of his ability to hang on to Jean if she continued to see Ronnie regularly as she was bound to do if they were to share the boy, was determined to minimize any chance of reconciliation. There were signs, but not until some eighteen years later in 1963, that the breach might be healed but David was then killed in a military accident in Germany where he was serving with the 11th Hussars. Ronnie never really knew his son and this tragic episode in his life had its final curtain when Jean died in 1969.

The army, having discussed Captain R. E. Wallace's medical condition at a number of Boards, decided that he was fit to continue his service until his turn came for demobilization. The Japanese threat had been removed by the atomic bombs at Hiroshima and Nagasaki and the RGH had been stood down from projected service in the Far East and were now in Austria on garrison duty. Ronnie, not fancying at all a spell in that notably non-foxhunting country, had found himself employment as Paymaster to prisoner-of-war camps in Shropshire and the neighbouring counties. He found his role a particularly congenial one as he was able to combine it with extensive calling on farmers in the Ludlow country in order to pay their trusty POW labourers. His first foxhound mastership was about to begin in earnest.

CHAPTER 5

MFH – The First Seven Years

IN 1945 the finances of both the Ludlow and of Captain Ronnie Wallace were in an equally parlous state. The £300 guarantee given to him the previous season was clearly not enough and there were the added complications of the Hawkstone and the North Ludlow Foxhounds, a pack which had ceased to hunt in 1940 and was now to be amalgamated with its southern neighbours, so increasing the master's responsibilities considerably. The new Ludlow Committee, recognizing the changed circumstances, decided that Ronnie was to be given £500 for the coming year, to be increased to £600 if at all possible. In return Wallace undertook to hunt hounds two days a week.

Mark Mainwaring, who lived in north Shropshire, volunteered to share the mastership of the Hawkstone (but not the hunting of the hounds) and he and Ronnie made an offer to the otterhound committee which suggested that they would see that those hounds also went out twice a week in 1946 against a guarantee similar to that made by the Ludlow. In fact, of course, the fortunes of the two packs were closely intertwined in that all the hounds were kennelled at Caynham and there were opportunities to share both labour and transport costs. In the event the details were quickly and amicably resolved so that Ronnie was able, at last, to embark on a full-time hunting career.

The staff situation at Caynham was eminently satisfactory. George Knight was a wonderful hunt servant, again of the old school, who had, as we have seen, kept both the Ludlow and the Hawkstone hounds going almost single-handedly during the war with the help of his unfailingly supportive, rather hen-like, wife who watched over what she considered to be her personal canine brood with dogged determination. In the background, as always, had been Eden, without whose administrative skills it is likely that neither pack would have survived. Charles Parker had found his way west, first to work on a farm (from which he was quickly sacked by his employer who discovered that he was subsidizing an unofficial hunt servant) and was installed in the stables at Caynham. The full complement was made up by Harry Evans, an elderly ex-stud groom who had been taken on to do the horses and act as general dogsbody.

Only one cloud darkened the otherwise promising horizon: the absence of the bubbling, enthusiastic Jean and the adored David. Outwardly, Ronnie had borne the ordeal of his wife's desertion with some equanimity but he felt the loss more deeply than he cared to admit. Furthermore there was an additional unsettling factor in his life because of his parents' forthcoming move away from Whitton Paddocks to Woodlands, a house on the Eardiston estate. The family home at Eardiston had by this time become flats but Woodlands had been left to Eden by one of the great-aunts and someone was needed to run the fruit and hop business which had sustained the estate erratically since the First World War but was now distinctly run-down.

The venture was not destined to prosper. Despite his administrative talents in other fields, Eden Wallace was not geared to making a success of a commercial enterprise. The farm was over-manned and under-machined to a degree and Eden was incapable of grasping the need to pay off the largely superannuated work-force and invest large sums in mechanization. In this he was, no doubt, guided by an admirable if impractical sense of loyalty and matters were not helped by Cecily's rather old-fashioned notion that the farm labour was in part there to provide help in the house and garden at the estate's expense. In short, the older Wallaces were ill-equipped to come to terms with the post-war social and industrial changes.

During the process of the move to Woodlands, Ronnie had gone to stay with Bill and Baba Evans at Stoke St Milborough. Bill, who was chairman of the Ludlow Committee, was a close friend of Eden's and had done much to educate Ronnie in the finer points of horse and stable management and Baba, by virtue of being a daughter of Sir William Curtis of Caynham Court, had great influence locally. The Evans's role in Ronnie's life was not, however, to be confined to hunt affairs for they had a young friend called Valerie Kemp-Gee, a prominent point-to-point rider in adjacent hunt races – almost the only category then open to lady jockeys – who had been lately divorced from her husband Peter. Ronnie and Valerie, although knowing each other slightly as children at Eridge where Valerie was born, met again at the bedside of Bob Champion, Will Freeman's successor at the Eridge

Hunt, who had broken his leg in 1945. Soon Ronnie was driving to Sussex to watch Valerie race, often combining the trip with going to a meet of the foxhounds before moving on to the point-to-point. On their way to the Romney Marsh fixture in 1946 they were lost for so long in some woods while ostensibly trying to keep in touch with the Eridge Hunt that they only narrowly made the start time of Valerie's race. Ronnie was in love again and Valerie soon found herself frequently in Shropshire, hunting with the Ludlow and the Hawkstone. In the summer of 1946 they were married and set up home with the Evans until, after a few months, they were able to acquire the Wood House, an eponymous structure on the Eardiston estate.

The Ludlow country is described by Baily's as 'lying in Shropshire, Hereford and Worcestershire, covering about 20 miles from East to West and about 20 miles from North to South. Best centres are Ludlow, in the middle of the country, and Tenbury.' It thus encompassed the Wallace family homes and was particularly fitting as a place for Ronnie to start his career. The Ludlow was (and indeed still is) a wonderful country to learn the craft. The coverts are big and very thick so that it is difficult to get hounds out and away. Wenlock Edge, a 22 mile long hanging wood, dominates the northern half and is shared by the neighbouring Wheatland. Along its whole Ludlow length there was at that time just one ride along the summit and perhaps two from top to bottom. Apart from this problem of mobility, there were two further challenges to test the aspiring huntsman: at the end of the war foxes were not over plentiful, largely due to the fact that rabbits were trapped in their thousands to supplement the meagre meat ration; and secondly it was not a great scenting country being both naturally dry on top and heavily populated with livestock.

To Captain Wallace MFH it was bliss. Where better to wrestle with such problems and come to grips with his chosen profession than among people who knew what they were about? The fields were small, hardly ever more than twenty strong and practically all the subscribers had been brought up in the country. There was a pleasing obscurity here in which he could thoroughly learn his trade away from the critical eyes of High Leicestershire and the equally fashionable packs of Warwickshire, Gloucestershire and Dorset.

He set about his task with relish, aided not inconsiderably by the presences of Charles Parker and George Knight. Charles lent his hand to all the tasks around the kennels, including the horses which he regularly exercised with Harry Evans and when the latter died in 1947 (helped on his way by a surfeit of the rough Hereford cider he loved) Charles, despite his lack of formal expertise, did them all by himself. Out hunting he often rode a chestnut of Cecily's and acted as an amateur whipper-in until the return to Shropshire from the war of Hugh Arbuthnot. Arbuthnot, an Old Etonian in the Wallace mould, had been appointed master of the ECH for the 1940–41 season but had decided to disband the pack and leave Eton early to join the Welsh Guards. (The ECH was quickly rescued by the Hon. J. R. C. (Bob) Manners who hunted a few couple in the country nearest the School.) Arbuthnot, now a civilian again, was keen to pursue a foxhunting career for himself and became a major help to Ronnie both with the fox and the otterhounds.

Charles Parker's real interest, despite his work at the kennels, lay in the behaviour of foxes. He had recognized the importance of organized earthstopping for the efficiency of hunting and for the showing of good sport but he was unable for the moment to give full rein to his theories, both because of his duties and because the owners of the estates which largely made up the country were loath to let a stranger wander freely about their coverts, preferring to leave the stopping to the keepers.

One such landowner was Sir Edward Rouse-Boughton of Downton Hall whose 5000 acres lay plumb in the middle of the country. Sir Edward had been master and huntsman of the North Ludlow from 1932 to 1940 and had now joined the committee of the joint Hunt. He was of the strongly held opinion that it was entirely possible to have ten good pheasant shooting days a season and still hunt across his land – an admirable attitude sustained by his formidable daughter Mary, who inherited Downton in 1963 but who effectively took over the running of the estate in 1946 when her father found that he was unable to break off a war-time romance and bolted to the Isle of Wight.

The growth in organized shooting had long exercised the minds of masters of foxhounds. By the end of the nineteenth century, the practice of driving grouse, pheasants and partridges towards a line of guns had become not only widespread but fashionable to an extent that rivalled hunting. It was grumbled that the money spent on a good shoot, its keepers and its hand-rearing paraphernalia, could well have kept a pack of hounds. The sport was attractive socially – it worked up an appetite, still left the gentlemen with enough energy to play cards, chat or even make love to the ladies after dinner, whereas hunting tended to produce an exhausted torpor not easily shrugged off without an early night's sleep. Worse, the elderly (and the old are often influential in these matters) were taking to it when age made hunting an effort and, worse still, their children were showing an unhealthy interest in this sedentary sporting alternative.

Friction arose in the rural communities as the two factions clashed. Foxes ate pheasants and cubhunting disturbed the birds' coverts. Landlords, although seldom going so far as to deny a hunt access to their holdings altogether, restricted the number of days across their land and often turned a blind eye to the activities of their keepers in destroying whatever vermin they perceived as a threat. High up on any keeper's list came the fox; often his very livelihood depended on its elimination. Foxes were trapped, poisoned and shot; their earths were stopped in daylight so that they starved to death underground. The hunts met this pernicious and growing threat with a mixture of diplomacy, social ostracism and hard cash. Good relations with shoot owners and keepers often produced an accommodation which both sides found workable. Attitudes against vulpicide hardened in some hunting countries to the extent that farmers would neither deal nor sit down with those they suspected of the offence, and keepers were paid to preserve litters in their coverts, often without the knowledge of their masters. Hunts found this an expensive exercise but it had a curious by-product in that where it was in operation, keepers replaced the paid earthstoppers which most hunts had employed to ensure that foxes lay out in gorse, woodland or kale after the night's feeding. So it was that the professional earthstopper had largely fallen out of fashion and it was the resulting lack of organization that Wallace and Parker were determined to put right.

The Rouse-Boughton view was that the earlier in the hunting year that hounds came, the better. The birds were let out of their pens in the mornings and collected again, using dogs, at night. When hounds were cubhunting, they spread the birds who thus learnt to fly and roost in areas not just immediately adjacent to the pheasant pens. The foxes, too, were disturbed, and those that were not caught learnt to run and not merely dodge about locally, avoiding the keeper. All this, the Rouse-Boughtons maintained, is mutually beneficial both to good foxhunting sport and to those who prefer to take on pheasants who can fly faster and higher than the 'slow and low' birds sadly favoured by modern commercial shoots. This wonderfully eclectic attitude was not unique but was decidedly unusual even in the 1940s when most shooting landlords preferred to leave their birds undisturbed until at least the beginning, if not the end of January. The careful management necessary to sustain both interests demands from landowners a committed involvement and from their keepers an open-minded tolerance.

The Rouse-Boughtons were prepared to go to endless trouble to ensure the best hunting possible by, for example, trimming the rides through their many wooded coverts so that the huntsman could get about unimpeded by the thick rhododendrons and sky-high brambles which would otherwise cause him to take a considerably roundabout route. It is said still of some of the coverts in the Ludlow that they are so thick that hounds, particularly young hounds, never see a fox in them at all.

For Ronnie, despite his own enthusiasm and determination to make things work, the helpfulness of the Ludlow landowners and farmers and the keeness of his team, that first full season was not at all easy. Not only were family and domestic matters weighty distractions, there was also the fact that he was still a serving soldier and bound to see to his paymaster's duties which, even though he was able to combine them with getting about the country, were still time consuming. Finally there were difficulties in finding suitable horses for himself, George Knight and Charles Parker and a lack of hunt transport, which meant that although the hounds would be taken to meets in an elderly van, Wallace and his staff had to hack, often starting out at 7.30 in the morning and not returning to kennels until well after 12 hours later. There hardly seemed to be enough hours in the day.

Cubhunting got underway on 25 August, the start having been delayed by a late harvest caused by a great deal of rain – a circumstance that the master bore with ill-concealed impatience, reinforced later by the fact that even after he was able to get under way there was little freedom of action for the first few weeks as the harvesters continued their labours. This relative inactivity allowed Ronnie to go to London for a couple of days to equip himself with hunting dress – an expedition that he found to be horrifyingly expensive, noting that – 'Although Locks now have some caps, they cost £4.'

By the day of the Opening Meet on Saturday, 3 November at the kennels, he had set aside his tribulations and was expressing himself well pleased with events:

This has been good cubbing; killing 6 brace in 23 mornings. There has been consistently good scent since mid-September and a most satisfactory show of foxes wherever we have been. The entry, with the exception of Lawyer who is not yet fit enough, have been hunting extremely well.

By today's standards those bald statistics are noteworthy only for the few days hunted and the small number of kills but given the slow start, the paucity of hunt horses and the frequency with which Ronnie had to perform his military duties, they constitute a most satisfactory beginning.

Ronnie's anxiety to show good sport at the Opening Meet was given added impetus by the excellent first day enjoyed by the Wheatland who had begun their season a day earlier with a field of around sixty. The Ludlow turnout, although to be consistently smaller, was perhaps more knowledgeable and certainly expected affairs to be arranged to their sporting satisfaction by the new management. Expectations were high and Ronnie was not to be found wanting. On a grand scenting day hounds began with a successful hunt of nearly two hours and, even in the much warmer afternoon, they managed to account for another fox after an hour's hard running. It was a pleasing day's entertainment for everyone.

Ronnie's close liaison with the farmers began to pay off in not only opening up bits of the country which had not been hunted for several years (shades of Eton), but also in financial terms when, after much encouragement from the master, a series of farmers' dances were held in town and village halls. Those more local to Ludlow were organized by Ronnie himself and often resulted in sums approaching £100 being available to swell the hunt funds.

For financial, as well as more esoteric reasons, Ronnie was also anxious to resurrect the Ludlow point-to-point (after all a hunt was hardly a hunt without such a meeting to round off the season). The principal difficulty was the lack of a suitable course. A government edict had been imposed to the effect that no damage to food production was to result from the holding of hunt races and this seemed to pose an insuperable problem until the Teme Valley, neighbours who straddled the Welsh border, offered their course at Brampton Brian, the home of Major Ralph Harley, the master.

Ronnie did not lack for support. There were many who were as keen as he to organize and take part in this essential adjunct to the English country scene. Numbered among them was a local celebrity, 73-year-old Charlie Edwards, a farmer from near Craven Arms who hit the newspaper headlines when he entered his horse

Elsich in the 1946 Grand National. That this, on the surface of it, unexceptional happening stirred up nationwide passions was due to the remarkable fact that Elsich had never won a race, nor indeed come closer than 400 yards to a winner except once, when he had finished third of three. Elsich's jockey for the big race was to be a wartime Lance Bombardier in the Royal Artillery, Wilf Balfe, whose experience closely matched that of his mount. Balfe had never ridden a winner and had been put up on Elsich only twice. He had one modest claim to success, however, being the only one of eight jockeys in thirteen starts to have completed a race on the unenthusiastic animal.

The appearance of Elsich in England's premier steeplechase so incensed a Newmarket blacksmith, Bob Todd, that he wrote to the sporting press ridiculing the horse's chances and chastizing Edwards for entering him. Edwards, who was not averse to a challenge, took a bet of £250 to £10 offered by Todd; not against Elsich winning or even being placed, but against horse and jockey finishing the course together. Sadly Edwards was the loser; they fell at the fourth and the Grand National qualifications were tightened up considerably as a result. Todd had made his point.

Charlie Edwards, who hunted regularly with the Ludlow, was eccentric in ways other than racing: on a hill overlooking the chimneys of Sefton Mount, his home, he erected a granite tombstone cut with an inscription of the usual details (less that of the date of his death), announcing to the world, via an eager *Daily Express* reporter, that he was going to be buried up there so that he could watch the smoke rise from the chimneys as had his father, mother, grandfather and grandmother before him.

Among all these excitements and peripheral activities, hunting continued twice a week on Wednesdays and Saturdays, with the occasional meet at the invitation of the Wheatland where Ronnie was keen to show his mettle to the much larger fields. The Wheatland even ran to a field master, then not as common a phenomenon among the smaller hunts as it is now. The Ludlow had no such refinement; all who hunted regularly knew the country as they knew the backs of their hands and indeed it was the huntsman who occasionally needed a word of advice on how best to keep up with his hounds – advice which was readily forthcoming and gratefully accepted.

The season finished with a children's meet organized by Eden (now a Lieutenant-Colonel and District Commissioner of the Pony Club) and it was pleasing both for Ronnie and his father that

Lindsay, aged fourteen and hunting regularly on his leaves-out
from Eton, was among the field. Ronnie summed up the year:

> Hounds were out for 77 days with one on foot (due to a hard
> frost in mid-January). Most of the farmers say it has been the
> best season in this country for many years. I don't think there
> have been many really outstanding days or hunts but there
> have been very few poor days either – five since the opening
> meet. Hounds and horses have done an incredible amount of
> work, both in number and length of days, and stood up to it
> very well; hounds do not look like the end of the season at all.
> Killed 17 brace.

A typically Wallace account – strong on both brevity and pertinent
evidence for the opinions he offers and short on fancy claims and
irrelevant detail. He had shown good sport to a knowing audience
who liked him both for the immense organizational effort he put in
to his first proper year of mastership and for the fact that he had
sprung from a local family. They were mightily intrigued by his
never-failing anticipation of the whereabouts of a hunted fox and
impressed by his quiet and absolute mastery of his hounds. They
were less excited perhaps by his horsemanship, becoming used to
seeing him hit the floor sometimes as many as three times a day,
but admiring his courage and his perseverance in picking himself
up and getting on with the job.

Wallace's relationship with the horse had always been, and
would remain, equivocal and it would appear reasonable to sup-
pose that had he not chosen hunting as a profession, he would never
have gone near one after childhood. The horse is, however, a
necessary tool of his trade, a vehicle on which to get about the
country as economically as possible so as to be up with his beloved
hounds. Not for him the pure love of riding hard across country for
its own sake nor the flowing of adrenalin when faced with obstacles
at the limit of the abilities of horse and rider – the hallmarks of those
who hunt to ride. To Ronnie, hedges, ditches, walls and the like
have to be taken as they come so as not to interrupt the free flow of
the chase and, most importantly, to give his subscribers – the
life-blood of any hunt – the enjoyment they both crave and deserve.
Even the most carping critic of his horsemanship would not claim
that he has ever been found craven in an attempt on any obstacle,
often jumping on a loose rein out of a trot.

In anticipation that the main business of the Ludlow would be
over for the season, the 1946 opening meet of the Hawkstone had
been planned for 20 April – now fixed, however, as the day of the

Ludlow point-to-point. This clash of dates provides an illustration of the difficulties of the conflict of interests between the two packs which Ronnie had to confront in the years ahead and which forced him to make up his mind in the matter of priorities. The decision was not a difficult one and although there was no hint at that time that otterhunting would eventually run into difficulties as modern farming methods polluted the rivers, foxhunting was already the clear winner. To Wallace, any matter to do with the sport, however peripheral, became as important and as inescapable as a military parade. The Ludlow point-to-point clearly fell into this category and the opening meet of the otterhounds was postponed until the following Monday. From then on Ronnie always saw to it that a deputy huntsman was available to the Hawkstone on the occasions that he felt he could not be with them – the first being the ever-willing Pip Stanier.

There were already many demands on Wallace's time. Spring and early summer saw point-to-points and puppy shows, with Valerie often riding at the former and Ronnie judging at the latter. In the autumn there was cubhunting to be started as hound exercise finished and as the otterhunting season reached its climax.

Valerie, who had started her racing career before the war, was now in some demand as a jockey. Owners came to her from far and wide and in her keenness she was perhaps not as choosy in accepting rides as she might have been. On one notable occasion watched by the whole Wallace family she was run away with to such a degree that Cecily, who liked and was always very kind to her daughter-in-law, shouted from a vantage point near a fence, 'Don't go so fast, you're miles in front.' The hapless jockey was quite unable to heed this well-meaning advice, it being all she could do to steer the animal at its fences, and eventually she fell off almost exhausted at the second-last. Recovering her breath and something of her strength, she remounted and was so far ahead that she was still able to win. But her troubles were not yet over, for having passed the post she was then carted a second time.

Life now fell into what most people would consider to be a satisfyingly fulfilling pattern. Ronnie had been demobbed from the army, had acquired a new wife who not only shared his passion for hunting but had interests of her own, and he had two satisfactory packs of hounds in challenging and well-run countries whose subscribers were both knowledgeable and agreeably supportive. What more could such a man want? His family and friends were soon to find out.

At the root of his mild dissatisfaction was the fact that the Ludlow was capable of hunting only two days a week. Despite the amalgamation, the country was quite restricted and thickly populated by shooting people, not all of whom were nearly as keen to share their land with the hunt as were the Rouse-Boughtons, and there was a shortage of affordable horse-power for the hunt staff. Ronnie was keen to do more hunting and for this he needed access to wider resources. In February 1947 he laid some proposals before the Ludlow Committee which, after some debate over the details, passed them unanimously. In essence it was decided that:

1. The Committee having heard Captain R. E. Wallace's proposal to hunt the Teme Valley Country (1947–48) as well as the Ludlow Country, agrees to his doing so, one day and two days in alternate weeks. The Committee agrees to the Teme Valley Hounds being kennelled in the Ludlow kennels at Caynham provided that the Teme Valley hounds are named during September in this year and each succeeding year whilst they are at Caynham; a list of the Teme Valley hounds to be sent to the Secretaries of the Ludlow and Teme Valley Hunt at the time.

2. The Ludlow Hunt Committee agrees to give Captain Wallace £400 for the season 1946–47 in addition to the £800 guaranteed. They agree to guarantee him £800 for the next (1947–48) season and to give him an additional £400 if the state of the Hunt Fund permits in the opinion of the Committee. Captain Wallace agrees to hunt the Ludlow Country two days a week. Captain Wallace also agrees that 25 couple of hounds, in addition to the Teme Valley and Hawkstone hounds, are to be the property of the Nominees of the Ludlow Hunt Committee in the following proportion:

Unentered hounds... 8 couples
1st season... 6 couples
2nd season.. 5 couples
3rd season... 3 couples
4th season or over.. 3 couples

Of the foregoing, seven couples to be doghounds and eighteen couples bitches.

3. Captain Wallace agrees that on giving up the mastership he will leave an equivalent number of hounds in the kennels as specified above, a representative of the nominees and the incoming master selecting the hounds.

This extract from the Hunt Committee Meeting proceedings on

11 February was later signed by all parties and reflects vividly the qualities of persuasiveness and diplomacy developed by the 27-year-old Wallace in the interests of getting his own way. He was now about to be master and huntsman of three packs simultaneously and, vitally, had increased his various guarantees.

He was also, by this time, a member of the Masters of Foxhounds Association which then shared premises with the British Field Sports Society in St James's Square and was chaired by the Duke of Beaufort. Ronnie was to have a close, continuing and influential relationship with the Association in the years to come but at that time, in common with most masters, he was content to leave its business to others, older and more experienced than he. He had been to its first meeting at the Cavalry Club after the war and had been welcomed by the Duke himself whose name was synonymous with foxhunting and who had already been master of the famous 'Blue and Buff' Beaufort Hunt at Badminton for over twenty years. The MFHA was concerned that the resurrection of hunting should be conducted along approved guidelines and members of the Association (that is all masters) were bound by its rules. A rise in anti-hunting feeling among those (mainly) on the Labour benches in Parliament had made it conscious of the need for both correct behaviour and for good, positive public relations. In October 1947 Ronnie was appalled to receive a letter from the chairman in which the Duke had written to all MFHs of an incident, reported in the *Oxford Times*, in which a fox marked to ground in a drain had been dug out, captured in a noose and presented to hounds while still alive. This was a direct flouting of the Association's rule that all such foxes were to be dispatched with a pistol before being broken up. The incident made a deep impression on Wallace of the need for hunting to keep its house in order and present a well-ordered and humane picture to a public largely ignorant of its methods but all too ready to believe tales, however ill-founded, of cruelty and barbarous behaviour.

Life for Ronnie and Valerie became very much harder when he started to hunt the Teme Valley. The sometimes long hacks to the Ludlow meets and back again at the end of a day were now supplemented by 60 mile drives in the old sheep lorry, which acted as a hound van and also carried Ronnie, Valerie, Hugh Arbuthnot (as first whipper-in) and Charles Parker to distant parts of the country once or twice a week. They would often not be home until getting on for midnight, having been given supper and quantities of potent elderberry wine by a sympathetic farmer on the way.

Usually they were wet, not just from the rain (although there seemed to be plenty of it that year) but from half-immersions in the Teme or some other river, which Ronnie had forded in hot pursuit of his hounds and their fox. There was little or no chance to enjoy the sort of social life led by others of what was still called the County Set. Both money and time were too short to provide for such niceties and Valerie in particular was always tired and often alone. The marital writing was again beginning to appear on the wall.

Even Ronnie was beginning to realize, through the mist of his boundless enthusiasm, that he had perhaps undertaken too much. The problems of time and distance were compounded by petrol rationing and by the fact that the unfortunate Ralph Harley had become one of the earliest victims of a collision between horse and motorcar (the latter driven by an over-enthusiastic hunt follower) and unable to give his joint-master the full support he had planned. Wallace was loath to dissolve his Ludlow-Teme Valley partnership so soon after setting it up but nevertheless began to think that, perhaps, it would be wise to make a clean break and move away. There was a natural successor available in Hugh Arbuthnot waiting only just off-stage and it was at this fortuitous moment that Bill Hicks Beach, who had been master of the ECH in 1925 and had taken an interest in the Wallace career since Eton days, let it be known that the Cotswold Hunt, of which he was vice-chairman, was looking for a new master who would also hunt hounds. Ronnie applied for the post in competition with Freeman Jackson the international event rider and was gratified indeed to be appointed for the 1948 season in preference to such an accomplished and well-known opponent.

His time at the Ludlow had been a success from both his own and the country's points of view. For Ronnie, it had provided a demanding school in which to learn his craft. For the Ludlow committee and subscribers the manner in which the threads had been picked up again after the war had been very satisfactory particularly as the reorganization and the administration had been in the hands of one they liked to look on as their own; and they had been happy in the knowledge that they had been shown as many a good day's sport as had been possible. He left then not with acrimony but with much goodwill, handing over to Arbuthnot who now knew the country well and was a popular choice with the farmers.

The Cotswold hunting country is roughly diamond-shaped, some 17 miles from north to south and 15 miles from east to west, with Cirencester a little south of the southern apex and Cheltenham at the most westerly corner. In 1948 there was a great deal of grass – and vast numbers of sheep. The scenting conditions were very different from the Ludlow, being essentially fleeting because of the light soil, so that hounds had to pick it up quickly to be successful. The country was open and, in the main, stone walls kept the boundaries of the fields so that getting about was relatively easy. There were many lovely wooded coverts which could be regularly relied upon to produce foxes which, Ronnie noted with astonishment during a visit, walked about openly as if they owned the place.

The Cotswold joint-mastership had been held for two years by the Misses Violet and May Wilson, twins who had hunted with the Cottesmore before the war. They were identical in face, form and dress, hunting side-saddle in flat chimney-pot hats, and had become something of a comic turn in the infinite pain they took to be inseparable and unidentifiable. They lived at the kennels, rarely leaving the house, except to hunt, and rumour had it that they would meet on the landing outside their bedrooms to compare their appearances to ensure that there was no distinguishing feature by which they could be told apart. A more indelicate story suggested that there was a way of telling the difference but that no-one had been brave enough to put the matter to the test. From the time that Ronnie was first appointed, the sisters did their best to discourage him: 'You won't like it, you know,' they twittered. 'They're all very deceitful down here, specially the Admiral and that 'Ocks Beach, he's worse.'

The Admiral was Frank Marten, a delightful man who had learnt his hunting with the Britannia Beagles at Dartmouth and was the Cotswold chairman. He had something of a running battle with the joint-masters for, quaint as they were, the Misses Wilson had not been a success in Gloucestershire – although they later went on to hunt the High Peak Harriers for seven years with some distinction. They had refused to hunt the Cotswold vale, then accounted the best of the country, causing a rift so serious that in 1947, the Cotswold Vale Farmers' Hunt was formed and they appear too to have been peculiarly unenthusiastic about killing foxes so that the total tally in their two seasons was five brace. Here then lay the reason why so many appeared unmolested and unconcerned: farmers and landowners alike, brought up to believe that vulpicide was an unacceptable solution to their problems, were desperate for a change in mastership.

In early summer Ronnie and Valerie moved into a farmhouse at the kennels at Andoversford and both George Knight and Charles Parker came too – moving in to the hunt staff quarters close-by. There were some 120 acres of land with the house, on which Ronnie planned to grow a little corn, leaving enough at grass on which to turn out the hunt horses. The Cotswold Committee was careful to warn him not to lose money in any farming enterprise, a caution of which Ronnie hardly needed to be reminded on a guarantee of less than £2,000 a year.

The Cotswold was peopled after the war by some endearing eccentrics – even by Gloucestershire standards. The Hunt Secretary, for example, was Colonel Lloyd-Harford who lived in great state in Cheltenham attended by uniformed maids as he dined every evening, alone or otherwise, in a black tie. It was also his practice to pay the hunt's bills in the town either by riding round to the tradesmen's premises on a horse or pedalling imperiously a machine he was pleased to call 'my velocipede'. He used to tell of the day when he was reproved by a past master for being in the wrong place, declaring to his berater, 'I'll have you know I'm not going to burst my bladder for the best fox in Gloucestershire.' He, and a number of others, were a great and encouraging help to the new young master who, it has to be remembered, had left home (and the constant and close support of his family) for, in effect, the first time.

Another local notable with whom Ronnie hit it off was Cecil Elwes who lived in some, but rather faded, style at Colesbourne Park in the south of the country. Cecil had long fallen out with the hunt hierarchy and discouraged hounds from crossing his land despite the fact that he used to have a pack of his own which, although officially confined to his estates, had often ranged over large tracts of the Cotswold, resulting in some spectacular rows. He drove a yellow Bentley, from the wireless aerial of which flew three foxes' brushes, and spent his now declining years in writing books about elk hunting in Finland, a subject on which he was a self-appointed (and unchallenged) expert.

As a huntsman Elwes had two distinct idiosyncracies. He refused to shoe any of his horses, instead keeping them in a corral in the park which, he reasoned, hardened their feet to such a degree that shoeing was wholly unnecessary. He tried hard to convert Ronnie to this way of stable management – without any noticeable success – as he did to his second pet theory that hounds should be bred like wolves; that is to say that the bitches should be free to mate with whoever in the pack took their individual fancy. This startlingly original approach to hound breeding proved successful in the short term and his pack was much admired by the cognoscenti, but it was never put to a more testing long term judgement. When he gave up hunting in dismay at what he considered to be the thoroughly restrictive practices of the Costwold and took his hounds to sell at Rugby Sales, they unluckily proved to have red mange.

Elwes's acquaintanceship with Ronnie was still embryonic when one of the famous brushes was lost and he asked that he should be presented with a replacement: 'After all, old boy, it would be a pity if I had to ask my keeper to shoot one.' Ronnie was happy to oblige and thereafter there was no problem about the Cotswold hunting over the estate, although Cecil was still determined to have the last word: 'Mind you, the rapprochement is entirely between you and me,' he said to Wallace. 'I'm having nothing to do with the riff-raff from the pump-houses of Cheltenham!'

The summer of 1948 was very busy. Not only was there a new country to get to know and people to meet, but an unknown pack of hounds had to be readied for the season. Ronnie still found time, however, to hunt the Hawkstone on over 50 days, with Pip Stanier being allowed only 10. He also found time to accept an invitation to judge at a show in Ireland, beginning a long relationship with that country, its hounds and its hunting people.

He had perceived, almost on arrival in Gloucestershire, a need to introduce a good deal of new blood into the Cotswold hounds and set about it with his usual energy. Ireland seemed to have the only drafts to spare so soon after the shortages of the war and from the Kilkenny, ruled over by the autocratic Major McCalmont who had been its master since 1921, came doghounds and from the Carlow a draft of bitches generously bought by Mrs Mary Mews, a keen supporter. The Cotswold pack, after some years of near dormancy as far as finding and killing foxes was concerned, was to be rejuvenated.

Cubhunting began on 21 August, hounds going out generally on Mondays, Tuesdays and Fridays to dovetail with the Hawk-stone which Ronnie usually hunted on the remaining days. By late September the Cotswold was out four times a week without any noticeable letting up of otterhunting, and the early starts necessary to effect the frequent duplication were invariably shared by Valerie and George Knight. Charles Parker, who had brought a horse with him from Shropshire, had begun to make a start on the mammoth earth-stopping exercise which was clearly necessary, indeed crucial, if there was to be the dramatic improvement in the quality of sport on which Ronnie had set his heart. Parker embarked on a two-year plan, carefully devised with the master as a result of their wide-ranging and frequent visits to the land-owners and farmers whilst exercising the hounds during the summer. In this neglected, under-hunted country they soon real-ized that they had underestimated the task – no sooner had one set of holes been stopped then others appeared. The project assumed some of the aspects of painting the Forth Bridge.

The opening meet was held at the Andoversford Hotel, the pack having already accounted for 26½ brace during cubhunting. A large, enthusiastic and, no doubt, curious field of around 150 turned out under the field-mastership of Raymond Barrow (a distant relative of Ronnie's through the Lindsay Hoggs) to inspect the new huntsman at work. As at the Ludlow they were not to be disappointed. On a beautiful sunny day with unpromising scent they were given several good hunts – the final run of the day lasting over an hour and a half.

At least one member of the field, though, was not easily impressed. Alan (Tubby) Martyr, late of the Royal Scots Greys and briefly master of the Cattistock before the war, had come from the nearby Vale of the White Horse Hunt where he now lived at Ablington to see what all the fuss was about. He was sceptical that anyone, however good, could effect a quick change for the better in so moribund a pack and was not inclined to be carried along on the wave of euphoria clearly infecting the majority of Cotswold subscribers. On his way home in the evening Martyr met a member of the Cotswold committee who asked him what sort of a day it had been. Martyr shrugged his shoulders and replied that as far as he could see nothing much had improved and doubted whether he would come again – a triumph of preconception over objectivity which in the event was short-lived. For come again he did, the following day, when he and Ronnie were the only two in on the kill at a hayrick. Huntsman and critic met head-on and thereafter became firm friends, so much so that Tubby often whipped-in for the Cotswold on the occasions when George Knight was unable to do so.

The year was an undoubted success. Hunting four days a week, except when interrupted as they were in early 1949 by frost, 62 brace of foxes were killed and as the word spread, large numbers of visitors were frequent. Ronnie's thorough sorting out of the hounds, his meticulous courting of the farmers and the new and sensible earth-stopping arrangements put in hand by the indefatigable Parker had paid handsome dividends. There were other successes too: at the Horse and Hound Ball in February 1949, the social highlight of the foxhunting year, Ronnie won the horn-blowing competition, beating Jimmy Delmege, his pre-war predecessor at the Ludlow, into second place.

On the day of the ball there had been a farmers' pro-field sports demonstration in London to protest against a bill being debated in the House of Commons that afternoon which sought to ban coursing, deerhunting and otterhunting. A number of the demonstrators were mounted and dressed in full hunting fig to the obvious astonishment of the urban onlookers. Among those on parade, but marching on his feet, was Charles Parker. The bill was defeated comfortably (214–101) but it was not to be the end of parliamentary attempts to impose bans of this nature and soon Ronnie was to be much involved in the politics.

As the Cotswold season finished, the Hawkstone round began again, to be briefly interrupted for a week in May (during which Hugh Arbuthnot hunted hounds) when Ronnie took his foxhounds to the Southdown in Sussex, where he and Valerie stayed with Arthur Dalgety, the master. This was hugely enjoyed by the Wallaces who were able to relive the familiar scenes of their youth – the Southdown country adjoined that of the Eridge with whom it was later amalgamated.

The Hawkstone continued to hunt regularly on two days a week, increasing to four during the three weeks spent on safari in South Wales. In addition to this heavy commitment, there were the Cotswold hounds to be got fit again after their month off, and puppy and other hound shows to be judged or attended. It was a schedule which, on top of the long days of the winter, would test the most dedicated and energetic of men, but to Ronnie it was the very meat and drink of life and he hardly noticed the pressure. The same was not true now of Valerie.

Valerie was game and she loved her husband but no longer could she take the pace. After the heart-breaking long days with the Ludlow and the Teme Valley she had thought that life in Gloucestershire would be a little easier and indeed perhaps it was in terms of time spent away from home. But there were still the long hours spent in holding horses while Ronnie and Charles Parker dug for a fox gone to ground or, worse, being made to sit on a hole while digging was going on elsewhere and being terrified of being bitten.

If there had been a little more money available to relieve some of the squalor in which they lived or with which they could pursue a more active social life, she might have found it bearable. As it was, on Ronnie's income and with little money of her own, they were forced to put up with living conditions hardly tolerable then and unthinkable by the standards of today. The farmhouse was in need of major repairs and redecoration, for neither of which was there money to spare, although Valerie was able to paint the kitchen in which they spent most of their few waking hours in the house. There were flag-stones everywhere, covered sparsely by a few rugs, and the guest-room, such as it was, had holes in the floor and was above the kitchen so that guests, of whom Vivian was the most frequent, at least knew what there was for breakfast! There seemed not to be time for much cooking and they lived mainly on shepherds pie supplemented by the occasional wild duck shot by a friend, and butter sent by Cecily. Next door to the farmhouse and very close, was the kennels' flesh house – an attractive gathering place for bluebottles which found their way into the kitchen larder and under the meat covers (no refrigerator), so that Valerie remembers always feeling sick. And then there was the loneliness, evening after evening, while Ronnie went about hunt business, and no comforts with which to soften this harsh and solitary existence. Perhaps the greatest deprivation of all, from Valerie's point of view, was that she very much wanted to have children, a wish resolutely opposed by Ronnie because of their penury and the resulting living conditions. Perhaps he was right, but that final straw had broken the camel's willing back and Valerie left Andoversford. At first it was a temporary separation, both of them believing that a break away from what to Valerie had become a dull grind, would recharge her batteries and enable her to come to terms with the hardships that both of them knew would not last for ever. But the very fact that neither of them could forecast how long they were to remain in this hand-to-mouth state and what then would replace it, eventually persuaded Valerie that she could take it no longer. By the end of 1949 she had left for good. Ronnie's two marriages had run similar courses and for very similar reasons.

Valerie remained a foxhunting lady and, as we shall see, eventually took on the mastership of the Heythrop from Ronnie in 1967. In 1952 she married Maurice Willes, a Gloucestershire landowner whom the Wallaces had met soon after their arrival at the Cotswold and whom she admired for his sense of humour and comfortable lifestyle. Willes had fallen in love with the attractive, fun-loving Valerie but they had not become involved (as the euphemism of the day had it) until after the separation. Valerie continued to be both a firm friend and admirer of Ronnie – a welcome change from his post-marital relationship with the Perkins' who, by unfortunate coincidence, also lived in Gloucestershire and through whose garden the Cotswold hounds sometimes ran – to Wallace's somewhat grim satisfaction.

Ronnie now threw himself into foxhunting with renewed vigour as if to prove to himself and to those inevitably interested observers of the human condition under stress, that domestic strife had not affected his appetite for sport. He took the hounds out at least four, sometimes five, days a week, weather permitting, hunting up until the end of April 1950. As the word spread that the Cotswold was now something special, yet more people flocked in from outside the country to share the fun. Even Monday meets were well attended, and on Saturdays there would be as many as two hundred followers, unprecedented for an essentially unfashionable pack which had acquired, at best, an unexciting reputation before Ronnie's arrival. The number of subscribers from within the country also swelled substantially so that hunt finances, never before better than shaky, took root and became almost prosperous.

George Knight, now getting on in years, also found the pace hard and was often not fit enough to hunt, placing an added workload on the master's shoulders – lightened a little by a willing Tubby Martyr. Charles Parker, too, rose to the occasion breaking new ground in earthstopping practices. For over a hundred years, following the example set by the 7th Duke of Beaufort, this essential facet of successful hunting had been the responsibility of the mastership who would issue instructions before each meet as to which would be stopped and when. Parker took on this work with serious and conscientious intent. Not only were there an enormous number of earths, largely uncharted, but a huge population of badgers and their setts, which had to be controlled in the interests of both sport and agriculture. Some were inviolate; badgers deep in the rocky ground of the Cotswold hills were inaccessible and anyway interfered minimally with the scheme of things, but there were large and intrusive colonies without traditional homes which constantly opened up foxes' earths and occupied the artificial drains, constructed usually out of stone and near to the surface of the ground to give a fox shelter in open country, driving the intended refugees away. These Parker called 'the extra badgers' and they, too, needed control. On his feet he roamed far and wide, stopping earths a day or so before a meet, and then getting up before daylight on a hunting day to check that they had not been reopened. He soon organized teams of farmers and other helpers to cover each bit of the country and took it on himself to send out cards to coordinate their activities, checking the work of his army frequently to see that they had carried out his instructions.

Despite this phenomenal keenness in the service of his friend and foxhunting god, Parker's first love was otterhunting which, he considered, raised the art of venery to the highest levels. In the summer of 1950 he again resumed his activities with the Hawkstone, helping Jack Stallard around the kennels, carrying a whip and digging out holts with his terriers when an otter went to ground. When otterhunting ceased in England and Wales in 1972, he began to spend his summers in Ireland, where there was no parallel shortage of otters, finding employment first as a gardener with Evan and Gill Williams. Evan Williams, whom Ronnie and Charles had first met in Limerick when taking the Hawkstone to Ireland, became master of the Tipperary in 1953 and was something of a folk hero among the Irish hunting and racing fraternity scoring a remarkable double by riding a Grand National winner in Royal Mail and training Supreme Court to win the King George VI Stakes at Ascot.

For Ronnie the summer of 1950 was a clear foretaste of things to come. His mastership of the Hawkstone and the calls made upon his time by invitations (always accepted) to judge at puppy shows were often in conflict and he was now forced to order his priorities even more formally than before. During his four years at the Cotswold he never missed a day that his hounds were able to hunt. The Hawkstone was a different matter; much as he loved otterhunting and his trips into Wales, he turned more and more to a deputy whose ability he respected. At this time it was Hugh Arbuthnot who had bought Whitton Paddocks and was thus well placed for the otterhounds in terms of both geography and expertise. In 1950 Wallace still managed sixty days (with Arbuthnot taking a further ten) as well as judging at the puppy shows of the Berkeley, the Old Berkshire (with the Duke of Beaufort) and the Crawley and Horsham, the first two in particular being prestige hunts and a mark of the growing respect with which those knowledgeable about hound breeding now held him.

At the end of the 1951 season Ronnie took the Cotswold to

Exmoor for four days, the first of many visits which he was to value more and more. There was a great deal of interest in this expedition and the *Horse and Hound* correspondent wrote enthusiastically:

> When Captain Wallace and his Cotswold pack met at Bluegate on April 17 there was a big field to meet him including visitors from all over Devon, with Masters of Hounds and their hunt servants making such an array of scarlet which I had not seen since 1939.

There follows a long list of notable west-country hunting people headed by Colonel Guy Jackson, the outstandingly well-regarded master of the Exmoor, who was then in the middle of a reign which was to last for fourteen years and who was to be an increasingly important influence on Wallace's career.

It is at best a partial truism that people make their own luck but at the Cotswold in the 1951–2 season the hunting was outstanding. Before Christmas, red-letter days followed each other as never before until, on Saturday 22 December, Ronnie was able to conclude his diary entry with the words: 'This day should be written in letters of gold.'

John Smith-Maxwell, the hunting correspondent of the *Field*, was there and in an article headed 'The Cotswold's Great Day' he wrote:

> Many packs of hounds have had their good days this season but I doubt – and I doubt very much – if any have had a better day than the Cotswold had after meeting at Marsden Manor.
>
> Finding in Rendcombe Deer Park, hounds went away and hunted slowly through Clifferdine and Iffcombe to Boy's Grove where scent failed. Hounds then returned to the Deer Park and put up a fresh fox at the far end in the exact spot that a brace had been found a fortnight previously; on that occasion hounds killed in the open after a good hunt and I cannot help feeling that this second fox was the one that, fourteen days before, had handed the responsibility to his less fortunate friend.
>
> Slipping through the Wilderness, the Cotswold bitches were into and over the Greenmeadow Valley in a flash and crossed the Whiteway to Chittle Grove where they checked for a moment before hitting off the line and hunting beautifully over Chedworth Manor Farm into the big wood. Forcing their fox through this stronghold, hounds crossed the railway at the Roman Villa and swung left-handed to re-cross the track. Then, running hard round Monkey Pen, they went

back over the Turnway with a fresh fox in front of them as well as the hunted one.

Hounds quickly killed the newcomer and the hunted one was halloa'd on close to Chedworth village. With all the hounds on bar five couple, which took somewhat longer to finish with their well-earned prize, the body of the pack was quickly away onto their original fox back to Chittle Grove.

At this point Colonel Alastair Gibb went on to the far end of the covert at the request of the Master, Ronnie Wallace, and was just in time to view the fox going away. Hounds ran on at racing pace by Ashwell to Calmsden Village to cross into Lord Bathurst's country. Swinging into the valley over the railway, they killed in the open below Foss Cross, after a hunt of one hour and fifteen minutes. Hounds had then covered 12 miles of good, bold hunting country, including two 4-mile points.

Since the days are still short it was necessary that no time should be lost in hacking on to the next draw back in Rendcombe Old Park, from which a fox was soon away above North Cerney. Hounds quickly hit off the line over the road and with a wonderful cry ran very fast pointing for Bagendon.

Hunting round the lower side of Moorwood, hounds continued to run very fast to Cotswold Park and on past Shewell Wood to Combend. Leaving Elkstone on the right, they crossed the main Gloucester road to Harcombe and at Syde they checked in a field tenanted by pigs.

The Field by this time was reduced to Colonel Gibb, Major and Mrs Fleming and about three more who were now obliged to give up due to lack of horsepower, leaving only the Master and Mr Dennis Perry who, luckily, had second horses.

Hitting off the line again, hounds continued to run hard from Syde to Stony Hill and Barnwood, crossing the Edgeworth and Bisley roads before going on to Througham Slad and Battlescombe where the Master and Mr Perry had sufficient time to get on terms and stop them in the pitch dark. This was a hunt of one hour and ten minutes, covering 14 miles as hounds ran, with a 7 mile point.

We can all remember wonderful hunts and good all-round days, but to have the ability to hunt hounds like this must be every foxhunter's ambition in the same way that the target of the steeplechase jockey is to ride the winner of the Grand National. Ronnie Wallace, as an amateur huntsman has had, like many others past and present, his full share of success but I cannot help thinking that this particular day will be entered in his hunting diary as one of the greatest in his career. To kill a brace of foxes in a hunt of one hour and quarter, covering 12 miles including two 4-mile points and to follow this with another, nearly as long in time over 14 miles of country with a 7-mile point only to be defeated in the dark, would seem hard to beat.

The fitness of the hounds reflects great credit, not only on the master, but on his first whipper-in, George Knight, who would appear to be an expert in this direction. To produce a pack of hounds looking well at the beginning of the season is difficult, but to keep them fit, keen, controlled and at concert pitch throughout a hard and open season is another matter.

Smith-Maxwell was right; the day will live for ever in the Wallace memory.

Among those two or three followers who had to give up because their horses were too tired to continue was Peggy Miller-Mundy, a lady who although living near Andover, did most of her hunting with the Duke of Beaufort's. She had been a friend of Ronnie's since the time they had met when he was at the Ludlow and that friendship was now gathering pace. It was to culminate in his third marriage.

Ronnie's spectacular success at the Cotswold had sharpened his appetite for further challenges. He regretted much the loss of the Vale and had he been able to hunt it the chances are that he may not have wanted a move, at least for a few more years. As it was he felt that he had outgrown the country and its stone walls and he yearned for the mastership of a really top pack which would test both his hunting ability and his growing knowledge of breeding. He cast his eyes at Leicestershire, thinking that should a vacancy occur he would apply. Fate, however, took a hand much closer to home.

Now that his time at the Cotswold was drawing to a close he was able to reflect on those who had first brought him there and on those who had now become influential in his life. He owed much, he felt, to Admiral Frank Marten who had died in office and been followed as chairman of the hunt committee by Bill Hicks Beach. Marten, a fine horseman who had tried hard to reunite his country with its lost Vale, had shown much faith in Ronnie and was gratified by his success. Hicks Beach, although occupied greatly with being the Conservative MP for Cheltenham, was keen and active in the field, hunting most Saturdays after his constituency surgery in the town, usually arriving late dressed in 'rat-catcher' order and having to endure the good-natured taunts of Philips

Price, the Labour MP for the Forest of Dean, whose expansive land-owning figure was always immaculately attired in scarlet coat and top-hat. Marten, Hicks Beach and the latter's successor as vice-chairman, Colonel Alastair Gibb, had been assiduous in making sure that Ronnie met the important and useful people in the country and the adjacent foxhunting worlds which would become an essential part of his social and professional grounding.

Gibb lived at Cotswold Park and was head of a leading company of consultant engineers. He had commanded the Wiltshire Yeomanry in the Western Desert in the same Brigade as both Sir Peter Farquhar, who had the 3rd Hussars, and Guy Jackson of the Warwickshire Yeomanry, who was now master of the Exmoor. All three were to be appreciable influences in Wallace's life. Farquhar was the highly respected master of the Portman Foxhounds and a leading authority on hound breeding. Although considerably older than Ronnie, he became perhaps his closest friend and certainly his most trusted guide and mentor.

Peter Farquhar was also close to the 10th Duke of Beaufort, the almost legendary 'Master', who as chairman of the MFHA and master of his own pack since 1924, was the unrivalled leader of the hunting establishment. Through Farquhar, Ronnie came to know 'Master' well and as often as time permitted he would have a day with the Beaufort in order to watch the great man at work. He was unfailingly impressed by the control the Duke exercised over his hounds and the single-minded fashion with which they hunted their chosen fox.

'Master', Peter Farquhar, and Guy Jackson all played prominent parts in educating Wallace the ever eager pupil and were joined in this during his time at the Cotswold by other leading figures of the day: Chatty Hilton-Green at the Old Berks (who had made his name at the Cottesmore before the war), Bill Scott at the West Waterford, with whom Ronnie and Valerie had spent part of their honeymoon and who came to live in Gloucestershire in 1949 and Maurice Kingscote at the Meynell.

There were professional huntsmen too who contributed to the learning process: Albert Buckle of the North Cotswold, George Gillson from the Warwickshire and Percy Durno at the Heythrop, as well as the vastly experienced George Knight. All had become friends of the young master of the Cotswold and all had helped to round off the Wallace apprenticeship to bring him, at the age of 32, to the brink of one of the greatest masterships in the history of foxhunting.

TOP LEFT 1929. The Bobbery Pack. In the background: brother Vivian; in the basket: Jon Trouton.   *TOP RIGHT* Eastbourne; September 1920 with his mother, Cecily. She wrote: "At 14 months he walked nine steps alone but he is a slow learner."   *CENTRE* 1926. The opening meet at Eridge Castle. From the left: Lord Ralph Nevill (in tweeds): Lady Camden: Lord Henry Nevill (later Marquess of Abergavenny): Eden Wallace.   *BOTTOM* The Eridge Hunt moves off circa 1930. On far right is Eden Wallace. To right of centre wearing a bowler hat is REW aged 11.

TOP The Eton College Hunt at Easy Bridge. The master (second from the left) is clearly laying down the law.
BOTTOM The Eton College Hunt arriving at the Burning Bush. The "Invisible Thread" is already apparent.

TOP The Eton boathouse lorry decants its load. On the right is Bill Perkins: on the left Mr. Hatch the window cleaner and a devoted follower.

BOTTOM The Christ Church Beagles at Horspath in 1939, led by a terrier. Walter Clinkard brings up the rear.

TOP The Hawkstone Otterhounds have just found in the River Arrow. The Master has shed his coat before the serious work begins.
CENTRE The Hawkstone Otterhounds checked on the rocks in Glanusk Park.
BOTTOM The Hawkstone Otterhounds at Pontrilas. Jack Stallard leads the way.

TOP The Hawkstone pose before moving off in 1946. Pip Stainer is centre, standing on the steps: George Knight on far right.
CENTRE RIGHT The opening meet of the Wheatland at Bridgenorth in 1946. The master, Miss Frances Pitt, became a member of the Scott Henderson enquiry into hunting set up by the post-war Labour Government. The Wheatland huntsman, George Dumble, is on the right.   *CENTRE LEFT* Jean Wallace and her son David, born in 1944.   *BOTTOM* Summer 1946. Marriage to Valerie, flanked by his brothers, Vivian (then a Captain in the Welsh Guards) and Lindsay.

TOP Public Relations. The Ludlow Foxhounds outside the cinema in Worcester on a Saturday morning, in 1947. George Knight is on the right and next to him is REW's successor at the Ludlow, Sir Hugh Arbuthnot.

CENTRE Winning the horn blowing contest at the Huntsman's Ball in the Grosvenor House Hotel in aid of the Horse and Pony Benefit Fund, January 1947.

BOTTOM The master of the Ludlow at Oaker Wood in 1946. Major General Victor Wakely, MFH of the Teme Valley in 1946-47 is on the right.

TOP Boxing Day meet of the Cotswold in 1948 in Cheltenham. The huge crowd lined the roads for three miles as the hunt moved off.
CENTRE LEFT Boxing Day 1948. The master of the Cotswold and His Worship, the Mayor of Cheltenham, drink a toast. It is evident which of the pair is enjoying the occasion the more.
CENTRE RIGHT The Cotswold with Mrs. Mary Mews, of whom it was once complained: "She's always filling my shoes with champagne!"   *BOTTOM* Valerie at the Cotswold.

TOP The opening meet of the Cotswold move off from the kennels at Andoversford in November 1951. George Knight (in the middle of the road) follows the pack. *BOTTOM* The end of the Cotswold years. The master surveys his field at the children's meet at Rossley Manor, January 1952.

TOP LEFT Percy Durno, huntsman and kennel huntsman at the Heythrop from 1937 to 1963. It was the Duke of Beaufort who first persuaded Percy to wear spectacles, having noticed him unable to read the programme at a Peterborough Show. From then on he was never without them. *TOP RIGHT* The Heythrop hounds arriving at Bourton-on-the-Water. Percy Durno encourages a stray. The master is amused. *BOTTOM* The "Invisible Thread". Heythrop hounds at Asthall Leigh.

TOP LEFT Some Heythrop notables. From left: Raymond Barrow: Darby Haddon: John Mackinnon: Simon Loder.   *TOP RIGHT* More public relations. Heythrop hounds at the USAF Base, Brize Norton in 1960.   *BOTTOM* Champion of Champions, Peterborough Show 1965. Heythrop Cardinal (on left, closely inspecting the Moor). From left to right: Bill Lander: Hugh Robards: Steve Roberts (Fitzwilliam): Clarence Webster (Warwickshire): Tom Bailey: name unknown: Percy Durno: REW: Pam McKinnon.

TOP Announcing the results at a Heythrop puppy show. Bill Lander on the left: Heythrop Wiseman on the extreme right.

RIGHT Rosie Wallace and her son David.

BOTTOM Cubhunting at the Heythrop. The master is accompanied by the ever present and legendary Charles Parker.

TOP Rosie and David Wallace ask the way from Lord Rotherwick.

CENTRE The master and huntsman of the Hawkstone up to his waist in murky waters.

BOTTOM The Heythrop meet at Spillars Farm, Middle Aston. Mounted from Left: Bill Lander; REW; Anthony Taylor; The Marquess of Blandford; Rosie Wallace, equipped for gate-shutting.

TOP Boxing Day at Chipping Norton. Mounted are the master, Anthony Adams (back to camera) and David Wallace.
BOTTOM A Serious Foxhunter. David Wallace.

TOP LEFT Fuelling gossip at the Heythrop. REW with a new blonde.   *TOP RIGHT* ''My God, that was a good day.'' On holiday with th
Eskdale and Ennerdale fell hounds.
BOTTOM March 1977. The Heythrop move off for the last time under Ronnie Wallace. Lavinia Jenkinson is wearing the bowler ha
immediately behind hounds. Tony Collins on the right.

TOP LEFT Keeping goal, at the age of 65, for the Exmoor Foxhounds football team against the Devon and Somerset Staghounds XI at Exford. *TOP RIGHT* "Well done, you are good girls!" The Exmoor Bitches. *CENTRE LEFT* Dressed for judging in Virginia, USA, 1988. *CENTRE RIGHT* Taking a break from judging in London, Ontario, Canada in 1988 with Martin Wood III, the President of the MFHA of North America. *BOTTOM* Exmoor.

A good sign – not a hound in sight.

CHAPTER 6

The Heythrop Hunt

SO much in modern foxhunting stems from Badminton and the Beaufort family that it comes as little surprise that the Heythrop Hunt was the creation of Henry, the fifth Duke, in about 1770. At the time that he succeeded to the title after a long minority he seems to have decided that the fox was now a quarry more deserving of the vast resources of the stables and kennels at Badminton than either the hare or the stag and to mark this decidedly non-Beaufort departure he presented his chaplain with the pad of the first fox killed by his hounds. So pleased was the Reverend Doctor Penny with this manifestation of ducal esteem that he hung it on his bell-rope in the estate church.

Henry formed a second complete pack of hounds made up from those available at home and set up an establishment first at Cornbury and then at Heythrop itself from where he began to hunt, alternately with that at Badminton, what soon became known as the 'Oxfordshire Country' of the Duke of Beaufort's. In 1803, the 6th Duke, Henry Charles, engaged Philip Payne from the Cheshire to hunt his hounds and the latter carried the horn for 23 years until handing over to William Long, the son of the stud groom at Badminton who had served an eighteen year apprenticeship as second then first whipper-in to Payne.

Foxhunting two hundred years ago was a far more serious business than now and those engaged in it had fewer distractions. It was not uncommon to be mounted on the same horse, from dawn until well after dusk. Vast distances were covered and accounts of their lives left by both Payne and Long often note, with considerable understatement, that horses were 'dead beat'. Sometimes this appeared to be the literal truth. It was normal to kill only one fox a day, but that after a hunt of ten, eleven or more miles, having drawn a covert for what now would seem to be an interminable length of time. Long records a memorable visit by the great Squire Osbaldeston from the Quorn (of whose hounds the

Beaufort huntsman had no high opinion – 'pretty, small and not particularly clever'):

> Mr Osbaldeston hunted with us. The meet was at Bourton Bridge; we had a very hard day and he tired his nag. He was mounted by Mr Evans of Dean and it was the first time I saw him. William Grace of Charlbury rode very foul at the hounds at a fence and had it not been for Mr Osbaldeston he would have ridden over them. I think he richly deserved what Mr Osbaldeston talked of giving him which was a flogging.

Visiting masters, or even those on their home ground, are rarely quite so fierce today although there are those who recollect that, during the Wallace years at the Heythrop, there were incidents which led to retribution every bit as agonizing, if not quite so physical, as that threatened to the unfortunate Mr Grace.

Will Long was a remarkable diarist of the contemporary scene, given his almost total lack of formal education and the fact that his days were fuller and longer than any in all but the wildest of modern nightmares. He was often required to ride the 50 miles from Heythrop to Badminton after a day's hunting, attend to duties there and then return to Oxfordshire the next morning to take his hounds out again at ten o'clock.

His writing covers many incidents arising out of the Luddite agitations following the Reform Bill of 1832 when the Duke of Beaufort, as Lord-Lieutenant of Gloucestershire and High Steward of Bristol, was prominent among those called upon to enforce the law. A number of rioters were hanged as the Heythrop and the adjacent countries, in common with the rest of the Kingdom, witnessed scenes of arson and the breaking-up of hay-making and other modern machinery. In 1831, Heythrop House itself went up in flames and although Long never attributes the cause of the fire to Luddites, popular received wisdom of the day had it that it was the work of those who bore a grudge against the master of foxhounds. The house was gutted and not rebuilt until Albert Brassey took possession in the 1870s. The Duke moved his kennels elsewhere and hunted for four more years before, on 25 April 1835, he announced his intention of abandoning his Oxfordshire Country and retiring to Badminton. The last service he rendered to the Heythrop Hunt before he died in November of the same year was to sell his successors some 30 couple of hounds cheaply. Thus it was that the Heythrop, as a completely separate entity, came into being in the care of a committee of resident landowners led by

Lord Redesdale of Batsford Park at Moreton-in-Marsh.

It also became a subscription pack, that is one whose members contributed to the hunt's expenses. In 1810 there had been only twenty such packs but by this time, there were twice that number and more. Soon they were to become, as today, the norm. Gentlemen taking a country without subscription were a dying breed although Sir Richard Sutton at the Quorn from 1847–56 swam against the tide and cancelled subscriptions so that he could hunt without interference from members inclined to disagree with his methods. Perhaps the greatest exponent of benevolent despotism was Squire Farquharson in Dorset who single-handedly hunted the country now occupied by the Blackmore Vale, Cattistock, South Dorset and Portman hunts. There were distinct disadvantages attached to subjecting oneself to propriety masters of this kind – they were wont to turn up late (sometimes not at all) and often inclined to indulge other personal whims. The more independent followers developed a preference for subscription packs where they felt they could pay their way without further debt to the master other than the gratitude due to a successful exponent.

The first few years of the Heythrop regime were turbulent in the extreme as master after master resigned either due to personal misfortune or to the uncertain state of the hunt's finances – usually the latter. The budget caused constant anxiety, so much so that in late 1841 the committee came to the conclusion that 'the hounds must be given up immediately unless further means can be provided'. Modern masterships will have no difficulty in recognizing these circumstances and they have echoed through the hunting world regularly in the intervening years; *plus ça change*. . . .

The situation was saved by Lord Redesdale. It is a truism indeed that if something has to be done efficiently and with a purpose then it is as well to go to a busy man. Lord Redesdale was certainly that: his estate, his business interests and his political career (the Duke of Wellington had appointed him a whip in the House of Lords) all made great demands on his time. But he was a passionate fox-hunter and brought a much needed firmness and common-sense to Heythrop affairs, which he had, until 1841, largely entrusted to the other members of his committee. He took office with a guarantee of £1500 and stipulated that the books were to be balanced. When, as was the case with sad regularity over his twelve seasons of mastership, the accounts assumed a lop-sided appearance, he would threaten to resign and remove his own not inconsiderable personal contribution. The members having been apprised in robust language of the 'imminent danger of his Lordship's resignation' assured him of their 'perfect satisfaction with the liberal and efficient way in which he hunted the country' and braced themselves manfully for a further lightening of their pockets.

Lord Redesdale's committee had appointed Jem Hills to hunt the hounds when Will Long retreated to Badminton with his master. Hills had served his apprenticeship with the Beaufort and had then gone to the Vale of the White Horse as first whipper-in. He was to prove a huntsman of exceptional ability with an almost magical intuition of the line a hunted fox would take – a quality which many have ascribed since to Ronnie Wallace. A well documented incident records how his hounds had run a pregnant vixen round and round for over an hour until Hills, bored with repetition, stationed himself in a ditch to head her. Perhaps recognizing a true friend in need, the fox jumped into his arms and he took her back to the kennels on the pommel of his saddle where she delivered six healthy cubs.

Lord Redesdale resigned the mastership in 1853 when pressure of business in the House of Lords precluded him from giving the Heythrop the attention he felt it deserved. He settled a subscription of £400 a year on his successors and the generosity of 'The Lord Dictator', as he had fondly become known, also extended to presenting the hunt with a stable full of horses and the use of his hounds.

For the next twenty years the Heythrop fell back into its precarious financial ways whilst continuing, under its professional huntsmen, to show the sort of sport that its gentlemen (and the occasional lady) expected. Jem Hills retired and was briefly succeeded by his son and then by the popular Stephen Goodall. It was at this time that the Heythrop made its one and only foray, until the advent of Wallace, into allowing an amateur to hunt hounds when Mr A. W. Hall, the sole master from 1864 to 1872, hunted the bitch pack for two days a week. This experiment ended in 1873 as the hunt entered the first of its two golden ages with the appearance of Albert Brassey.

The Brasseys had made their money out of building railways, not an occupation which readily commended itself to a keen foxhunter of the nineteenth century. It was not so much the physical presence of the railways which bothered the sporting fraternity – canals probably caused more practical difficulties as obstacles to crossing a country – but the fact that they provided increased accessibility to the countryside. Coupled with the other regrettable manifestations of the industrial revolution, notably the growth of the large manufacturing cities, the railways, it was gloomily predicted, would surely spell the end of the self-sufficient rural communities by bringing in dangerous outside influences and changing aspirations.

The more pernicious manifestations of industrialization happily passed the Heythrop by. There was no urban sprawl within easy distance and even the railways themselves were few in the rolling Cotswold hills. The Duke of Beaufort, fifty miles away in his fiefdom, had countered the threat of having his estate bisected by the London to Bristol line by refusing permission to the builders of the Great Western Railway to traverse his land except by tunnelling underneath it, coming up for air at his private station at Badminton where trains were stopped when the ducal whim deemed it necessary.

Albert Brassey, the founder of the 'Brassey faction' which was opposed to Wallace taking on the mastership nearly eighty years later, was a success in every sense and aspect of that word. He was both immensely rich and remarkably generous. He bought the hounds from Lord Redesdale, in whose nominal ownership they had remained, and accepted office with a guarantee of £1500 a year – a sum which remained unchanged until the end of his regime 35 years later – and he paid all the additional expenses himself at a time when it was calculated that it cost £1000 for every day in the week that hounds hunted. He was devoted to the sport. He was capable and energetic and kind and genial to a fault. He was lucky too: all the social conditions were favourable to hunting – income tax was negligible, death duties unknown; farmers were prosperous and even the agricultural recession which begun in 1879 took many years to be felt in the Heythrop.

The country was still one of large estates. At Blenheim and Sarsden, Glympton and Great Tew, Cornbury, Eynsham, Swinbrook, Farmington, Batsford and at Heythrop itself (where the house was being rebuilt by Albert's father as a wedding present to his son), the great manors were maintained to the highest of standards. The farms and coverts were looked after with the interests of foxhunting in mind by still flourishing tenants and friendly game-keepers who knew on which side their bread could be more thickly buttered. Wire, although starting to put in an appearance in 1860, with the barbed variety following some twenty years later, was strangely absent from the compliant farms of Heythropia: the Hunt did not find it necessary to start a wire fund until 1913.

Brassey and Goodall, however, did not hit it off. The huntsman was of a wild and dashing, not to say an extremely gregarious, disposition and sometimes kept his boots on for three or four days at a time, seeing no reason to remove them in such an hospitable country. He was a courageous horseman who tried his master's patience more than once by jumping the expensive horses with which he was provided over both the railway level crossing gates at Chipping Norton. That he was popular in the country was not in doubt – the generous master and subscribers providing him with a handsome annuity when he was retired within two years, but the clash of temperaments was too marked for them to be able to work together.

His successor was the more sober and pliable Arthur 'Jack' Hazleton, a steady man much more suited to Brassey's ways, who lasted 15 years being himself succeeded by Richard Stovin, Alfred Watson and then Charles Sturman (from 1901 to 1922) whom some still remember as having no equal in his time.

Ronnie Wallace, by virtue of his age, never hunted with Sturman but either unconsciously or knowingly, from stories he had heard, he came to model his performance in the field on this ex-Whaddon Chase professional. Existing descriptions of Sturman's technique at the Heythrop could have been written about Wallace, taking into account the differing constraints of an amateur's and a professional's lifestyle. Charles Sturman was a quick thinker with marvellous powers of observation and an unusually retentive memory. He lived for his hounds and never left the kennels except to hunt and although clearly he could, like Wallace, have been a success in a more intellectually demanding profession, it was in hunting that he developed his natural talents. His use of the horn, although sparing, was an art form; his hounds had unbounded confidence in him and were as one in the field. He could pick them up and lift them and they would hunt again as he dropped his hand. He always pressed forward hard after his fox and used his whippers-in, as Wallace does, as intelligence agents and not as 'dog wallopers' engaged only in helping control the pack.

Wallace, too, has many of the qualities displayed by Albert Brassey during the latter's mastership. Brassey was as methodical as he was energetic and exercised a benevolent despotism over his country. Both laid down a system, a method and routine which ensured the maximum of satisfaction and the minimum of discord.

But in two essential facets of their masterships there were distinct differences. Brassey was content with the agreeable domesticity of his Heythropian kingdom. He sat in Parliament for eleven years but otherwise played little part in the national arena of public life. Wallace, on the other hand, was quick to enter into politics albeit with a low, almost concealed, profile when the well-being of hunting was in any way at stake. Perhaps more starkly, Albert Brassey was a man who spread his abilities and administrative talents widely in his local community: he was a member of the County Council, served a term as High Sheriff and as Mayor of Chipping Norton, was a JP, a force in the Territorial Army and a notable breeder of Oxford Down sheep as well as being a member of the Coaching Club, the Four-in-Hand Club and the Royal Yacht Squadron. His resources were, of course, vastly in excess of Ronnie's but the fact is that whereas both entered into life with a whole heart, Wallace channelled his energy and talents into only one field, rotated round only one sun, worshipped only one secular god. The Wallace impact on the Heythrop and, more importantly, on foxhunting in general was to be all the greater for that single-mindedness.

Albert Brassey had three sons, five daughters and five sons-in-law, most of whom and their children and grandchildren followed him into the hunting field. One of the sons-in-law, Captain (later Major) Denis Daly became his field-master in 1898 and when the old man died peacefully in 1918, having steered his beloved Heythrop through the rigours of the war, his one surviving son, Robert Brassey, took over the mastership. Robert left his home in Northamptonshire and came to live at Heythrop and Denis Daly soon joined him as hunt secretary. The brothers-in-law and Charles Sturman set about reviving the fortunes of a pack sadly depleted by the war with the help of a healthy bequest from the far-seeing Lord Redesdale who had, in his will, set aside securities for this very eventuality and which proved a financial god-send in a time of severe scarcity of good hounds and thoroughbred horses. But Brassey fortunes were on the wane: death duties and the need to provide for so many children had taken their toll and in 1921 Robert found it necessary both to sell the Heythrop estate and resign the mastership. Sturman retired in the next year after 21 years as huntsman and his place was taken by Jack Lawrence, also from the Whaddon Chase.

So, temporarily, the Heythrop passed out of the hands of the Brassey family until, in 1925, Edwin Brassey, a nephew of Albert, took on a joint-mastership with Daly. Times had changed however and hunting could no longer be considered the effortless recreation enjoyed during the golden age of the paternal Albert. It now became a serious business, success in which entailed considerable organization and administration to combat costs which had escalated alarmingly with the general increase in wages and prices. The guarantee, although now at £4000, hardly began to meet the true price of mastership and various economies had already been introduced, including the end of the unique, but expensive, plush coat worn by hunt servants. The wearers of that singularly inappropriate material were, perhaps, the only wholehearted approvers of this sartorial change – plush is a great retainer of water and at the end of a day in the rain a coat could weigh in at up to four stones – although the green colour of the livery was retained to continue the link with the Beaufort family.

There were changes in the country, too. Estates were broken up – notably those at Heythrop and Sarsden plumb in the centre – and sizeable bits of Blenheim, Sezincote, Ditchley, Batsford and Sherborne were sold off either to speculators or to tenant farmers. The former were not, as a rule, influenced in any way by the requirements of foxhunting and the latter soon discovered that it was one thing to be protected from the financial ravages of damage by a hunting landlord and quite another to maintain hedges, walls, fences, ditches and gates at their own expense, especially in a time of falling crop prices. Wire made a significant appearance as a cheap way of closing gaps and farmers' wives turned to poultry farming as a way of increasing the family income – thus incurring heavier liabilities for the hunt poultry fund.

At about this time, too, the delights of living in the Cotswolds were being discovered by city-dwellers who started to turn farm-houses and cottages into either commuter residences within acceptable motoring distance of London, Birmingham, Oxford and Gloucester or into hunting boxes. This certainly had the effect of swelling the hunt subscription list, not an altogether undesirable by-product in a relatively poor scenting country, but few of the newcomers were landowners and had neither stake nor influence in the country. This was to be a continuing problem and one which Ronnie was to tackle, some 25 years later, with both energy and a certain amount of guile.

Daly and Brassey continued their partnership until 1934 when Daly's health failed, thus ending some thirty years of unbroken service to the Hunt. Edwin Brassey was then joined by Lord Ashton of Hyde, a knowledgeable breeder of hounds along 'English' lines whom Ronnie later met in the RGH during the war. Ashton was the sole master from 1936 to 1948 and in 1937 was responsible for employing Percy Durno as huntsman, an astute move as there can be few in any walk of life who were as universally loved and respected by all who came in contact with him as that twinkly little Yorkshireman. Loyal to a fault and untiring in both the hunting field and the kennels, Durno and Lady Ashton carried the Heythrop through the difficult war years during which he was, luckily for the hunt, prevented from doing military service by a physical disability. A neat horseman from a hunting family, both his sons were to enter hunt service, Joe being tragically killed in a road accident shortly after joining the Warwickshire and Bruce who became the Fernie huntsman in 1965.

In 1951 Lord Ashton announced his intention to retire and it was this move that precipitated the crisis that was to bring Ronnie Wallace across the border to the Heythrop as an alternative to a possible move to Leicestershire which he had been contemplating as he outgrew the Cotswold. That the opportunity to move to the Shires had not yet arisen was probably fortunate for the Heythrop because although he recognized that a hard riding country, such as the Quorn or the Belvoir (where he might have been frustrated as Meynell had been by the thrusters who yearned only to cross the country at breakneck speed), was not best suited to his talents he may not have been able to resist the challenge of the Cottesmore.

In 1948 Ashton had been joined by Colonel Humphrey Lloyd, a connection of the Brassey family by marriage and when the former finally retired four years later, the so-called 'Brassey faction' was anxious to preserve and reinforce the family tradition by persuading Mrs Pamela Mackinnon, Edwin Brassey's daughter, to join Lloyd who was her brother-in-law, in the mastership with Percy Durno continuing to hunt the hounds.

Others thought differently. Major W. E. (Ted) Lyon, the editor of the *Horseman's Year Book*, and an ex-master of the Atherstone as well as a previous field-master of the Heythrop organized a pro-Wallace lobby which envisaged a joint-mastership: Ronnie hunting hounds with Raymond Barrow as field-master. The Heythrop Committee having argued the matter for the whole of the summer (during which Wallace, as usual, busied himself with the Hawkstone) presented a united front by August 1951. Not so the country at large.

There were a number of factors over which fierce differences emerged. There were, as we have seen, those who wished to preserve the Brassey tie, almost at all costs. Then there were many who worried over the position of Percy Durno – he had hunted hounds more than satisfactorily for fourteen years and it might appear to be a pretty poor reward, not to say an abrogation of loyalty, to ask him now at the age of only 49, to step down and accept the relatively lowly position of kennel-huntsman. Thirdly there were those traditionalists who saw no reason to abandon the Heythrop habit, tried and in their view not found wanting, of always having a professional huntsman. And then there were the moralists who, while recognizing the startling success at the Costwold and anxious to transfer it to the Heythrop, were not ready to accept what they regarded as Ronnie's rather unsatisfactory marital arrangements – or lack of them. Lastly there were the straw clutchers who just did not like the man and who fell back on an innuendo that 'he had a bad war'.

The committee, finding none of these objections to be valid and discerning that the opposition was anything but united, called a General Meeting to decide the matter in good time for the 1952 season (the hunting year for purposes of employing of masters and staff runs from 1 May). The tense atmosphere rapidly became heated and then acrimonious as the various views were aired in downright opposition to, or variations from, the committee's recommendation. The latter, in the face of this vocal, but divided hostility, remained firm and when the vote was taken Barrow and Wallace got home with a comfortable majority which, however, was far from overwhelming.

Ronnie was in Ireland, staying with Lord Daresbury, then at the beginning of his thirty year mastership of the Limerick, and Barrow telephoned him with the news and with an account of the meeting. Daresbury, taking the view that a less than unanimous vote was insulting to his guest, advised Wallace to turn down the Heythrop's invitation but Ronnie was not of a mind to quibble or stand on his dignity. He accepted the decision (as he would have done if the majority had been just one) and sailed for England.

CHAPTER 7

The New Broom

THE Heythrop country – sometimes known as Heythropia – is a mixture of bare wild uplands and green wooded valleys through which run the rivers Evenlode and Windrush and their tributary brooks. The land rises gradually from the upper Thames valley, north of Oxford, to the Cotswold Hills. Much of it is above five hundred feet where the soil is light and lies on the oolitic limestone which has for centuries provided the distinctively mellow building material known as Cotswold stone. In the little vales, dotted about with small woods, the earth is of holding clay which gives up the fox's scent less readily than its thinner cousin on the high ground. Large tracts of the land are still at grass, feeding sheep on the uplands and dairy herds below, although, as is common throughout England, there is considerably more plough than in the earlier years of this century. The villages, once the homes of farm workers, craftsmen and those tradesmen and small shop-keepers responsible for servicing the infrastructure of an agricultural community, now house commuters who work in London and the great cities of the Midlands. In the summer tourists flock to the Cotswolds from both home and abroad to revel in what must still be one of the most picturesque collection of pleasing communities in the land. Despite the changes wrought by the mechanization of farming and the improvement in communications it remains, in truth, a most agreeable place 'to ride to a meet in'.

The hunting boundaries of the country have changed little over the last two hundred years and encompass about 15 miles (north to south) of Gloucestershire and Oxfordshire and 30 miles from east to west. Chipping Norton, about midway between the east and west extremities and slightly towards the north, is the home of the Heythrop kennels which stand on a hillside about a mile from the centre of this market town. The huntsman's house has a sweeping view and there are a number of cottages and stable flats

101

which must make it one of the most well-equipped and comfort-
able establishments of its kind.

In May 1952, Percy Durno lived there as he had done with his
wife Nellie since 1937 and there were those, led by Lord Ashton,
who cared greatly about the state of mind and the future of the
pair of them. It was, of course, essential that Wallace and Durno hit
it off, not just in the interests of the Heythrop Hunt but for the
happiness and well-being of them both.

Percy was in a very difficult position. He was a close friend of
George Knight and had made several trips to the Ludlow as
well as frequently seeking permission from Ashton to visit the
Cotswold: 'I'll just be out for a few hours, Milord.' 'A few hours, be
blowed,' His Lordship would reply, in good-natured exasperation.
'No such thing. You'll be out half the bloody night.'

Percy had thus come to know Wallace well and admired both
his talent and his methods so that when the committee made its
final decision he knew that here was a man with whom he could
work; nevertheless he was deeply hurt at being supplanted. Not
for one moment did he make his feelings evident, except to his
closest farming friends whom he could rely upon not to make
them known. To Ronnie, who had taken the trouble to consult the
huntsman before letting his name go forward, he had given an
absolute assurance, never since modified or regretted, that he
would be happy to serve under him and he pursued the same line
with those of the Heythrop hierarchy who anxiously enquired
about his feelings.

Percy Durno continued to serve the Heythrop as kennel-
huntsman and first whipper-in for thirteen more years and only
rarely during that time did he have the opportunity to hunt the
hounds. He did so for a month at the beginning of one season
(characteristically telling everyone that he couldn't wait for the
Captain's return) when Wallace broke a vertebra while cubhunting, but for the most part Wallace appeared to be physically
indestructible. There would have been one further chance when
Housewarmer, a Grand National horse that Ronnie had brought
with him from the Cotswold, was killed in a traffic accident one
morning, writing the master off for four days, but as luck would
have it Percy himself was laid up, having himself had a fall from a
young horse he was 'bringing on'.

The kennelman, Tom Bailey, who now became Percy's deputy
but whose duties in the kennels were largely unchanged on
hunting days because Durno invariably acted as first whipper-in,

had been in post for four years and was clearly the tops to the extent that Wallace describes him 'as the kennelman of all time'. He had been in hunt service since a boy and his wife came from a staunchly hunting background. As is so often the way in such families, their son Sidney became huntsman of the Vale of the White Horse in 1966. Tom Bailey was in the Durno mould, loyal, hardworking and fun, despite his rather forbidding appearance which occasioned those that did not know him well to give him plenty of room to pass on a dark night.

The stables were run by Stella Prideaux-Brune (later Towler) and Anita Krott, both of whom Ronnie had imported from the Cotswold – giving rise to delicious but unfounded scandalous speculation on the parts they played in his life – where they had been such a success in the days when girls were not readily acknowledged as best fitted to look after horses in hunt establishments. Both settled easily and efficiently into their grander surroundings and increased responsibilities.

The more formal Heythrop hierarchy appeared as strong as the staff but the division of some of the duties undertaken by them was not to Ronnie's taste. The immensely supportive Edwin Brassey was still chairman and the secretary was John Chamberlayne whose elderly and irascible father, Ed, ran the hunt's damage fund. Under the Ashton mastership it had been the practice that the secretary did much of the visiting of farmers – recruiting, enthusing and, where necessary, placating them in the interests of the hunt. John Chamberlayne had carried out this onerous task as well as running the damage repair organization (based on one elderly land-rover) but this had never been the Wallace way and he immediately set about taking it on himself. Another habit of the Heythrop with which the new master disagreed strongly was that Percy Durno sent out the earth-stopping cards which prefaced each meet. This is a very complicated and time-consuming business which, to be carried out properly, is hardly within the compass of a man hunting hounds four days a week, being a hangover from the days when a professional huntsman had domestic help as a matter of course, even being provided with a man to clean his boots, breeches and coat. Other than Percy the Heythrop had hitherto neither a focus nor a checking system for earthstopping activities but now with the arrival of the indefatigable Charles Parker, things were to change. Parker travelled the Heythrop extensively and produced a comprehensive list of both earths and those who could be called upon to see to the stopping of them before a day's hunting, following the system that he and Ronnie had first devised at the Ludlow and refined at the Cotswold. The Earthstoppers Lunch, which had always been held before the annual puppy show and at which the volunteers had been paid off in cash by the huntsman, was stopped. In its stead Wallace introduced a Feast and Clay Pigeon Shoot during which the army of willing helpers received a cheque for their services – in those days of few bank accounts a startling innovation which met some resistance but one which won almost universal wifely approval in that it enabled the hard-earned money to be saved rather than spent in the pub on the way home.

Charles Parker was not universally popular. Like his friend and mentor he was eyed with some suspicion by the more conventional Heythropians who thought that his intimate acquaintance with the habits of the fox extended well beyond stopping their earths. Dark hints were dropped to the effect that the remarkable change in the fortunes of the Cotswold Hunt had been due, at least in part, to the purported fact that Parker transported foxes in a bag (some even essayed that they travelled down his trouser leg) so that there was always one available to be found by hounds. These rumours were soon shown to be absurd when the new Heythrop team, under close and expectant observation, wrought a considerable improvement in the number of foxes killed and the distance they were pursued without resort to skullduggery; soon Parker became something of a treasured institution – indeed a living legend.

The reorganization of the earthstopping arrangements, in themselves a seemingly trivial (but in fact an all too often underestimated) adjunct to the efficient running of a hunt's business, gives a further clue to the Wallace drive for perfection in all his endeavours and his obsession with the importance of sound organization as being the key to success. Nothing must be too much trouble in ensuring that those who provided the land should be repaid by the effective killing of the countryside's major predator or that those who paid for the instrument that did that killing should get the best of sport as a dividend for their not inconsiderable investment. These important prerequisites demand a plentiful supply of huntable foxes, the one essential ingredient which cannot be brought to the meet.

Ronnie next turned his attention to improving the means by which he and his subscribers could cross the Heythrop country. There were few, if any, hunt jumps – artificial fences introduced into otherwise uncrossable hedges or other boundaries. All the impassable obstacles which impeded the swift and smooth progress of hound, horse and rider were natural except where wire (by now plenty of it) had been put up to stop gaps or reinforce hedges. There was clearly much to be done if the Captain and his followers were to regain the six to ten mile points which were a feature of Albert Brassey's day.

Wallace tackled the problem with energy: post-and-rail fences were erected; wire was removed and the gaps closed by timber rails; in places tiger-traps were introduced, a novelty then at the Heythrop, which in themselves could be formidable. Jimmy Edwards, the comedian and no light-weight, found himself and his horse under a notably robust example during one of his frequent excursions with the hunt, much to the amusement of the rest of the field. Edwards, who was something of an expert on the hunting horn, became a very popular adornment and would entertain the guests at Heythrop childrens' dances, inventing calls which characterized hunting in other, less favoured, parts of the country; a particular favourite being the 'Sussex' which, he explained, meant 'drinks, sandwiches and four hours steady digging!'

The aim of this daunting exercise was to ensure that the field could always get out of whatever enclosure they found themselves in and it was clearly necessary to persuade farmers and landowners not only that the work was necessary, but to do most of it themselves. Ronnie set about the business of getting to know them all; no small undertaking in a 450-square-mile patch. By a mixture of persuasion, cajolery and occasional judicious bribery he had largely achieved his objective in the first two years. Remarkably his process of enlisting the support of those who had influence strayed into by-ways not often explored by masters of foxhounds: the manager of the sewage pits became a friend ('good place for foxes'), as did the Fire Brigade chief in Moreton-in-Marsh who happened to have a promising covert behind his headquarters. It was a meticulously conceived plan carried out with drive, determination and tact.

Ronnie made the cultivation of his relationship with the farmers a very high priority indeed. He got to know each of them and their families and after hunting he made his visits, paying particular attention to those whose land or fencing had been damaged. His interest in them was deep – much more than going through the motions dictated by good manners or expediency. George Smith, whom Wallace introduced to hunting and who has since become one of the most respected of farming subscribers, remembers that Ronnie always inquired after the welfare of his friends and relatives and never forgot either a name or a face. Smith also recalls the sincerity with which the young master always dealt with both 'the high and the low' so that everyone knew where they stood in their dealings with him.

> He didn't mind that the odd farmer was not well disposed towards hunting but he didn't like those who pretended they were – said one thing and then did another. He hated that.

As with George Smith, a number of young sons and daughters began to hunt under the Wallace influence and many remember how he found them their first pony so that they would enjoy the experience from the very beginning. Others recount that when they were a little older, Ronnie found them a steady and proven old hunter or organized a day's shooting for them.

His attention to this, perhaps the most important of all aspects of hunt organization, paid off a thousandfold. His talent for tact and diplomacy ensured that he quarrelled with very few and where he found it impossible to deal with a particularly truculent individual, he would find someone better equipped to act persuasively on his behalf. The farmers appreciated that he would never let them down and in return were straight with him. If one did not want the hunt on a certain day they would make sure that the master knew and there were few cases of lack of communication or crossed wires.

The importance of these good relations had both a general and a particular aspect. It was very much in the interests of hunting in general that harmony should prevail and the word be spread. Closer to home the Heythrop country would be open and free for hunting with the minimum of rows, recriminations or bad blood. To this end, the repair of damage to fences and the care that stock did not wander from their proper enclosures was paramount. A more efficient and timely method of damage repair was required and to achieve this Ronnie exercised shamelessly another of his talents – that of his fascination for women. His quick rise to the forefront of his profession, his youth, his dark good looks, energy and determination had already won him two wives and a number of affairs and now ladies with perhaps only a passing interest in foxhunting suddenly discovered a passion for the sport and explored ways in which they could become his trusted lieutenants. As a result a number of them became known as 'The Adorers', a faintly malicious sobriquet coined by some of the more cynical, and perhaps slightly envious, Heythrop followers.

Among those loosely included in this group was Lavinia Jenkinson. Intelligent, cultivated and a naturalist to rival Charles Parker, she was an Oxford graduate who taught at Tudor Hall Girls School. She had a deep and technical interest in hunting and a love for the countryside and all that lived in it, human, animal, bird and plant, which made her activities unusually wide in scope. Lavinia was enlisted in the service of the hunt to lead the damage repair teams, a duty which John Chamberlayne was happy to relinquish and now was to be increased both in importance and in work-load by the employment of a full-time man and two land-rovers permanently based at the kennels. Lavinia knew every field and had a sketch map of each; she knew everyone, they knew her and, above all, she was liked enormously. Wallace had once again picked a winner. The combination of Ronnie's ability to record mentally every occurrence during a hunting day ('eyes in the back of his bloody head,' muttered more than one follower caught at some misdemeanour), remember every broken rail or unhinged gate, and Lavinia's dedication in setting things to rights every evening after hunting with her mobile teams was a potent one, the like of which for sheer efficiency had not been seen before, certainly not in the Heythrop. And if Lavinia's teaching duties or Pony Club activities precluded her from personally performing her self-imposed tasks, then there was another Adorer poised to stand in. Diana Hastings, for instance, a lady with an impeccable hunting pedigree at the Pytchley had moved house in order to hunt with the Heythrop, and did sterling and unstinting work on the kennel accounts as well as coping with the damage in Lavinia's absence. It was not unusual for one of these ladies to pick up Ronnie at the end of a hunting day in a car where the division of the evening's labours would be made and then for the pair of them to spend hours leap-frogging from gate to gate (one in the car, one on foot) to check that no stock had wandered. Ronnie would not return home or embark on a social engagement until all was as it should be. As a result he was the despair of many a hostess with a delicate dinner spoiling in the oven.

Wallace's first two years at the Heythrop were spent as a bachelor in Bettridge Cottage, a rented house in Salford about a mile from the kennels. From there he began to put his careful plans into effect and somehow still found time to conduct an energetic affair with Peggy Miller-Mundy who was to become his third wife in 1954. Born Peggy Clarke, she came, like Valerie, from Sussex and was a little older than Ronnie. Her husband, always known rather curiously as Potter, had been a senior and rather eccentric boy at Eton when Wallace arrived there and a 12th Lancer in the war. The Miller-Mundys had come to a dance in Shropshire when Wallace was hunting the Teme Valley in 1947 and Peggy, whose marriage was on the rocks, had fallen for him then. By the time Ronnie reached the Cotswold and his own marriage to Valerie was beginning to flounder, Peggy was divorced and living in Pewsey from where she hunted with the Beaufort as well as making frequent appearances first at Andoversford and then at Bettridge Cottage. She was wildly attractive and Ronnie, never one to resist such constant attention (unless it came from a married lady on his doorstep) was smitten. They married and rented Rignell, a house at Barford St John which belonged to the appropriately oft-married Derek Jackson who had ridden in the Grand National before the war and now owned the *News of the World*.

Rignell was built at the turn of the century in the style of a Canadian ranch-house – indeed the whole property was a microcosm of a ranch, being bounded by a sea of post-and-rail fencing. It was some ten miles from Chipping Norton, a situation which pleased Ronnie greatly – he had become averse to living either over or close to the shop, believing both that the staff would rise to their duties with a more effective will if he was not always near and that the kennels were a prime target for droppers-in with nothing more important to do than drink his whisky. His marriage to Peggy was to last eight years and did much to make Wallace conventionally acceptable to the more old-fashioned (and often influential) members of Heythrop society.

The hunt committee had offered Ronnie and Raymond Barrow a guarantee of £5000 a year to hunt hounds four days a week, that is excepting Tuesdays and Thursdays which Lord Ashton, after several glasses of Madeira, had once confessed to the Duke of Beaufort were, as far as he was concerned, the best days in the week; the Duke thought he was joking but Ronnie was never sure. This sum, although hardly munificent, turned out to be adequate initially, supplemented as it was by additional forage, earthstopping and damage funds. From this and their own resources, the masters had to buy and maintain the horses necessary for themselves and their whippers-in, pay the staff and keep themselves in a style commensurate with the social obligations expected of a master of one of the smarter packs of foxhounds. Horses were always a worry; some twenty to twenty-five were needed and members of the committee were generous in their assistance, notably Lord Leigh who offered to help mount Percy Durno.

Four days a week were not enough for Wallace and he soon began to hunt on the occasional Tuesday and then every Tuesday leaving only Thursdays free for the more dedicated subscribers to carry on their businesses and other obligations. For a brief period he attempted to go out on all six days but the infrastructure was not quite up to such a sustained effort. Such was the influence of the foxhunting community in the early fifties that Thursday became the day when the magistrate's bench sat and the district councils met in deference to the importance of killing foxes on each of the other days of the week.

All in all most things were now progressing to Wallace's entire satisfaction, but there remained two further pieces of groundwork to be completed before he could feel with every justification that he had carried out all that he had privately determined was necessary if the Heythrop was to be transformed into the complete hunting paradise. The first, that of uniting the factions that had opposed his appointment was relatively easy. His organizational brilliance, his constant showing of good sport, the lack of complaints and the paucity of the friction which often bedevils hunting politics had done much to silence his critics. There was now only the die-hard Brassey faction to pacify and these he satisfied by persuading Pam Mackinnon to join the mastership in 1954; not that she needed much persuasion for she had become an unwavering friend who did nothing to rock the boat and everything to heal the breach. The second was a much more complicated and delicate matter, that of producing a pack of hounds better than any other in England. His ambition in this respect was to make the Heythrop hounds not only the best practical hunters of foxes but to produce show champions which would vindicate his belief that they were one and the same animal.

The evolution of the modern English foxhound has been a complicated affair which can be traced back to three main strains. The Normans introduced the Talbot for the formalized hunting of first the deer and then the hare. Slow and persistent, with plenty of voice or 'cry', they were renowned for their steadiness and resistance to riot. In the north of England, the influences were different. Here hounds were generally smaller, probably derived from the Irish Kerry Beagle mixed with greyhound, and were quick, sharp-nosed but often mute. In Wales hounds derived from an indigenous Celtic breed, woolly and rough-coated. The monks of Margam Abbey had crossed these natives with French hounds from the Ardennes, resulting after years of carefully kept records which show the occasional admixture of other types, in the so-called Gascon strain of Welsh hounds which began to be introduced into England in the late fourteenth century for their fine noses and musical voice. The inter-breeding of these three types remained a pretty haphazard business, mainly because of the general absence of proper stud-books until the eighteenth century when Hugo Meynell first applied a scientific approach. His imperative was the need to breed hounds that were faster than the horses which followed them and quick enough, too, to stay close to the speedier, healthier foxes which by a process of natural selection were by his time the norm.

Meynell took as his model the 'in-and-in' breeding methods used by a neighbouring sheep farmer. To his own hounds, brought from Derbyshire where he had first conceived the need for an increased measure of speed, he added blood lines from the Brocklesby in Lincolnshire and the Wardour in Wiltshire in an effort to produce, successfully, the fastest pack in England. The days of practically walking a fox to death were gone for ever.

Hard on the heels of the master of the Quorn came Peter Beckford. Like Meynell, he was rich and far from a country bumpkin. Fond of music and the theatre, he had done a Grand Tour before joining his Jamaican sugar baron father on their estates near Blandford in Dorset in 1776. Enforced idleness whilst recovering from a fall in 1779, enabled him to write *Thoughts on Foxhunting*, in which he expounded his own theories on hounds and their breeding. For the most part it agreed with Meynell (whose views were already received wisdom): Beckford looked for 'straight legs, deep chest, broad breast, small head, clean neck and cat feet'. The pack should be 'all of a size' and the ability to hunt together for ten miles was looked upon as far more important than the speed of one individual. Nevertheless it was emphasized that speed and dash were the qualities that distinguished the first-class hound.

Beckford's hounds, like Meynell's, were walked all summer to get them steady and not prone to riot, especially among the sheep with which Dorset abounded. In the autumn he entered them in woodland cubhunting and only to the fox. Peter Beckford looked upon a fox, once found, as half killed and returned home after an indifferent run ending in a kill in far better humour than after a ten mile chase and the loss of his quarry. In this he and Wallace would agree wholeheartedly but the latter had always to temper his inclinations with the wish of the subscribing ladies and gentlemen to cross the country at speed as a first priority and kill foxes very much second. Beckford also had strong views on the use of the horn, urging huntsmen to leave hounds alone whilst they worked and remarked that the true genius in this respect was he who could recognize the moment to assist them; he would have been proud of the master of the Heythrop.

A *Foxhound Kennel Stud Book* was first produced in 1800 but became the breeders' bible only in 1886 when it was taken in hand by the Masters of Foxhounds Association. Proper maintenance of such records and guidelines are essential but its formalization in this way had the effect of encouraging rigidity of selection which rapidly became a fashion to which too many masters became slaves.

By the end of the First World War hounds had become too big, not active enough, lacked drive and intelligence and were short of both nose and tongue in the view of many, including a clutch of prominent young masters led by the Duke of Beaufort and Peter Farquhar. They had noticed that Frank Freeman at the Pytchley had, as early as 1910, begun to introduce a strain of small bitches which the foxhunting establishment had dismissed as 'harriers'. They may have been small but they produced a pack capable of sticking to a hunt of over 13 miles and lasting for well over two hours on one red-letter day still talked about in the Midlands. A prominent critic of Freeman's methods was out that day and rather grudgingly congratulated the huntsman on the performance of his hounds. 'Yes, sir,' said Frank. 'Not bad for harriers.'

Curiously the man to whom Farquhar and the others turned to for help was not an Englishman but an American citizen with no family hunting background who had been brought up in Paris.

Ikey Bell was born in 1878 and had hunted the Galway (The Blazers) and the Kilkenny before becoming master of the South and West Wilts in 1923. He was a vocal dissenter who went a great deal further than sniping from the side-lines. He and his adherents believed that the blood in the approved lines was thinning and urgently needed an outcross, preferably Welsh, which would add a nose and physique which could better cope with tarmac roads, more and deeper plough and the other manifestations of the machine age. The traditionalists, led by Lord Bathurst, were outraged and saw to it that the prizes at Peterborough – the premier hound show – went always to the classic hounds which

Bell's supporters now saw as almost misshapen, being straight-shouldered, short in the back and knuckled over at the knee. 'Not fast enough to keep themselves warm,' sniffed Mr Bell.

He went to Wales to consult with Sir Edward Curre who hunted his own pack of pure Welsh hounds around Chepstow. From there he also sought the advice of the other great local breeders, Jack Evans at Brecon, Lord Coventry at Carmarthen and David Davies who hunted a private pack. All four had kennels recognized by the MFHA and Bell produced a first outcross of breeding from the Welsh and entered them in the stud book. By the time the foxhunting oligarchy woke up to what was going on it was too late; notable kennels such as Badminton and Farquhar's Portman had already started to use Bell's revolutionary outcrosses. By the time that a committee of the MFHA, chaired by Bathurst, changed the registration rules to read that grand-sires and grand-dams also had to be 'in the Book', the damage, as the reactionary but influential senior members of the MFHA saw it, had been done.

Those who favoured the English type were not at all pleased that this departure could now continue unchecked and the hunting correspondent of *The Times* fuelled the flames by welcoming Bell's initiative by pronouncing the English foxhound 'as slow as the Durham Ox'. Among those who indignantly took him to task were some of the Brasseys and the formidable Lord Leconfield as well as the furious Bathurst who wrote, when Bell retired in 1932: 'He has done no end of harm. Now that he has gone I hope that this propaganda will cease and in time they will breed out the Welsh – the little sharp bitches that he likes will cure themselves by killing rats.'

Lord Bathurst was to hope in vain but the debate continued for years, consuming the writing-paper and the after-dinner hours of masters and huntsmen alike as well as ensuring immortality for Ikey Bell. Bell was a good example of what original thought and enthusiasm, backed up by intelligence and drive, can achieve even in the most hidebound areas of society – and the average early twentieth-century hunt was certainly in that category.

Ronnie had been brought up on the breeding controversy almost from the days when Frank Freeman had started to visit his brother Will and the Wallaces at Leylands. By the time he came to the Heythrop only four packs in England and one in Ireland were free of Welsh blood – the Belvoir, the Brocklesby, the Hurworth in County Durham and the York and Ainsty South; in Ireland the Limerick, hunted for thirty years by Lord Daresbury, remained virtually pure from the time that Daresbury imported hounds from the Belvoir where he had previously been master.

Wallace set about improving the Heythrop hounds having first closely observed the methods used by the Duke of Beaufort and Peter Farquhar and then by applying his own ideas and flair to the breeding process. He had come to believe that what was necessary in the female line were 'good plain cooks' and this was certainly the case at the Heythrop where the bitches were exactly that in the shape of a line going back to a remarkable hound called Lady, bred by Sir Thomas Mostyn in North Wales in 1801. Mostyn, far from home, hunted the Bicester and it was his practice to send his pregnant bitches to Wales to whelp. Lady was never keen to be sent away and on at least one occasion she produced her litter and then walked alone from Wales to Bicester to resume her hunting.

The main problem with the Heythrop pack was the doghounds who were also of the plain, honest but unexciting variety which damned them as definitely run-of-the-mill. This, to the new master's mind made them ripe for development. On 1 May 1952, the first official day of his mastership, he discovered that Peter Farquhar's stallion hounds Portman Lorimer and Portman Lovelock – both of them descended from the brilliant Meynell Pageant 35 – were lodging nearby and he sent to them a number of Heythrop bitches, two of which he had brought from the Cotswold (one had been with him at Ludlow). This fortuitous beginning laid the foundations and in 1953 Ronnie began to produce the results at hound shows. For the first time ever the Heythrop Hunt entered the competitive lists, thereby beginning the intense rivalry with the Duke of Beaufort which was to be a feature of the next two decades and more.

Successful hound breeding, like that of thoroughbred horses, cannot be accounted an exact science. Many in search of excellence – the perfect hound – have tried the simplistic approach, logical in its way, of putting a leading show bitch to a champion stallion hound. Seldom does that seem to produce the desired answer. The missing ingredient, possessed by Ikey Bell, the Duke of Beaufort and Peter Farquhar, seems to be the sort of intuitive flair analogous to the green fingers of the great gardeners; Wallace, as we will see, has it in abundance.

CHAPTER 8

The Wallace Way

FOXHUNTING runs in some families in much the same way as politics permeate the Churchill and Asquith dynasties. Prime examples are the Fanshawes whose contemporary connections frequently appeared in the Wallace orbit. Sir Peter Farquhar's sister Ruth married Major Dick Fanshawe and they became joint-masters of the South Oxfordshire, later moving to the North Cotswold where they were followed, in due course of time, by their son Brian before he assumed his distinguished, if a trifle noisy, mastership of the Cottesmore. In 1952 Mrs Fanshawe had been joined at the North Cotswold by the Hon. F. A. H. (Tony) Wills, whom she later married, and who was soon to succeed to the barony of Dulverton at Batsford Park, the very cornerstone of the Heythrop country. In 1963 Lord Dulverton took on the mastership of the Heythrop, an action that greatly pleased his wife who had first noticed Wallace's hunting skills under rather trying circumstances.

In the early spring of 1938 the Christ Church Beagles had invited the ECH to hunt for a day over the part of their country allowed to them by the South Oxfordshire. The Fanshawes watched with some interest as hounds were put into one of their best coverts – one that they themselves had planned to draw the next day. They made a mental note that the young master of the Eton Beagles was to be commended on his single-mindedness if not on his tact and geography. In short they concluded that Ronnie, who was having a wonderful day and was oblivious of his misdemeanour, was a great poacher. Two years later their paths crossed again when Ruth Fanshawe (like Lady Ashton of Hyde) was struggling to keep her pack going in the absence of her husband away at the war. She was standing on a hillside in company with an elderly, taciturn and immensely experienced hunting farmer watching the Christ Church Beagles working in the meadows below. The time passed in companionable silence; eventually the old boy spat and turned away: 'I'll tell you what, Missus,' he said at length, 'that young feller down there, he do know what he be doing.'

Wallace had given himself two years, from the day that he assumed the mastership of the Heythrop, to get people to understand that he did indeed know what he was doing. If he failed within that time to make his mark on the country in a way which was generally approved, then he would move on.

The painstaking groundwork laid down in the first two years and covering every possible aspect of hunting, attracted interest far beyond the boundaries of the Heythrop. The number of people wanting to see for themselves the results being achieved by the new mastership grew as alarmingly as it had done at the Cotswold five or six years earlier. Applications to subscribe regularly or to have an occasional day, poured in from afar and although to begin with (when there appeared to be plenty of room for all-comers), this was clearly beneficial, bringing a much needed financial flush to the treasurer's books, numbers soon became so great that the farmers expressed their justifiable concern. Rules were introduced to try and limit the size of the fields and the Heythrop became among the first to insist that visitors should obtain the permission of the secretary and negotiate a fee before being allowed to come out for a day. Up to that time it had been the general practice to welcome anyone who turned up and charge them a standard cap, but quite clearly something had to be done when 200 people turned out on the purportedly unfashionable Fridays. There was already a widespread view that 'every day you go out there's something worth coming for'.

There was also a rule, observed more in the breach than in the observance, that members were allowed three guests a season, but only if they spent a night with their host or hostess – a condition that was sometimes interpreted as a splendid licence for immorality. More serious were the attempts to limit the number of regular subscribers who lived outside the country. Those within adjacent hunts could apply with some chance of success and even some from further afield, if they were in Ronnie's opinion 'persons of consequence'. But even if they passed this rigorous social examination they would be expected to acquire, within a reasonable period, some stake in Heythropia – a farm, some land (a covert or two), or take some shooting to ensure that it stayed in friendly hands.

As far as this last was concerned, Wallace was lucky. The explosion of commercial pheasant shooting, let to teams of tycoons to reward the upper echelons of company staff or for the corporate entertainment of particularly profitable clients, was not a feature of the two-and-a-half decades of his mastership, so that during that time the problems were minimal. Where conflict was likely to arise, he adopted the oblique but effective ploy of persuading the wives and children of the potentially difficult to hunt with him so that husbands and fathers were shamed into giving the Heythrop some sort of consideration, if not priority. Where shooting land came up for sale he tried to ensure that it passed into actively pro-hunting hands.

Despite the anxiety of the farmers and the efforts to restrict numbers – or perhaps because the latter were only half-heartedly applied – the size of the field grew steadily until, on Saturdays, it peaked at around 300, causing substantial difficulties for successive field-masters and an increasingly busy time for the damage repair teams. Every huntsman since Hugo Meynell has been faced with the conflicting needs of providing a good run for the field (the vast majority of whom are there for the haroosh of the chase) and allowing hounds to hunt properly, which inevitably means that they need to check occasionally to re-discover a lost scent. There has always been the temptation to pander to the more impatient followers by lifting hounds when they have paused in this way and canter quickly on to the next covert to find a fresh fox. At the other extreme are those, often amateur huntsmen, who will sit about at the head of a fuming field while hounds cast around a sheep enclosure for twenty minutes without a realistic hope of picking up the line again.

The Wallace way was to strike a balance: to give his hounds a chance; to slow up when they needed a minute or two to recover the scent but never to sit about unnecessarily. Put in this ultra-simplistic manner it is difficult to comprehend why any huntsman should ever fail to apply such a basic technique. What seems to have raised Wallace out of the ruck in this respect is a superior instinct and a shared mutual trust with his hounds that tells him that the moment to move on has arrived and tells his hounds that they will not be disappointed at his actions. This is the often referred to invisible thread which binds huntsman and hounds together so that each anticipates the other's needs – a gift which few if any of Wallace's contemporaries possessed in quite such a high degree and which, if it is not to be wasted, presupposes hounds of such conformation and fitness that they are able always to press their fox close so as never to lose its scent unnecessarily.

Wallace, despite his occasional public protestation that hunting cannot be tailored to suit the whims of the field, has, in fact, its collective needs very much in the forefront of his mind – but strictly on his own terms. They are hurried from one draw to another without wasting a second; they are moved on from the successful conclusion of one hunt to the beginning of a new without pause for breath, a draught from their flasks or an opportunity to discuss the pleasures of the fences they have just jumped and dwell deliciously on the discomfort of fallen friends. This 'hurry, hurry on' attitude is not to everyone's taste and many experienced foxhunters have criticized it as detracting from their fun, preferring the more relaxed atmosphere generated by those who allow plenty of time for gossip, drinking and self-congratulatory reflection. Nevertheless they almost invariably came back for more, knowing that the dedicated professionalism of the man assure them of the very best of conditions in which to realize their dream to be part of an unforgettable experience which could take them flying over ten and more miles of Heythrop country without let-up. For that they were prepared to put up with a great deal more from their increasingly autocratic master than merely being hurried along.

Misbehaviour was punished unmercifully in the time honoured fashion – by sending the offender home. Dashing young men from Leicestershire trying to emulate 'Flying' Childe, who (it will be remembered) had caused Hugo Meynell such anguish at the Quorn by getting too close to his hounds, were dispatched for committing similar offences and, for good measure, were advised to have a hair-cut before applying to the Heythrop again. Titled ladies of impeccable foxhunting pedigree who knew the country as well as they knew their drawing-rooms and, as a result took an occasional short-cut through a forbidden field, were summoned forward 'to have a word' and within minutes were bound for their horse-boxes complaining that they had a sudden debilitating headache which precluded them from taking any further part in proceedings. On one never to be forgotten day, remembered with much relish by those who saw the incident, a party of four senior members of the hunt, in the wrong place at the wrong time, saw the master and his hounds trotting up a lane towards them and fearing the worst, turned aside and locked themselves in a disused but handy Nissen hut, until the danger had passed. The rest of the field, properly following their leader, were astonished to see what appeared to be the early stages of a smoking fire, so great was the volume of steam issuing forth from the four hot and agitated thoroughbred horses through gaps in the corrugated iron sheeting. Maurice Willes, one of those firmly in the 'I only hunt to have a laugh' brigade hardly ever completed a full day and recalls that: 'I never really ever hunted with Wallace; he always sent me home!'

Sometimes the field would suffer collectively. One season Ronnie had noticed that more and more people were coming late to the meets, an unfortunate habit which could seriously interfere with the success of an early find of a fox by latecomers inadvertently crossing its line whilst riding to the appointed place. A number were very tardy at a meet in the little village of Cornwell on a day when there was no whipper-in, and arrived only just in time to see the remainder of the field disappearing in the wake of hounds who had found in the covert known as Quarry Wood. It was a magnificent hunt of 1½ hours which took them through Daylesford, Oddington, Broadwell and the Sezincote Vale before a successful conclusion near Hinchwick – perhaps 15 miles or more as hounds ran. Ronnie then took his hounds home, a punishment that was not lost on the miscreants who had also to suffer the acrimonious comments of those who had been properly on time.

Once the Heythrop followers became used to the fact that the one sure way to stay out of trouble was to learn the ways of the man they now called 'God' (except, that is, Bill Lander, Percy Durno's successor, who – out of earshot – always referred to the master as 'Dad') and act promptly and accurately when required to perform a service for either himself or his field-master, they were quick to warn visitors, however distinguished, that they would be unwise to take liberties.

Field-masters were chosen for their ability to cross the country speedily and, perhaps more important, for their minute knowledge of its geography and the idiosyncracies of the farmers and landowners over whose land they were passing. In this office he was well served. Raymond Barrow, the first, owned property in the country without ever really being part of the recognized establishment and this slight detachment from the social scene, together with his outstanding horsemanship in navigating his pony-sized mounts over any obstacle which presented itself, made following him both a pleasure and a challenge as he executed his duties meticulously without fear or favour. Barrow retired in 1962 and was followed by Anthony Taylor, a retired cavalry officer, Lord Dulverton and Ted Marsh (who both became joint-masters) and finally by Simon Loder and John Kirkpatrick, both ex-guardsmen. All were equally successful in this demanding task, so that the unwieldy fields were, for the most part, kept both under control and happy.

Despite the iron discipline which in itself became a *cause célèbre* and something which people became anxious to witness for themselves, it has to be remembered that the outbursts were often tempered by an underlying humanity and understanding – above all, perhaps, by a desire not to leave a lasting rancour. No-one was expected to bear a grudge and Ronnie often went out of his way the same evening to call on those who had received the rough edge of his tongue, to put matters right. Not that there was often an apology, just a passing reference aimed at smoothing ruffled feathers and soothing hurt feelings. A small boy who had mistaken one of the master's directives and ended up under his pony in a wet ditch, would be visited and he and his pony's welfare anxiously inquired after. An experienced hunting lady and great friend of Ronnie's who, with helpful intent, three times tried to point out to the master that she could distinctly hear his hounds over on the left, was told in an angry roar: 'If you know so much about it, you bloody-well hunt the hounds and I'll go home,' and who then burst into tears and took herself hastily off, was to be later mollified with a disarming: 'But you knew quite well, my dear, that I didn't mean it.'

Few days were without their humour, some of it undoubtedly of the *schadenfreude* variety, occasionally because Ronnie did not appreciate how unintentionally funny his imperious ways were to a few of the more irreverent members but often because he himself would allow his sense of humour to get the better of him.

A characteristic of the British temperament (perhaps English would be more accurate) is that we are often perversely jealous of success, much preferring the keen, hardworking tryer or the good loser. Such attitudes are particularly prevalent in foxhunting where unstinting praise for one practitioner from another is rare. Indeed it is not unknown for retiring huntsmen, amateur and professional, to try and ensure that their successors are of a low enough calibre to allow they themselves to continue to bask in a benevolent light. Ronnie's brilliant organization of the Heythrop and his early success made him an obvious target for those wishing to find a chink in his armour and the one aspect of his activities which some critics found an easy target, was his horsemanship. We have already seen that to some extent he considered the horse to be a necessary but complicating accessory to the sport and it is undoubtedly true that he is not a natural, despite the good pair of hands inherited from his mother. Lady Dulverton and many others describe him, not unkindly, as scrambling over the Heythrop country.

Wallace never allowed this lack of talent to hinder his performance, although it probably explains why he never applied for the mastership of a Leicestershire pack, being intelligent enough to realize that he just would not be able to compete with the 'Shire Flyers'. Quite simply he was an adequate horseman who took a number of steps to see that any shortcomings in this respect never hindered a day's sport. Firstly, he had good horses – or, anyway, suitable horses (often found for him by Lady Daresbury in Ireland), well schooled by Jack Stevens, a Banbury farmer and keen foxhunting man, Bill Lander and then by Clem and Di Barton, whose main business was the importing and making of top grade polo ponies and who were also keen Heythrop followers. Ronnie's horses were required to have stamina and go on for hour after hour, relentlessly. High quality, more delicate, blood horses could not have managed, particularly in the later days when he had put on weight. Secondly, he knew his country and almost exactly what the hunted fox was likely to do, so that he was always up with his hounds when it mattered, often to the surprise of the thrusters at his heels. Thirdly, he was brave. John Chamberlayne, one of the earlier critics of Wallace's horsemanship, would not hear a derogatory word on the subject after seeing the new huntsman fly over a huge obstacle in the Evenlode Vale where the hedges are as formidable as any in England. True, he was always selective, again more so as he became older, and he would not jump a fence unless it was necessary, but he was never found wanting.

Occasionally he would alarm even his hard-riding hunt staff in his determination to jump out of the most awkward places. The young Anthony Adams, a second whipper-in, tells a story of finding himself in company with Wallace and Tony Collins (itself an unusual occurrence for Ronnie rarely travelled in company with one, let alone both, his whips). Hounds were hunting hard and the three of them were in hot pursuit down a steep hill towards the biggest post-and-rails fence that Adams had ever seen. Tony Collins clearly shared his apprehension and they exchanged startled glances of the 'Bloody hell, he can't be; surely he can't be?' variety, as the master deliberately began to line himself up in as boggy and poached a take-off route imaginable. At that moment providence intervened in the shape of an out of control lady subscriber, who hurtled through them – an offence which would, under normal circumstances, have meant instant dismissal. Ronnie slowed to a trot as she tore into the fence. Her horse rose not an inch and destroyed the obstacle, at the same time decanting its owner in a deep quagmire of mud and splintered timber. Getting shakily to her feet, she prepared herself for a major Wallace blasting which, she was sure, would now be her unfortunate lot.

'Thank you, madam,' he said, as he trotted through the gap, 'Thank you. That was just what we wanted.'

Perhaps the definitive judgement on Wallace horsemanship comes from Percy Durno: 'He'd jump a bloody house if he had to.'

Ronnie's equivocal relationship with the field was very different from that which he enjoyed with his hunt servants. With the exception of Percy Durno and Tom Bailey, whom he had the good fortune to inherit, he chose them all with extreme care. They had to be intelligent, receptive and be capable of exercising their own initiative when the occasion demanded. Most of all they had to be entirely reliable to do things the Wallace way without supervision and having been shown that way only once. He was a hard taskmaster; Percy Durno believed that he required a man made to measure for each day's hunting and that, of course, was very difficult to live up to. But they were always encouraged to act in a given situation in a manner which they thought was right at the time. If they got it wrong they were left in no doubt, but the incident was then forgotten and no grudges were ever harboured.

His three principal henchmen during the Heythrop years were Percy (until 1963), Bill Lander (1964 to 1970) and, finally, Tony Collins. All three were devoted to him and took their sometimes horrendous tellings-off in the field in differing ways. Durno would smile sweetly, muttering, 'My word, the kettle isn't half boiling over this morning'; Bill would pull out his old pipe and suck it reflectively whilst Tony, perhaps not as hardened as his predecessors, would determine to put into practice one day the lesson he had learnt. On some aspects of their master they are all agreed: he was a just if demanding boss. He was the master of his trade and one from whom they all continually learnt and above all he was intensely loyal to them personally. There is also a strong consensus about the absence of any form of patronizing paternalism, unusual in a dictatorship (for that is what the Heythrop had become): hunt servants, farmers, landowners, nobility, all were treated the same; the face presented to each was the only face.

Adams, who became the professional huntsman to the Heythrop in 1989 and who had served seven seasons as second whipper-in before moving with Ronnie to Exmoor in 1977, remembers particularly the care that Wallace took to see that the staff were not treated as servants in the old-fashioned sense of that word. On tour with the Heythrop hounds in Somerset, the master and some of the remaining members of the field out that day were asked in to tea through the front door of an imposing residence whilst the whippers-in and the local hunt staff were invited to go round to the back and thence to the kitchen where a fine spread awaited them. Within minutes Wallace had appeared to join them and eventually everyone else followed, so that the party, in the hunting way, became an entity and not the 'upstairs-downstairs' affair that the host had clearly envisaged. Wallace, having characteristically made a point in which he passionately believed, then proceeded, equally characteristically, to make the most of the party by quizzing the locals closely on how the country was run, about farming attitudes, earth-stopping and many other aspects of how the hunt was organized. He was always willing to learn.

Another good example of Ronnie's caring attitude in this respect was evident when Bill Lander announced his intention of leaving the Heythrop because he and his wife found the five-day-a-week programme too much for them and their young family. When the decision was made it appeared that the only available vacancy was at the now defunct North Warwickshire. Lander was not keen ('all barbed-wire and bedsteads') but there seemed to be no alternative. Patiently Wallace negotiated, instead, a move to the Wynnstay (Sir Watkin Williams Wynn's) – one of England's best and most sought after countries. A contributory factor in the move was that Bill, unlike Percy Durno, had found it irksome that the master of the Heythrop never missed a day. Asked by a visitor how he got on when he was allowed to hunt the hounds he answered that he had never done so.

'But what about when Captain Wallace is ill or something?'

'Ill? Ill? I've never heard the bugger cough yet.'

Hunt servants occasionally found themselves in the firing line when Wallace judged that his own presence would not be beneficial – such as the day a hunted fox sought refuge in a supermarket in Chipping Norton and ran up and down the shelves, much to the consternation of both staff and customers. This is the sort of high-profile event which is the substance of a Master of

Foxhound's nightmare; headlines in the tabloid dailies can be imagined with little effort and would certainly be a thousand times more lurid than those that followed the affair of the Eton Beagles in Mrs Amelia Harris's kitchen copper. Ronnie turned to Tony Collins, who was trying hard to make himself invisible, smiled and said:

'I think you'd better go in there. I don't know very much about these places.'

Critics were quick to argue that this appeared to be tantamount to cowardice in the face of the enemy. A more dispassionate view would be that, as Tony Collins was certainly acquainted with at least some if not most of those within, it was common-sense that he would be better placed to defuse a potentially serious public relations disaster than the imposing, not to say portly, Old Etonian figure of the master. And so it proved.

A different decision had been made in a previous year when a fox bolted into the playground of a primary school and thence into the headmaster's study where the latter was engaged in a meeting with some of his staff. Percy Durno quickly made himself scarce; Wallace considered the situation and (pausing only to tell his grinning brother Vivian to take the fag out of his mouth and comport himself with a decent dignity befitting an officer of the Welsh Guards) called for a sack. The members of the field looked at each other helplessly. No-one, it seemed, went hunting with a sack tucked beneath their hunting coats. No-one that is except Mr Peglar, a baker from Tetbury, who with the air of a conjuror producing a rabbit from his top-hat, trotted up to Ronnie and handed him the required receptacle. The master heaved himself off his horse, strode into the school and entered the study. The huge figure encased in its green coat caused, if possible, more alarm than the fox which had now gone to ground behind several piles of arithmetic books. Ronnie swept off his cap.

'Good morning ladies and gentlemen. I am terribly sorry and I do apologise. I believe that there's a fox in here.'

Speechlessly they indicated the pile of books.

'Perhaps if you would be good enough to pop out for just a minute and I'll deal with it.'

They filed out to be followed, seconds later, by Wallace clutching his sack. He had stunned the fox with his whip ('Didn't seem right to shoot it in there') and it was terminally dealt with later in the approved fashion.

He did not quite get away with it for a kitchen lady had seen at least some of the incident from her window and telephoned the local press where the story flourished briefly. But what might have been a major scandal in newspapers always keen to make much of such matters was averted by Wallace, first making sure that hounds were kept well away from the school and second by his immediate telephone call to the Chairman of the Education Authority to ensure that the facts were properly and accurately presented and, of course, to apologize.

If Wallace was successful in his choice of hunt servants and field-masters so too was he both successful and lucky in his joint-masters and hunt chairmen. Pam Mackinnon, who was instrumental in uniting the country by mollifying the Brassey faction, stayed for 12 years and was succeeded by Lord Dulverton who also acted as field-master for two days a week. Unlike Raymond Barrow, both Mackinnon and Dulverton put up money to supplement the guarantee, as did their successors, Ted Marsh, an outstanding three-day event international in the 1950s, and Lord Rotherwick, the shipping magnate. Inflation and the increase in hunting days from four to five a week saw to it that the guarantee more than quadrupled in the Wallace era and the gap between it and the legitimate expenses of running the country grew ever wider. That gap was largely filled by the generous contributions of Ronnie's joint-masters.

Lord Rotherwick became a master in 1974 having moved to Cornbury from Bletchington, a house over the boundary of the next-door Bicester Hunt with whom he had enjoyed a slightly uneasy relationship because of the priority he sometimes gave to his pheasants at hunting's expense.

It is far from unknown for landowners to refuse a hunt permission to draw or even cross their properties during the pheasant shooting season and then to take themselves off to hunt elsewhere; few are as enlightened in this respect as the Rouse-Boughtons in Ludlow or the Dulvertons at Batsford. The master of the Bicester, Miles Gosling (whose father, Squeaker, hunted side-saddle) was infuriated to discover that Lady Rotherwick, whose husband had temporarily refused to allow hunting over his land, was proposing to have a day with the Heythrop. He telephoned Ronnie and when her Ladyship appeared at the meet, Wallace took her aside to explain the difficulty. She, in turn made a telephone call to Rotherwick, as a result of which she went home. This determined and principled action by Wallace appeared not to affect the delicate negotiations he was then engaged in with Rotherwick concerning the latter joining the Heythrop mastership – indeed it was treated with great good humour by all concerned, Lady Rotherwick relating it to her hairdresser with some relish, from which source it rapidly acquired suitably lurid embellishments.

Wallace demanded very little from those who shared his mastership, except money to keep things going and improve matters where necessary – Marsh, for example, was phenomenally generous; buying farms and coverts as they came on the market to prevent them falling into the 'wrong' hands. Joint-masters were not required to play any part in the organization of affairs – Ronnie saw that as entirely his own responsibility, backed up, where necessary, by the ever-faithful Lavinia Jenkinson and the hunt chairman. The latter's duties are multifarious and difficult to list tidily, but as the head of the committee which, in the final analysis, is responsible for hiring and firing the huntsman, it is essential that the chairman and the masters understand, agree and then support each other on all matters of policy: financial, organizational and landowning, for example.

Again Ronnie was lucky in the men appointed to this position. After Edwin Brassey came Philip Fleming, a much loved member of the banking family, widespread in Heythropia, who lived for hunting and resided in Barton Abbey where Wallace's only amateur predecessor had lived in the mid-nineteenth century. When he died he was succeeded by Cyril Kleinwort, another banker in the very first flight and an able administrator who may have lacked Fleming's deep roots in the country but undoubtedly shared the former's single-minded appreciation of the importance of hunting to the rural community. Both Philip Fleming and Kleinwort were put to a severe loyalty test – which, in the event, they passed with flying colours – as Ronnie went through yet another marital crisis.

He had first met the beautiful Rosie Lycett-Green shortly after the war when he fell into the same Exmoor hole as she when they were both hunting with the Devon and Somerset Staghounds. She was then a sixteen-year-old schoolgirl and made no impression on him other than his embarrassment, as a visiting Master of Foxhounds, in being ignominiously dumped alongside a mere child. They met again in 1958, during the Heythrop's regular spring visit to the West Country, and from that moment began to see each other often and in secret. He and Peggy had already begun to grow apart and for much the same reason as before: Ronnie's wholehearted approach to hunting and organizing the country in the winter, otterhunting and an ever-increasing round of shows in the summer, meant that they hardly saw one another. Like Jean and Valerie before her, this punishing routine was more than Peggy could bear but, unlike her predecessors, she determined to stick it out growing ever more miserable. They eventually divorced in 1962, Peggy going to live first in London, and then briefly in the United States, before returning to the Heythrop that she loved. She eventually killed herself in a motor accident – a tragic end to what had been a largely sad and disappointing life. Her Miller-Mundy sons asked Ronnie to give an address at the funeral and this, after some hesitation, he did, both because towards the end of her life they had become good friends again and, by doing so, he partly assuaged the guilt he carried for adding more unhappiness to an already unhappy lady.

The Lycett-Greens, Rosie's parents, maintained establishments in Yorkshire, Eaton Square and at Ashwick Manor Farm near Dulverton between which Rosie fluttered like an unsettled butterfly. They were not happy with their daughter's growing closeness to the master of the Heythrop: not only was he sixteen years her senior, he was a master of foxhounds (a notoriously unfaithful breed in their judgement), and he had a track record with women that confirmed their worst suspicions that hunting was a den of marital iniquity. Rosie herself naturally felt rather differently and, tiring of her girl-about-town ways, decided that it was time she settled with the man with whom she had fallen in love.

After leaving Peggy, Ronnie had moved out of Rignell and had gone to stay with Eric Towler at Glympton Park, near Woodstock. Towler, who later married Stella Prideaux-Brune, was both kind and generous to the errant couple and when Rosie became a permanency he lent them a house on the estate. They married in 1964, shortly after David Wallace was killed whilst serving with the 11th Hussars in Germany, and in 1966 they bought Eyford Knoll, a farm of 800 acres near Stow-on-the-Wold. A year later they had a son who was also to be christened David, in the circumstances a most singular choice of name but one which Rosie believed might help to replace for Ronnie the son he had never been allowed to know.

Rosie had never hunted regularly outside Exmoor but took to the Heythrop country with a relish which soon endeared her to the members. This was just as well as there had been a good deal of malicious gossip over the period of Peggy's final departure and it was during this time that Philip and Joan Fleming and Betty and

Cyril Kleinwort were so supportive. They enthusiastically endorsed Rosie and became firmly convinced that the proper ending to the saga for the sake of not only the principals, but also for the continued well-being of the Heythrop, was a clean break and then another marriage.

Wallace's success during his first ten years at the Heythrop was solidly based and apparently unaffected by his complicated (and much criticized) private life. Three factors contributed to his quite clearly pre-eminent domination of his profession: his absolute dedication – to the exclusion of all else – his mastery of organization and his control over hounds. It is to the last that we now turn.

Like all intelligent beings, Wallace was keen to learn. Indeed he had, throughout his life, soaked up knowledge of his sport from those very first talks between the Freemans and his parents in the kitchen at Leylands. But it was from Bill Perkins at Eton that he first became aware of the importance of control. To Perkins, absolute mastery of his pack of beagles was a creed and, by example, he passed on this simple tenet to his eager young master. The streets of Slough, navigated without a whipper-in, were both the training and the testing ground and Wallace, having passed with honours, never forgot.

To Perkins, George Knight and Percy Durno, Ronnie owes much in his pursuit of knowledge. All possessed the talent to get their hounds fit and teach them the basic essentials of their craft; above all, they were quiet men who obtained results by patient training, scolding their charges only when they seriously transgressed. Knight, Durno and the latter's successors at the Heythrop were absolutely to be relied upon, so much so that after his first two years at the Ludlow, Ronnie never again walked-out his hounds with a pocket full of biscuits in an effort to court popularity; indeed he rarely took them on exercise in the summer, so demanding were his other commitments.

It is during hound exercise that the groundwork is done. Hounds, and particularly the young entry, are brought to a peak of fitness to be ready for cubhunting in the autumn and taught the essence of togetherness – to act always as a team. The Wallace way has it that the most important single ingredient of this process is a quiet atmosphere. The first step in training a pet or a gun-dog, is to teach it to be calm and to be there at heel or wherever without constantly having to turn and shout for obedience. So too it has to be with hounds. Hounds, like all dogs, love quietness and, conversely, hate a constant nagging which leads them to feel insecure and not confident in their own ability. Importantly they must never be allowed to get away from the huntsman and will never forget such a victory once they have won it. Some experienced masters hold to the theory that to teach hounds the biddability that is required, it is essential to expose them to deer or to hare or even sheep so that they can be taught a sharp lesson, perhaps even a whipping, should they show untoward interest in anything other than a fox. Ronnie believes strongly that this is to take unnecessary risks and that the patient work of weeks can be undone by ten minutes rioting. The Wallace test, one always applied by his kennel-huntsmen, is to take them to a cross-roads and pause there to see what happens. Some, especially the young dog-hounds, may turn away and if so they can be allowed to move a little way off and the mass of the pack is then taken in a different direction. The wanderers return and are scolded, not just by the whipper-in but by the older members of the pack. Scolding by the huntsman should be done by fixing the errant hounds with the eyes, pointing the whip at them and telling them sharply what fools they have been. That is not to say that hounds should never be physically beaten, a shrewd smack with a stick at the right one at the right time can do a great deal of good but they have much more respect for their master if they are spoken to severely when they do wrong. Silence, though, is the key; silence means that they have done right.

Hounds brought up in this way hardly need further disciplining. They are in touch with their huntsman, a part of his life as he is a major part of theirs. There is a link between them – the invisible thread – an almost mystical experience which never fails to impress and uplift a casual observer. At its highest level it is found rarely. Far more often seen is the tightly bunched pack, held together by a pair of anxiously watchful whippers-in and a constant cackle of remonstration, rather as school monitors hover about a recalcitrant crocodile of children eager to escape.

The three most important influences on Wallace's performance with hounds were the Duke of Beaufort, Sir Peter Farquhar and, at a most important time when Ronnie arrived at the Cotswold, Major Chetwynd Hilton-Green; all possessed the gift of the invisible thread. They also had the talent (and the intelligence) to know exactly when to leave their hounds alone to regain a temporarily lost scent and when to pick them up and give them a hand. The Duke of Beaufort's hounds ignored fresh foxes as if they were rabbits and stuck to their task unharried and unhurried by

'Master'. Peter Farquhar would pause and light a cigarette when his hounds checked, a signal to the eager field, keen to come to grips again quickly with the big, black hedges of the Portman Vale, that they would have to be patient. Chetty (often further corrupted to Chatty) Hilton-Green was generally acknowledged to be the finest amateur huntsman of his generation when he was master of the Cottesmore in Leicestershire from 1931–46 and his imperatives were similar to Wallace; both had to combine proper hound hunting with the need to push on to please a fashionable field in a way that the autocratic 'Master' did not feel was necessary. Hilton-Green was not only superlative with hounds but, being a strong and effective horseman, was well able to keep the thrusting, well-mounted Shire fields at bay and away from his tough, fast hounds without betraying their trust in him. He became something of a legend in his lifetime, not least because he arrived home after hunting one day to discover that his wife had left him, emptying his house of all but a brass bedstead and a portrait of Ikey Bell.

Wallace's relationship with the Heythrop hounds was extraordinary even to his kennel-huntsmen. They would walk them all the summer, sticking faithfully to the methods laid down by their master. Ronnie, himself would appear perhaps only twice between the puppy show (held in May) and the first day's cubhunting in September. Percy Durno, Bill Lander, Tony Collins and the second whippers-in all commanded instant obedience from them during this time. Yet, having been taken to the first cubhunting meet by a huntsman they had seen so little and having walked the last mile or two to settle down, hounds would do only Wallace's bidding, fixing him with their eyes, eager and ready to go. None would wander, none would take any interest in anything or anybody until he gave the word; then they would move off with him, purposeful and alert, to the first draw where they would go into action like lightning. After that moment, the kennel-huntsmen all agree: 'We might just as well talk to a brick wall. They listened only to him.'

Nowhere is the absolute control of hounds so important as when they have checked. Wallace, in a seminar held by the American Foxhound Club, explained:

> I think one needs to realize that 49 checks out of 50 are not discernible by a member of the field; hounds put themselves right. It is at very few that the huntsman is required and great concentration on his part is then necessary in order to choose the right time. If a huntsman is not the jolly fellow that some

followers think he should be on a hunting day, then that is a
very good reason indeed for hunting with him; it means that
he is attending to his job.

If he is good, he will know that the hounds are going to
stop before they in fact do so because he will have spotted a
sign: he sees a herd of bullocks galloping two fields away; he
notices that hounds are coming to a road and that the road is
empty of people and cars so that the fox could travel it in
apparent safety; he sees sheep in the distance which will soil
the scent or he knows that there is freshly worked arable land
up ahead which again will make scenting conditions difficult.
He is anticipating a difficulty.

He then has to make his mind up as to why hounds have
stopped and whether they need help – whether they have to
be picked up or not. Sometimes the decision he comes to is
inexplicable in rational terms.

I remember one of the best hunts we ever had (at the
Heythrop). We had a point of over 10 miles, rare enough in
these days, and had come down off the hills on to a lovely
stretch of grassland and hounds stopped. I couldn't see why
but I just felt the fox must have gone on and we crossed
another four grass fields, still hunting but hounds were
snatching at the scent and not very confident. Then I saw a
man and asked him whether he had seen the fox. He said 'No'
but he said it not very convincingly. Then suddenly hounds
hit the line again and ran into a very big wood. I just knew
that the fox was going on so I picked them up and went
round to the far end where they found the scent again and we
ran for miles.

I found out a week later that the man's dog had chased the
fox and he hadn't liked to tell me.

That high degree of instinct cannot be learnt; nevertheless every
huntsman, even Wallace, needs cooperation. Illustrating this point,
he continued:

The field can do so much to help by remembering that the
hounds are all important. They must not be galloped off the
line; people must stand absolutely still and give them space,
give them a chance to come back to the line and try to take it
again. If they can they will always try it for themselves; they
are used to it, bred to it. They have learnt more in 3 years of
hunting than any human in 33. But if the field is close enough
to tread on them, hounds won't bother; they will say to
themselves: 'Let these fools have a go; they think they know
better than us.' So then you have a huntsman trailing about

when what he should be doing is ensuring that the unlikely ways have been tried first to eliminate them – foxes do, quite often, turn short. So the huntsman must have room to do so before he takes his hounds on. Otherwise he will get it wrong and they will lose confidence in him.

Hunting is a scientific business. It costs a great deal of money. For that money, members deserve a professional approach.

Wallace has equally cogent and decisive advice to offer on the matter of halloa-ing. Halloa-ing produces a problem for the huntsman in that he has to decide whether to lift his hounds and move them straight to the point where the fox was apparently seen or whether he should allow his hounds to hunt on undisturbed. Halloas are not always reliable and may have been made when seeing a fox other than the one being hunted. Ronnie explains his view:

I don't mind a halloa; I think everybody enjoys it. After all it must be better to proclaim that you have seen the fox than to keep the information to yourself until the next day.

If I react to a halloa I like the person to stand still and not gallop off with his hat in the air trying to point out the direction the fox has gone. That can lead to misunderstand-ings. I like him to be precise and tell me: 'He went through the hedge a yard or two to the right of that oak tree,' and I like him to position himself very close to the heel way (the direction from which the fox has come) so that hounds having been lifted, don't set off back down the line. I have seen that happen so often. And people should never stand actually on the line they saw the fox take; that way they foil the scent and hounds can only find the heel way. If it is a bad scenting day and hounds seem unsure, the huntsman will doubt the veracity of the halloa and that will be the time to reassure him and be precise about exactly where the fox went.

If it has been a bad day with difficult scent and hounds are settled with a fox, I leave them alone and ignore a halloa. There will be few followers left and they will deserve a good hunt.

Most of all I would never try to lift hounds unless I was absolutely certain that I could grab them all. If they are hunting a long way away, this may not be possible. They should then be left to hunt on however much I trust the halloa. The very worst thing you can do to your hounds is to give them an order which you cannot enforce.

The key to the Wallace way with hounds seems to be control but not slavish control. The Heythrop hounds were allowed, encouraged even, to do their own thing during both a draw of a big or difficult covert and when having checked. Perhaps the most graphic description of Wallace's unique skill comes from Michael Clayton, the Editor of *Horse and Hound* who, having hunted with practically all the 196 packs of foxhounds in the United Kingdom, is better placed than most to make comparisons:

> It was towards the end of the day and there were not many of us left. Ronnie stood at the side of wood and said, 'Shut up all of you. Stand absolutely still and I want to hear no halloa-ing. Not a sound.'
>
> With that he disappeared into the covert with his hounds. Foxes came out in all directions but not a single hound. I was astonished; this was quite incredible. Eventually a fox emerged, presumably heading in the direction that Ronnie wished it to go and then came the pack; hunting as one they swept off like a carpet. I don't remember seeing Wallace and we had a fast and brilliant 25 minutes round the Evenlode Vale, hounds catching and killing their fox just in front of us. I looked up and the master of the Heythrop trotted through a gateway, dismounted and told the bitch pack that they'd been 'rather good girls'. It was an astounding performance and one that I have never seen matched. I asked him how he did it; how it was that all the other foxes had been ignored; nobody else could do that. He said: 'You just wait your chance.'

Bill Lander, that most generous of men who went on to hunt the Wynnstay Hounds with much distinction, sums up this aspect of Wallace's talent: 'I don't know what the bugger does. I do the same as him but it doesn't work for me.'

The production of a pack of foxhounds which will perform in the superlative way required by Wallace is a long drawn out and patient business. When that kennel is also required to produce show winners to beat the best in the world, the difficulties are compounded. It would seem self-evident that the two demands should go hand-in-hand, that the qualities needed by the best working hounds should also be those that make a champion and it is Wallace's belief that it should be so; but others have felt differently. We have already heard of the coterie of influential men who, in the 1920s and '30s banded together to impose a fashionable, show-winning type almost irrespective of performance in the field. This attitude has sometimes been taken to even greater extremes in the interests of pot hunting. A stallion-hound in great demand in the 1950s was never allowed to go hunting for fear that he should become injured in some way. A kennel in Wales kept a separate lodge for show hounds who were also never able to enjoy the hurly-burly of the chase for which they were bred.

As in all competition at the highest level, there are often incidents which at best cause the eyebrows to raise and at worst give rise to speculation of downright skulduggery. Ronnie, like all successful practitioners of an art, has been by no means free of innuendo directed at his methods and, as his influence grew, at his alleged manipulation of hound show judges. Some comments are, there is no doubt, manifestations of plain jealousy, others are more constructive and refer to Wallace both complicating and, perhaps, compromising his position as a leading judge and chairman of the MFHA by showing hounds himself.

In 1952 hounds, especially good hounds, were still scarce so soon after the war but it was clear that the 'good plain cooks' of the Heythrop clearly needed both smartening up (for showing) and sharpening up (for hunting). The Wallace plan was to meld both these improvements so that the hounds that won the prizes were unarguably those who performed best at their job. He began, as we have already seen, by using the two brilliant Portman stallion-hounds, Lorimer and Latimer. He also started to cull the Heythrop pack of its disruptive influences, notably the tendency to skirt caused by the surprisingly rascally off-spring of a fine hound called Kilkenny Teacher whose progeny had also permeated the Duke of Beaufort's kennels. A hound prone to skirting is one which cuts corners instead of following the exact line of the hunted fox and this attribute is one which breaches the mutual trust between huntsman and hounds which Wallace placed very high on his list of priorities. He culled ruthlessly, not necessarily by putting hounds down (although in extreme cases this had to be done) but by drafting out those who were not up to the standard he had set himself to other packs now eager for some Heythrop blood.

He began to upgrade his pack by judicious use of stallion-hounds from the Portman and from Badminton and introduced some new female lines which he had admired at the Ludlow and one emanating from a bitch from the Carlow in Ireland which he had drafted into the Cotswold. It was clearly important to stick generally to the 'Heythrop sort', that is those that performed best on both the thin soil of the Cotswold hills and on the more holding ground of the Vales. But this, he felt, had to be tempered by the need to adapt to changing conditions: the increase in farm machinery and road traffic (whose fumes added to the scenting problems) and the spread of arable farming which reduced the proportion of grassland to plough considerably.

With all this in mind he decided that the influence of the Welsh blood, introduced by Ikey Bell and his principal disciples, Farquhar and 'Master', had gone far enough and there was no need for more. Speed, nose, tongue and fox-sense had certainly been improved but Wallace felt that some of the stamina required to keep going all day, as well as the essential biddability which, together with fox-sense could be described as intelligence, was lacking. It was not that he felt that those who continued to show good sport in Leicestershire, or even in the less fashionable packs such as the Taunton Vale, should be criticized for their breeding policies, but he felt that affairs could be better arranged. In short, he believed that where Old English blood predominated, hounds would often be strung out, a little short on discipline; and that where Welsh blood had too much the upper hand, stamina and speed were lacking so that catching foxes slowly and efficiently became the be-all and end-all at the expense of the enjoyment of the ladies and gentlemen who, after all, provided the funds. Huntsmen with hounds which were 'too Welsh' were prone to keeping people still while hunting methodically on their own and this, Wallace felt, is not what the sport should be about; he has a marked dislike of killing a lot of foxes without the attendant haroosh.

He cast about for answers to these two problems and concluded that the tough fell-hounds of Cumbria would provide both the endurance and speed that he sought, and that a touch of American blood would add stamina and an inclination to chase almost anything which, in moderation, could be harnessed into a proper keenness to press affairs to a swift conclusion.

This triple combination of conventional breeding using Heythrop blood, that from the two most successful kennels in England and the more adventurous out-crossing with Fell and American, eventually resulted in dazzling triumph in the show ring as well as in the field. But in the latter case it has to be remembered that it was Wallace's handling abilities that set the Heythrop apart. His hounds, as time passed, were all beautifully bred with good noses, fine voices, speed and stamina. They were all of a size – important because a hound that is too big has difficulty passing through sheep wire and thick hedges and those that are small tend to breed even smaller – and they hunted as one. But Heythrop hounds, bred in just the same way, were constantly drafted to other packs and did not necessarily show such good sport. Careful breeding is not the only criterion. The other essential is the trust between huntsman and hounds which leads to high morale on both sides. The Heythrop hounds (not to mention the followers) expected every day to be a good one; they expected to catch foxes and they were not disappointed. Apart from the first two years of Ronnie's mastership, over one hundred brace were killed every season, his record being 151.

In the show ring the Heythrop, having never having competed previously, soon began to make an impact. In 1953, an unentered hound won its class at the West of England Show at Honiton and Percy Durno was tickled pink at this unaccustomed public glory. Soon he was as enthusiastic as his master and the following year they won the Novice Class at the Peterborough Show, a prelude to carrying off both the Doghound Championship and the Stallion-Hound Class with Harper 53 in 1955. From then on the Heythrop became a major force in the premier shows all round the country and the Duke of Beaufort, who had considered winning championships to be his own divine right, became first alarmed and then rather cross. He was extremely competitive and would rock to and fro in his seat as judging approached a climax, exploding in a flash of fury if his hound was beaten. This much amused his close friend, Queen Elizabeth the Queen Mother, who once asked those around her at Peterborough: 'Is it always like this?' She knew perfectly well that it was!

The Heythrop won as many championships as the Beaufort in the 22 years from 1955 to 1977, including 17 dog and bitch hound winners at Peterborough alone and now, from a standing start, the hunt lies second to their greatest rivals in the all-time lists. The rough tough Heythrop Brigand 54 became the most valuable stallion-hound of his time – perhaps the greatest ever – and his progeny have had enormous and widespread influence. Both he and his mother, Ludlow Bangle, hunted in their tenth season, another quality which Wallace prizes highly. Longevity enhances the much sought after 'fox-sense', for a hound learns and retains more in three years hunting than a human in a life time. How much wiser then is an animal in its eighth, ninth or tenth season, and how useful that experience is to the younger members of the pack.

Ronnie Wallace's quarter of a century at the Heythrop not only attracted foxhunters from all over the world anxious to see the sport at its very best (including members of the Royal Family, notably that most enthusiastic afficionado, The Prince of Wales) but also attention from the press. Eulogies from *Baily's Hunting Directory*, *Horse and Hound*, the *Field* and other publications devoted to field sports at home and abroad were only to be expected, but his fame spread much further and led, among others, to a perhaps surprisingly sympathetic profile of him in the *Sunday Times Colour Supplement*. That article made a point of highlighting yet another of Ronnie's contributions to the fabric of hunting in its allusion to his relationship with the all-important (and frequently forgotten) foot and car followers:

> Ronnie Wallace is unfailingly courteous to people on foot and in cars. Many masters treat them with contempt, but they are a source of income which he has organized into a very profitable supporters' club. Followers come from Birmingham, Coventry and Derby, jamming the lanes, spoiling the scent with their exhausts, but they are always welcome. It is with hunt members that Wallace can be crushing. . . .

The Heythrop were among the first to acknowledge and encourage the formation of a supporters' club and the concept was enthusiastically embraced by the new master at the very beginning of his tenure. He saw it as a way of not only raising money but of spreading the word and widening the interest of the community in hunting. In another address to the American Foxhound Club, Wallace enthused:

> What it (a supporters' club) really means is that the hounds are not just the property of the master or the committee. They become the property of anyone and everyone who wants to be interested. The whole basis of hunting in England is to be able to do so with the consent of the community. I believe that instead of hunting being just an exclusive sport for people dressed up in fancy clothes it is far better to make it a sport in which all can have a part if they want it.
>
> Supporters' clubs are not, however, things you can push. It is no good persuading people to join if they are not interested; they must do their own recruiting at their own pace. Most important of all it has to be their own show. They must organize their own party and ask you, as a master or a subscriber, to join them if they wish it. Let it be their performance.

These are wise words indeed and those of a man who has the survival of foxhunting truly at heart, not just for the pleasure it gives its mounted followers or the practical help it provides to those whose interests it serves as a method of controlling the fox population, but to a much wider community.

In 1952 there was no possible way that the Heythrop Hunt could guess exactly what it was getting when, after so much wrangling and heart-searching, it appointed Ronnie Wallace to be joint-master and huntsman. The subscribers knew, of course, of his reputation at the Cotswold and even those who had not nipped across the border for a day or two with the young prodigy, might well have seen him in action as he penetrated deep into Heythropia in hot pursuit of his quarry. They might even have suspected that he would be a tartar in the field, that he would reorganize the country and that he might even break new ground by putting the Heythrop hounds up in competition with the best in the land. But they could not know that they were to experience a second Golden Age under a huntsman whose regime would stand favourable comparison with any in the long history of the sport.

Neither could they even guess at the phenomenal energy of the man who led them in the field for five days a week for twenty-five years, and for most of those years was master of the Hawkstone Otterhounds as well. They had no idea that they were taking on a whirlwind of activity which would be harnessed to the business of satisfying them all – subscribers (both old and conservative and young and eager), farmers, landowners, supporters and hound breeding enthusiasts. They could only learn to marvel at the hours spent at the end of a long and tiring day, soaked to the skin through the heavy green coat, seeing that a missing hound had been retrieved, that damage was being repaired, that a hard used piece of land was apologized for to the farmer in person – and then attend a quiz at the Supporters Club or visit the kennels to see that the staff, horses and hounds were safely tucked away. They could not believe, until it proved incontrovertible, that this man could also be playing a major part in the central direction of the sport (as he was from 1970 onwards) and that he never turned down an invitation to judge at a puppy or hound show, at home or abroad, unless he was double booked.

It would be impossible and even tedious to attempt to recount here the many red-letter days of the Wallace regime or even those that his diaries describe as deserving to be written up in 'letters of gold'. One example, though, is necessary and was recorded, with many a patent understatement, by Richard Fleming on 27 February 1971 following the meet at Stockbridge:

The field-master had some difficulty in penning his unruly charges in the corner of Wing Commander and Mrs Mackie's twenty-acre field and when our scout gave us the signal, the thunder of hooves as the large field swept down towards the small hunting gate was worth hearing. As each rider shot like a cork from a bottle through the creaking gate-posts they searched anxiously for sight or sound of the pack and as luck would have it, hounds had been brought to their noses on the railway and gave us a few moments to get on terms.

The first part of the hunt that followed was enjoyable enough but there was nothing to show what lay in store. Over the railway and in and out of the Evenlode road, we were soon jumping Gim Laurence's inviting fences on our way to Stupples. A broken bridge here caused some confusion but hounds ran on steadily past Stupples and then at a better pace back over the railway and up to the Fosse. Our pilot turned here and gave us a good ride, with the brook claiming one or two victims, over to Frogmore. Once again we crossed the railway (thanking our lucky stars that we have such good friends among the engine crews on this line) through Mr Worlock's covert Yells Osier and Evenlode Mains and out at a smart pace over Mr Arthur Lane's nice grass as if for Warwickshire.

Competition was keen among our young thrusters but it was one of our senior ladies on her grey cob who pounded us all over the iron gate which had turned our treasurer over earlier in the season. Then to everyone's disappointment hounds turned back into Stupples and a most unwelcome silence descended on proceedings. Out came cigarettes; horses' legs were inspected and a few – a lucky few – changed to second horses. But the respite was short. No doubt our pilot hoped to shift his responsibilities to one of Gim Laurance's strong foxes, two of which emerged before our pilot, showing distinct signs of work, broke boldly out and set his mask for Wolford Wood. Hounds now really settled down to run, taking some of us quite by surprise and it was all one could do to get on terms with them by the time they reached the Four Shire Stone.

Crossing the Wolford road they dived into the depths of Wolford Wood, running with a great cry. He who hesitates is lost and the only thing to do was to dive in after them and take each ride or path which led towards the ever diminishing cry in the hope that one would not finish up at a dead-end. And then suddenly we were out in the open with Richard Sumner halloaing our fox away and the leading hounds silhouetted on the skyline. Once again the field was favoured for on the edge of Great Wolford, hounds were brought to their noses and we had a moment to catch up. After that we had a real touch of pre-war foxhunting over the wide Warwickshire enclosures, all green pasture, good strong fences which you could jump anywhere (or as some seemed to prefer, good strong gates), and plenty of customers ready to try conclusions with them.

As we swung left over the old railway line and the uninviting Knee Brook to Ditchford, some of us wondered if we were going to repeat the historic Meon Hill hunt of 38 years ago but to most this was unknown territory and all the more exciting. Mrs Freer's strong fences took their toll and there were frequent cries of 'loose horse' to be heard (and all too frequently ignored) as we swept down over the hill past Stretton-on-Fosse and, more slowly now, into the outskirts of Ebrington. The fox had run through Mr Stanley's lambing ewes, crept through several cottage gardens and then lain down among the sheep. Fortunately he was seen (though thought by many to be a fresh fox) and hounds worked out the line slowly but surely along the brook and crossed it close to Chipping Campden Station; we were firmly in North Cotswold territory.

They ran on better now and hunted with a great cry up the brook below Broad Campden; it was the sort of moment when Mr Jorrocks would have wagered a hundred guineas to a pound of tea that they would catch him in a moment. Suddenly all was quiet; had they caught him? We heard a horn and, turning a corner, we found ourselves face to face with Andrews the huntsman and the field of the North Cotswold who had themselves just brought a fox into the village. There was a halloa across the road and both packs ran well up to the Five Mile Drive and then to Westington Hill. By this time the Heythrop horses, and certainly that of our huntsman, had had enough but, as Robert Bartlett said, 'We can't allow the North Cotswold to have it all their own way,' and Mrs Annesley suited the action to the word by sailing over a very uninviting gate.

Fortunately for our horses, an open earth put an end to a very remarkable hunt to have taken place in 1971. For some two hundred horsemen and women to be able to travel unimpeded over 24 miles of fair hunting country; for a pack of hounds to stick to their fox for 3 hours and 25 minutes in two different points of 7½ miles and for an equal number of car followers to enjoy the fun as much as their mounted fellows is an event well worth remembering for those that had the luck to take part. It was a remarkable achievement on the part of our master and huntsman who handled the hounds so skilfully and had bred them for just these conditions. Among the unsung heroines of the day, Mrs Dammers' feat in gate-shutting for all those 24 miles deserves our thanks and admiration.

An Oxford undergraduate once described the Heythrop as 'a nice lot of old gentlemen in long coats who don't curse you so much as the Bicester'. Wallace changed more than the quality of the oath. He moulded his environment in a way not seen before or since.

CHAPTER 9

The Battle for Hunting –
and the End of an Era

FOXHUNTING, like all sports, has a governing body which formulates its rules and attempts to see that they are carried out. What sets it apart from football, cricket, bridge and the rest and also adds a crucial dimension to the preoccupations of its law-makers is that it is continually fighting for its life against the menaces of some politicians and the anti-hunting bodies whose causes they espouse.

The organization charged with the proper conduct of England's leading country sport is the Masters of Foxhounds Association, formed in 1881. Before that time hunting disputes had been arbitrated by a committee of Boodle's Club in St James's under the long-term chairmanship of Lord Redesdale; a committee which functioned for 24 years in a reasonably effective way but which suffered considerably from the fact that it had no powers to enforce its decisions. This lack of teeth was highlighted by what became known as the Great Quorn Dispute, precipitated in 1853 by the action of Sir Richard Sutton, master of the Quorn, when he handed over the Billesdon portion of his country, essentially that around Market Harborough, south of the Leicester–Uppingham road, to his son (also called Richard). Three years later, with permission from the Suttons, a Mr Tailby formed a pack and hunted the area successfully for nearly a quarter of a century, towards the end of which the Quorn decided that it should be reclaimed. The ensuing furore divided farmers and landowners and tempers ran high when the Boodle's Committee ruled that the country should indeed be returned to the Quorn. Tailby and his successor Sir Bache Cunard, backed by a powerful and vocal body of tenant farmers, took not the slightest notice and the committee fumed impotently on the side-lines. Eventually the influential Earl Spencer, master of the neighbouring Pytchley, stepped in to try to save something of the committee's face by announcing that in his view Cunard should continue to hunt but that on his retirement the country should then revert. In the event Sir Bache hunted happily on, retiring in 1888 to be succeeded by Mr Fernie who, during his 31 years of mastership gave his name to the new hunt which now continues to enjoy some of the best grassland in Leicestershire. The Quorn's claim had faded into oblivion.

The Boodle's Committee had been seen to fail so dismally in its efforts to solve this dispute that a number of people felt that a body more representative than the twenty-four past and present masters who constituted it, was clearly needed to manage the sport more effectively. An opportunity presented itself when the management of the club quarrelled with its foxhunting members and the 8th Duke of Beaufort seized the initiative, sending the following letter to every serving master:

Badminton
May 14th 1881

The Committee of Masters of Foxhounds of Boodle's Club having ceased to exist, in consequence of the withdrawal from the club of most of its members, it is thought desirable that all the Masters of Hounds in Great Britain should form an Association and from their body appoint a committee to settle any disputes that may arise between Masters or Countries.

To effect this object you are invited to attend a Meeting on Thursday, June the 2nd at 4 pm at Tattersall's; Messrs Tattersall having kindly intimated that their Large Room shall be at the disposal of those who will respond to this Circular, and that a Committee Room shall also be always at their service.

All details as to constitution, number etc. of the Committee to be settled at the General Meeting. It is suggested, subject to the alteration that may then be agreed to, that a Committee of Nine, with a Quorum of Five, would be a workable number, and that three Members should retire annually, any of whom should or should not be eligible for re-election.

It is also suggested that valuable assistance may be derived from ex-Masters of Hounds of long standing being invited to join and that all those who come under that description, and who belonged to the Committee of Boodle's, be especially invited to do so.

Any Gentleman receiving this Circular and unable to attend the General Meeting, is requested to signify in writing to the Hon Secretary, MFH Association, Tattershall's, whether he will join or not.

A subscription of 10s per head, annually, will more than cover all expenses.

BEAUFORT

Forty-seven serving masters responded by turning up at the meeting with a further 105 signifying that they would wish to be included in the Association. The list of those present is a reminder in itself of the great names of hunting, among them Beaufort, Grafton, Portman, Watkin Williams-Wynn, Coventry and Yarborough as well as the redoubtable Mr Tailby (now retired from the Billesdon) and his adversary at the Quorn, Mr Coupland.

Matters proceeded much as envisaged by the Duke of Beaufort and on 20 June the new committee met for the first time under the chairmanship of Mr W. E. Oakeley to formulate its rules. The guidelines then laid down, although refined and supplemented over the years to keep pace with modern developments, have changed little and even today remain the basic framework by which the Masters of Foxhounds Association conducts its business.

All masters are members of the MFHA and ex-masters too are eligible, provided that they have served their hunts in that capacity for not fewer than five consecutive years. The much needed teeth are provided by the fact that unless a hunt's master (or masters) are members, the hunt is not 'recognized' and the privileges that go with that recognition are withdrawn. Perhaps the most telling of these, financially anyway, is the right to hold a point-to-point race-meeting for which the Jockey Club will only grant a licence to a recognized hunt – the Jockey Club and the MFHA having a Joint Liaison Committee to administer the sport which is run strictly under the Club's rules. Expulsion of a master or a whole mastership from the MFHA means, therefore, that either the hunt has to appoint a new team acceptable to the Association or its recognition is withdrawn.

Ronnie Wallace first became a member in 1944 and went to his first Annual General Meeting at the Cavalry Club shortly after the war, under the chairmanship of the 10th Duke of Beaufort. In 1952, at the instigation of his principal mentor, Peter Farquhar and proposed by another old friend, Bill Scott, he was elected to the committee. At that time the secretary of the Association, Toby Fitzwilliam, was located with the British Field Sports Society in London and this close marriage of the two bodies was to remain in force until 1967 when the MFHA and a full-time Secretary, by now John Chamberlayne, who figured so importantly in Ronnie's

Heythrop life, moved to Chamberlayne's Oxfordshire home.

In the years since its inception, until well after the Second World War, the Association largely confined itself to the internal regulation of the sport, settling disputes over boundaries, amalgamations and hound ownership as well as seeing that its members conducted both themselves and their hunting according to the law and the MFHA's own rules and recommendations. Rarely did it involve itself in the wider political issues, leaving the defence of hunting in parliament and in the country to the BFSS which had been set up in 1930 in response to political moves against country sports in general and hunting in particular. In this it had been wholly successful – despite its lamentably low and unrepresentative membership, not one Act of Parliament contrary to its main interests had been passed since its inception.

Since the 1950s the balance of MFHA business has shifted considerably so that latterly only a minute fraction of its time is devoted to solving foxhunting disputes. The defence of hunting in the face of increased pressure from its opponents as expressed in opinion polls and encouraged by the popular press and the occasional television programme; the proliferation of anti-hunting organizations, the sometimes militant activities of their members and the consequent need to oppose them effectively, obliged the Association to come out of its rather cosy rural retreat and meet the criticism head on.

Wallace was in the front line of this fight at a very early stage beginning with a notable foray into high visibility public relations on the subject of myxomatosis. This cruel and lethal disease was introduced into the United Kingdom as a means of controlling the rabbit population at about the same time as he joined the MFHA Committee. Once the British public had begun to take in the ghastly pictures of the effect on rabbits it began to speculate on the effect that the disease might have on the ecology in general and foxes in particular. What, it wondered, would the fox eat when deprived of its major prey. More domestic hens, no doubt; many lambs, indubitably. And then what? Would they venture out of the countryside and into the towns? Were cats safe? What about babies being sunned in their prams in suburban gardens? Clearly nothing and no-one would be immune unless something was done. Foxes must be caught, shot, gassed, poisoned, wiped out – anything to prevent them becoming a menace. Difficult as it is to believe, such speculation amounting to near hysteria, fanned as it was by newspapers battling for circulation, began to appear to be a serious threat to the very existence of the fox and, therefore to hunting. Action was required urgently to stabilize the situation and, characteristically, Ronnie provided it. He wrote a piece for the *Sunday Times* laying out the evolutionary principles involved and proven over the ages by the survival of other species threatened by similar dire changes of environment. Matters, he pointed out, would find their own level. The fox's nocturnal habits and instinctive dislike of human habitation would not easily be changed; a more vegetarian diet would be cultivated; there was no need for panic; things would soon return to normal. Hunting was still, and always would be, the best way of controlling the fox population without endangering the species. It was expensive, of course, no-one would deny that, but it was not public money that was being expended and hunting was unarguably selective, ensuring that there would be no distressing incidents of foxes and other animals injured and left to die in slow agony by any of the wholesale methods of destruction now being urged on the government. It was a sound, well presented case and brought a strong whiff of common sense back into an argument which had threatened to get dramatically out of hand. He had made his point and successfully defused the situation. The media lost interest and moved on to more pressing affairs.

The myxomatosis saga had two profound effects on Ronnie Wallace's life: it made him aware of the power of the press and how it could be manipulated both for and against his beloved sport and it raised public consciousness over the issue of hunting, sparking in Wallace a vague, as yet unformed, realization that positive steps would need to be taken to secure its future. Nothing should be taken for granted.

Organized opposition to hunting had started in 1891 with the formation of the Humanitarian League, founded and run by two Fabian pamphleteers, Salt and Williams, who were also active members of the RSPCA. In its brief existence, the League made three major impacts on society. It first attacked the Royal Buckhounds – which hunted carted deer – on the grounds of both cruelty and because they were supported by money from the Civil List, and in this campaign it had some success. In 1902 it launched an attack on the Eton Beagles which, in common with subsequent similar assaults, was singularly unsuccessful, failing even to gain the support of the local branch of the RSPCA. Finally, in 1915, it published a collection of anti-hunting essays under the title 'Killing for Sport'. This gathered together the various arguments against hunting, emphasizing the alleged cruelty and stressing that it was the duty of humanity to protect other living creatures. The pamphlet also made the fundamental error, often repeated since, of trying to introduce a decidedly class element into the arguments, claiming that because of the expense involved, hunting could only be for the rich. George Bernard Shaw, in an otherwise sympathetic preface to 'Killing for Sport' sounded a notable word of caution about the dangers of similar generalizations: 'I have known many Sportsmen,' he wrote, 'and none of them are ferocious. I have known many Humanitarians and they are all ferocious!'

The League's short life ended in 1919. It had been unable to resist expanding its condemnation of hunting to include attacks on other aspects of the imperfect society in which it believed it lived: it espoused pacifism and vegetarianism among other un-fashionable causes, shedding support in the process and withering away in a social climate which had little patience with what it came to perceive as a collection of cranks.

It was not until 1924 that a new anti-hunting body was formed with the emergence of the League for the Prohibition of Cruel Sports, later to become the League Against Cruel Sports. This considerably more single-minded institution was the brainchild of Henry Amos and Ernest Bell who, like their humanitarian forerunners, were disgruntled members of the RSPCA. Acrimonious criticism of the world's leading animal welfare association was not, however, to the unanimous taste of the members of the embryo LACS and the League was able to preserve its unity for only eight years – internal dissension appears to be endemic among such organizations – for in 1932 a breakaway group formed the National Society for the Abolition of Cruel Sports. Among the prominent defectors were Ernest Bell and Henry Salt.

The NSACS, although launched on a wave of optimism, was soon outstripped by the LACS in terms of membership and income but it was to be some time before its influence evaporated altogether. Both concentrated their efforts on obtaining a political platform and during the Second War strenuous attempts were made to drag hunting into the limelight on the grounds of the unpatriotic nature of continuing such activities during hostilities and times of deprivation but these somewhat strident calls were unheard in Parliament, partly because of the suspension of Private Members' time but largely because MPs had more weighty matters to consider. Both organizations, however, believed with some justification that a post-war Labour government would be sympathetic to their views. In 1947 the NSACS published a Bill to protect British wild animals from cruelty in which it proposed the abolition of all forms of hunting and cast about for a Member of Parliament willing to promote it. In this it was helped by Anthony Greenwood (later a President of the Society) who secured the services of a Labour MP, Michael Cocks, whose name had come near the top of the Private Members' ballot. After wide consultation the original terms of the Bill were modified (in an attempt to increase support) to exclude a ban on foxhunting and in the 1948–9 parliamentary session it was debated in its new form. To the intense disappointment (and no little surprise) of the sponsors, it was defeated when the Government Front Bench withdrew its support after taking advice from the Minister of Agriculture, Tom Williams, and the Home Secretary, Chuter Ede, despite the fact that each had sponsored abortive anti-hunting measures in the 1930s. At the same time, a separate Prohibition of Foxhunting Bill was withdrawn whilst still in draft. This twin defeat signalled the end of the NSACS as an effective lobby.

During all this activity the position of the largest and easily the most influential animal welfare society in England and Wales, the RSPCA, remained equivocal. Founded in 1824 and given its Royal Warrant (and consequent respectability) by Queen Victoria in 1840, it was not until the 1880s that it began to wrestle with the strains of trying to carry out its role and yet approve (or anyway, not disapprove) of hunting in any of its forms. The struggle to resolve this dilemma has been one of a leadership – drawn in great part from the field-sport establishment – trying to avoid the need to take executive action on regular anti-hunting resolutions passed by activist rank and file who pack Annual General Meetings. In 1908, for example, a motion was passed which instructed the governing body, the Council, to draft for parliament a bill to abolish otter hunting. In 1929 and 1939 respectively, similar votes were won on measures to ban deer hunting and coursing. None were acted upon; the pro-hunting majority on the Council being adept in shelving the hunting issue while always continuing effectively to promote action against all forms of cruelty to tame, captive and domestic animals.

The publicity attendant on the progress of the 1949 Bill heightened public and parliamentary interest and led to a government appointed inquiry – the Scott Henderson – into all forms of hunting. No member of any abolitionist body was invited to serve on the committee but the evidence offered by the RSPCA leadership to the effect that the cruelty involved in controlling foxes by means other than hunting (including shooting) would far outweigh any suffering inflicted by hounds, was decisive. In 1951 the Inquiry made its report and unequivocally rejected any notion of abolishing either hunting or coursing.

The Scott Henderson Report has been a much quoted document by those charged with the preservation of hunting and was a further grevious blow to the abolitionists. The BFSS saw an opportunity to go on the attack, particularly in its attempts to convince journalists (and through them the general public) that hunting had a positive contribution to make, both to the countryside in general and to the conservation and balance of nature. By the end of the decade the Society was declaring that the unfavourable publicity generated by anti-hunting incidents was a 'thing of the past'.

That this proved to be a somewhat over-optimistic prediction was due to two developments. The apparent loss of initiative by the LACS drove its extremists to form the Hunt Saboteurs Association whose members dedicated themselves to bringing the issues once again before the public – this time by direct action. In this it was successful and its activities soon began to enrage hunting people – and in particular masters of foxhounds – by their disruptive, sometimes violent demonstrations. These, in turn, provoked reaction both physical and verbal from the more volatile of masters so that once again the press found the hunting field a fruitful source of dramatic copy. Fights frequently broke out between saboteurs and hunt supporters and the BFSS was obliged to issue guidelines to masters on how they should deal with the adverse public relations that such incidents were engendering. The unease of the BFSS was, to some extent, shared by the LACS (now by far the strongest of the anti organizations), who felt that strong-arm tactics did nothing to recruit respectable citizens to its own cause and indeed might lead to a positive falling off in middle-class (and therefore monied) support.

The distancing of the MFHA from the BFSS in 1967 was, to begin with, confined to the geographical separation – the Society still continued to lead in directing the campaign in defence of hunting. The balance started to change, however, in 1970 when Wallace assumed the chairmanship of the MFHA. The process was a gradual one as Ronnie slowly immersed himself in hunting related politics and public relations. He had, by this time, formed a strategy which was soon to become a firm (if unstated) tenet of both MFHA and BFSS policy: 'Hunting has to be kept off the agenda.' Despite opinion polls, the activities of the antis, the shrinkage of hunting countries and all the other difficulties, the only real threat to hunting was, and always would be, through parliamentary legislation, and the best way to avoid that, Wallace insisted, was to see that hunting maintained a low public profile whilst cultivating and developing influential contacts capable of diverting trouble, if not avoiding it altogether. The importance of knowing the right people and getting them to act at the right time first became apparent to him during the 1949 Bills when the National Farmers' Union and the senior civil servants in the Ministry of Agriculture were instrumental in persuading Tom Williams that, 'The nation depended on the goodwill of all classes of the rural population; to ban hunting would alienate the very people now so critically engaged in providing the nation's food' and that, 'Field sports were not the exclusive preserve of the leisured classes but a traditional feature of country life, patronized by large masses of the rural population.'

By the mid-1960s Ronnie, as a prominent member of the ruling bodies of both the BFSS (of which he was to become a vice-chairman) and the MFHA, had extended his contacts considerably, cultivating MPs of all parties including Marcus Kimball, John Morrison (later Lord Margadale) and Edward Du Cann from the Conservatives, and Reggie (later Lord) Paget from the Labour benches. All were committed hunting men and indeed there were many other active supporters in parliament, including a number of Labour MPs who preferred not to have their sympathies made widely known. A major study into Predatory Mammals in Britain saw him involved with senior representatives from the Home Office, the Ministry of Agriculture, Nature Conservancy, Forestry Commission, the Council for Nature, the Fauna Preservation Society and the Society for the Promotion of Nature Reserves, among others, and did much to extend his network of potentially influential and sympathetic allies as well as giving him an invaluable insight into the attitudes of those who would work against hunting. It was at this time, too, that he first got to know a young BBC Lobby Correspondent, Michael Clayton, who was later to take on much of the PR work for the MFHA and then to become editor of *Horse and Hound* – an apolitical, almost apathetic, magazine which Clayton was to turn into an informed and powerful voice in the cause of hunting.

When Wallace became chairman of the MFHA in 1970, he

followed a distinguished line, succeeding Lord Halifax (who as the Hon Charles Wood had been a predecessor in the mastership of the ECH), Sir Peter Farquhar and the Duke of Beaufort. He had understudied Halifax when the latter had taken a central role in Whitehall two years earlier in minimizing the effects of Foot and Mouth Disease on hunting and had revelled in the chance that gave him to display his talent for diplomacy and patient negotiation. He immediately set about making his mark at his first AGM by changing the format of the Chairman's Address, traditionally the centrepiece of the meeting. It had been the custom for his predecessors to read out a prepared statement. Wallace spoke from only the briefest of notes and delivered a wide-ranging survey of the present state and the future of foxhunting. The audience, a mixture of the most distinguished practitioners of the sport and those who hardly knew how to wear their breeches properly, were transfixed as he outlined the need for political awareness and impeccable standards in the conduct of hunts. The Duke of Beaufort described it as the greatest exposition on hunting that he had ever heard – praise indeed from Master himself.

Wallace was expected to hold the post for the usual three-year term, but between 1973 and 1991 he had been re-elected annually nineteen times and made the Association very much his own. When first appointed – and apart from stepping up his political initiatives – he turned his attention to two internal matters which seemed to be less than satisfactory. Firstly he was concerned, as he had already made plain, that standards had slipped in the field and in kennels among both amateur and professional huntsmen. Accordingly he extended the system of training weekends, first implemented by Farquhar, to be held periodically in the summer at which huntsmen and other hunt servants could come together to be reminded of the basics of their profession and talk over their problems. The first was held at Pendley Manor, the Tring home of Dorian Williams, a former headmaster of Hawtreys Preparatory School, and master of both the Grafton (1951–54) and the Whaddon Chase as well as a prominent writer and broadcaster on matters equestrian who shared Ronnie's enthusiasm for a less introverted approach to the sport's problems. An average attendance of around 200 in the years that followed is a testimony to the success of the venture.

Wallace also felt that matters were not all they should be in the point-to-point world (in which the MFHA also represents Harriers, Drag and Staghounds) and tackled the Senior Steward of the

Jockey Club on the matter. This led to an enquiry by Lord Leverhulme which resulted in a structure that has also stood the test of time. The modern organizational format, which Wallace was instrumental in initiating, is hierarchical: at the grass-roots, representing the Hunt Committees is an Association of Hunt Point-to-Point Secretaries (of which membership is compulsory) which reports to a number of Area Secretaries who, through their Chairman, answer to the MFHA Sub-Committee and thence to a Joint Liaison Committee (two Jockey Club Members and two from the MFHA). This may seem cumbersome but the formalization which it brought about has all but eradicated the constant differences of opinion which arose between hunts, Weatherbys (who control the qualification and registration of the horses) and the Jockey Club over the running of individual meetings. Wallace, although far from a racing man, has always chaired the relevant MFHA Sub-Committee and has been active in promoting the view that hunting (through point-to-points) is essential to the well-being of National Hunt Racing – a perspective that the Jockey Club and Weatherbys have not always shared – and that point-to-points are a useful part of the hunting year.

In 1970 there was one other problem which exercised him greatly – that of the future of otter hunting – and the happy resolution of it remains one of his most singular pragmatic triumphs. Wallace had continued to hunt the Hawkstone Otterhounds until 1969, some 30 years in all, and had stopped doing so in that year because he perceived that the time was approaching when there would be so few otters that they would die out altogether in England and Wales. The glimpses of the Hawkstone that we have seen show that otterhunting was a very different sport from its foxhunting cousin and perhaps the most apparent of these differences concerns organization: in contrast to the complicated, labour and time-intensive work necessary in say the Heythrop, the otter was hunted from most locations only once a year and little planning had to be done other than the sending out of meet cards. This infrequency of visits and the consequent opportunity for clear comparisons year by year had made it obvious to Ronnie that otters were disappearing and it was equally plain to him (although, it seems, not to others) that hunting, although contributing to the scarcity, could hardly be wholly to blame. Research proved him right. The principle detrimental causes were the increase in the use of pesticides which polluted the rivers and made some stretches uninhabitable by otters, and the lowering of the water table which denied them the cover and isolation they craved. There were subsidiary factors too – the growing popularity of canoeing as a sport and the alarming number of feral mink with whom the otter could not co-exist, are but two examples. Unlike the fox, which when under ecological pressure, turned the enforced change of habitat to its advantage by exploiting the proximity of human beings, the otter shunned such society and was completely unable to cope with the manifold disasters overtaking it.

Wallace has always felt strongly that there is no point in hunting a species unless some good comes out of it. He has, in a sense, always hunted by the book – if the quarry species is rare then fewer should be taken. He, himself, has generally hunted where foxes are numerous and has encouraged their habitat to keep affairs in equilibrium. Now he foresaw a time when the otter would become endangered to the point of extinction, and believed that those engaged in its hunting should set an example to others by curtailing their activities. It was not a universally popular view (although the number of active otter hunts had declined from 32 to 19 in the previous 40 years), especially among his otterhunting friends who, for the most part, seemed to believe that given legislation against pollution, the problem would go away.

In the face of much criticism and above all by personal example, he got his way. By careful and persistent persuasion he achieved the voluntary cessation of otterhunting before the species became officially protected in 1978. As a panacea he talked many packs into turning their attentions to mink and coypu, unpopular breeds with the general public, not least because they had been introduced and, rather like the grey squirrel, had supplanted an attractive native.

There can be little doubt that Ronnie's far-sighted perception of the otter problem did much to make him and the views propounded by him in defence of other forms of hunting, much more credible in the eyes of conservationists than they otherwise would have been if he had not taken this stand. Many, among them Michael Clayton, believe that the likelihood of legislation against other forms of hunting in the late 1970s and '80s would have been greater, perhaps irresistible, if Ronnie's view had not prevailed.

As politics and the battle for hunting took up more and more of the Wallace time – with no compensating reduction in hunting days and an ever-increasing demand for his presence at puppy and hound shows both at home and abroad – he began to contemplate his future. His beloved annual pilgrimages to Exmoor with first the Cotswold and then the Heythrop hounds, Rosie's family connections in Somerset and his advancing years in a demanding country all led him to look to the West Country. In 1975 he made his decision and gave the Heythrop committee eighteen months notice of his intention to move to the Exmoor Foxhounds and a wholly different, perhaps purer, form of hunting.

Wallace had given a great deal of thought to his successor at the Heythrop and had come to the conclusion that he would best be followed by a professional huntsman – if one could be found of exceptional calibre. But eighteen months is a long time for consideration and decision making, let alone consensus, and well before it was up internal dissensions became apparent in the hunt committee, much as they had done twenty-four years before. There were two immediate problems: who would hunt the hounds and who would take on the mastership (Lord Rotherwick having announced that he would be giving up at the same time as Ronnie). Loyalty dictated that Tony Collins, who had been first whipper-in for eight years and who was well liked, should become huntsman but in the very nature of the Wallace regime he had not hunted hounds a great deal so there was a clear risk and many had their doubts, preferring to look for an experienced outsider. In the event, internal preferment prevailed and Collins was appointed.

The mastership was a more complicated matter altogether. Not only was the guarantee for the 1977 season forecast to be £22,000 – a substantial increase – but there was the not inconsiderable matter of who was to try and emulate the Wallace talent for superlative organization and devote the long and dedicated hours involved in carrying it out. This side of affairs was exacerbated by the fact that Anthony Adams, the second whipper-in, was also planning to move to Exmoor.

Ronnie's search for a suitable joint-mastership started with Jaime and Di Aladren of Oddington. Di was Victor McCalmont's daughter and thus had a formidable hunting pedigree (as Di Turner she became joint-master of the Quorn in 1991). The Aladrens appeared to have the means to inject substantial funds and, equally important, they were already doing much of the work hitherto carried out by the estimable Lavinia Jenkinson and doing it so well that Wallace confessed himself both surprised and delighted.

The centrepiece of the jig-saw eluded him until he heard from the Ballards, the joint hunt secretaries, that Valerie Willes had confessed to them at a dinner party that, if asked, she would be prepared to join the Aladrens. Ronnie was pleased at this further evidence of hatchet burying as well as recognizing that here was the answer to the Heythrop's prayer – no-one could have held better hunting credentials. He was round to see her within an hour, much to the surprise (and secret gratification) of the cynical Maurice who steeled himself to chip in what seemed to him an inordinate amount of cash. Valerie's particular responsibilities in the mastership would be to look after the south-west of the country – that around her home at Aldsworth – and more vitally, to supervise the breeding of the hounds, advised from afar by Ronnie who would continue to be a Trustee.

The final partner was John Kirkpatrick of Little Rissington, an experienced Heythropian who, as field-master on Wednesdays, had already proved himself as a brave and dashing (some would say almost too dashing) horseman over the stiffest of obstacles.

This reorganization, promising as it seemed, was not destined to last for more than a year and perhaps, in retrospect, it would have been remarkable if it had done so. There was a gloomy and pervasive air of doom about. People were freely forecasting that things would never be the same again and were bound to fall apart when Wallace left. Such resigned attitudes often result in prophecies becoming self-fulfilling, and so it proved. The Aladrens, on whom so much depended, were in the midst of a domestic crisis which led to divorce and not only were they unable to get on with each other, they also had difficulty in getting on with Tony Collins. The huntsman, through lack of true, un-supervised, experience at the very sharp end of hunting and the high expectations of a field now used to superlative sport on almost every day, irrespective of conditions, failed to deliver. It was hardly his fault.

There were other factors too: the energetic and efficient Hunt Vice-Chairman, Richard Fleming, died suddenly and with him went the accumulated, precious and irreplaceable knowledge of the Heythrop imbued in the Fleming family. In the country itself, more corn was grown and more wire was appearing; shooting was beginning seriously to encroach upon traditional hunting preserves and some of the older and staunchest supporters were coming to the end of their active careers. Characters like Colonel Johnnie Godman who, if shooting but hearing hounds get closer, would instruct his guests to lie down and hide, were becoming few and far between. This unfortunate combination of circumstances conspired to ensure that the Heythrop was on a hiding to nothing and in the end it was Valerie Willes who was left to shoulder the administrative burden until another new mastership could be formed and an amateur, Stephen Lambert, engaged to hunt hounds.

At his last official meet, Ronnie and Rosie were driven in a carriage and pair (with the Crown Equerry, Sir John Miller, in attendance) to join the rest of the field and his beloved hounds. A silver rose-bowl and a pair of equally magnificent silver foxes' heads were presented to them and hunting started at ten, ending with a successfull kill at two-thirty after a hunt of three hours and fifty minutes. A champagne reception at Batsford was attended by the Duke of Beaufort and was followed by dinner with the Flemings at Leygrove complete with speeches and appreciations from a number of distinguished guests. It was an emotional time and Ronnie was relieved to be out again on the Monday with a Children's Day – a fitting final appearance at the Heythrop for one who had always taken immense trouble to see that the young were encouraged to enjoy their hunting.

The final curtain on Ronnie Wallace's epoch-making tenure was lowered at the Heythrop point-to-point in May 1977. On a brilliant blue summer's day, hunt servants in full livery from all the neighbouring packs had brought their hounds and were joined by the Duke of Beaufort's and by Tony Collins with a scratch collection from the home kennels – not even this momentous occasion could be allowed to interfere with the annual pilgrimage to Exmoor. Hounds and huntsmen drew up in a guard of honour to pay homage and Wallace was joined on a dais by Lord Halifax, the Lord Lieutenant of the county and a host more of his admirers and colleagues from all over England as he reviewed the splendid scene. The horses wheeled away as if hunting, jumping a wall as hounds responded to a halloa from a nearby covert. It was a deeply moving spectacle in salute of the man who had done so much in twenty-five triumphant years to raise the art of foxhunting to undreamt-of levels. The thousands of Heythropians present, from the most nobly born to the humble, had come not, perhaps, to honour him but to say a simple thank-you to 'The Captain'.

CHAPTER 10

Star of the West

THE 1991 Cattistock hunt puppy show was held at Melbury House, the splendid Dorset home of one of its joint-masters, The Honourable Mrs Charlotte Morrison. The puppy show is among the more important dates in any hunt's calendar, at which hounds born in the previous year (and therefore unentered) are shown off to an audience of puppy-walkers, admiring subscribers and many guests. The youngsters, who have spent most of the previous winter and spring boarded out at the homes of their walkers, are also to be judged on their looks and potential – a serious and formal business invariably undertaken by a pair of experienced masters or huntsmen drawn from elsewhere – and at Melbury on a grey day in June, that task fell to Captain R. E. Wallace of the Exmoor Hunt and E. R. Hanbury Esq. of the Quorn. Jos Hanbury had, for many years, been a master of both the Quorn and the Cottesmore and, although the more junior of the two, was hardly likely to be overawed by the formidable reputation of his partner. A competitive standard of judging was eagerly anticipated.

Melbury House is quite one of the most lovely and imposing houses in the Cattistock country, its mellow stones and soaring turrets giving the day a sense of stately occasion not easily matched by less well endowed hunts who, at their own shows, might well have to make do at the kennels. At precisely three o'clock, the crowd gathered in the spacious stable yard around a show-ring set up for the day. Mrs Morrison, her joint-masters and some one hundred of her friends, neighbours and visiting hunting dignitaries who had been enjoying lunch (and entertaining the judges) in the house, joined perhaps three times that number, also there by invitation, who would later take tea on a grand scale as a fitting conclusion to the afternoon's proceedings. For those who wished to sit, chairs had been placed around the ring and on one side were assembled two rows of particularly welcome guests – hunt servants in dark suits and black bowler hats, settling down good-humouredly to criticize the arrangements, the Cattistock young entry and, of course, the judges' final selections.

Hounds were introduced into the ring in couples and put through their paces by the young kennelman and first whipper-in, Charles Watt (a nephew of Tony Collins), who had spent his formative years under the demanding regime of Michael Farrin, the Quorn's professional huntsman. Watt and his assistant, Richard Sherwood (whose father had been kennel-man to the Cattistock), both wore white coats and grey bowlers as is the long established custom in the smarter countries.

Twenty-one dog-hounds were first looked at, five of them sired by Exmoor Rapier '88, a stallion-hound bred by Wallace. Six of the others, however, had been sired by Quorn Wildman '88, adding a certain piquancy to the filtering process as the less favoured were dismissed from the ring. When only five remained, Watt was asked to take them to a lawn in front of the house so that their movement and conformation could be better observed as they galloped and gamboled against each other, chasing biscuits thrown for them from the kennelman's capacious pockets. Back once more in the stable-yard, the decision was announced by the Cattistock's amateur huntsman, Martyn Lee: 1st, Raider (by Exmoor Rapier), 2nd, Lazerus (by Exmoor Rapier), 3rd, Wessex (by Quorn Wildman). The crowd murmured agreement, the more knowledgeable drawing each other's attention to the breeding of the prize-winners.

The bitches (twenty in number) produced a surprise for those who had cynically expected a similar final tussle between Exmoor and Quorn blood. The first prize went to Fourpence, sired by The Duke of Beaufort's Forester '87, a popular decision as this endearingly active young lady had been walked as a puppy by Charlotte Morrison. Fourpence was also awarded the championship for the best hound of the day – a most satisfactory conclusion and one referred to in both the short speeches made by the judges before the throng headed for tea in the library.

Wallace, in his address, made the usual congratulatory comments on the quality of the hounds and the excellence of the arrangements before taking the opportunity to stress that it was important for all those present to be continually aware that hunting was still under threat – most recently from the National Trust. Everyone who loved hunting, he urged, should join the Trust and play an active role in its affairs to help counter the anti-hunting noises being made by some within that organization.

The Cattistock puppy show was, in its way, a microcosm of the Wallace life during every summer since he had become Chairman of the MFHA 21 years earlier: a continual round of shows, both at home and abroad (particularly in the United States and Ireland), punctuated by frequent forays into the corridors of power to pre-empt or fight the occasional assaults on his beloved sport. There were those who had prophesied in 1977 that so demanding had been the pressures on Wallace that he would choose to go into some form of semi-retirement when he left the Heythrop, either to devote his time to hunting hounds in a less demanding country and doing a little judging in the summer or, perhaps, to hunt fewer days which would enable him to deal with MFHA affairs at greater leisure. They could hardly have been wider of the mark.

Ronnie and Rosie sold Eyford Knoll to Cyril Kleinwort's daughter and moved in to Mounsey Farm at Ashwick, near Dulverton at the end of July 1977. Ashwick had been Rosie's home and the Lycett-Green family once owned all the land thereabouts. The Wallaces were able to take on some 900 acres of the Manor Farm but Mounsey itself had to be bought back and there was a short but frustrating period of disorganization whilst it was redecorated.

The Exmoor Hunt was founded in 1869 by Mr Nicholas Snow of Oare in the Doone Valley. It was first known as the Stars of the West in recognition of the pale colour he favoured in his hounds. Only at the end of his mastership, twenty years later, when the Hon. Joseph Bathurst (younger brother of the foxhunting Earl) took it on, did it become known as the Exmoor. It is a wild country, some 20 miles from east to west and 12 at its widest from north to south, straddling the Devon-Somerset borders. At its heart lies Exford, a hunting village, a Melton Mowbray in minia-ture, whose hotels and businesses are largely devoted to satisfying the demands of those locals and visitors whose lives revolve round the Exmoor Foxhounds and the Devon and Somerset Staghounds. There is no jumping here – what hedges there are dividing the small grass fields from the moor proper are planted with beech and banked high and wide, beyond the scope of even the most optimistic of horses. The gradients are steep and the going is rough; enormous distances are covered, making a day's hunting a test of stamina for the fittest of horses and their pilots, especially during the driving rain and near horizontal sleet for which it is accurately famed. When the weather is good, as it often can be during cubhunting (which begins on Exmoor in early August) and in the Spring when hunting goes on into May, there is no grander or more spectacular country in England; seemingly limitless horizons of rolling moorland, rushing rivers, neat emerald green fields and the sea all blend effortlessly in a slowly changing but always dramatic kaleidoscope.

Ronnie's boyhood holidays, his honeymoon with Jean and, more extensively, his annual excursions to the Moor with the Cotswold and Heythrop hounds meant that he had come to know its vagaries well and he had formed close friendships with a number of its distinguished masters. Among them had been Peter Wood and, most notably, Colonel Guy Jackson who had taken the Exmoor in 1946 after a war in which he lost both legs, making it necessary for him to teach himself to ride all over again using a special saddle. Ronnie, then at the Ludlow, had toyed with applying for the job himself but had been advised by Jackson and his wife Audrey that the Exmoor was not a young man's hunt. He would do better, they urged, to spend a few years in good galloping countries, gaining experience. Since that time the Jacksons had done much to encourage his spring visits and the Colonel had been a constant friend and mentor until his death in 1960. Guy was succeeded in the mastership by his widow who spent a year in partnership with Jack Hosegood, a joint-master since 1956 who was still officiating, with only a three year break when Audrey was the sole master, twenty-one years later. Hosegood was a local auctioneer, born and bred on Exmoor of an immaculate hunting family (father, mother and grandfather had been either master or huntsman of the Minehead Harriers) and he knew every inch of the country. During his long tenure he had become very popular with both the farmers, with whom his business brought him into close contact, and the growing number of spring-time visitors whom he always greeted with evident pleasure. In 1976 he shared the hunting of the hounds with Alfred Dyer, the kennel-huntsman, and it was Jack who first conceived the notion of asking Ronnie to take on the Exmoor, first writing to him in 1975 suggesting that should he wish to give up the Heythrop, he would be welcome as the principal master and huntsman. This brought together two men united only in their love of hunting; each had an implacable determination to have his own way and clashes were immediate.

Events during Ronnie's first three seasons made it difficult to discern easily just what had prompted Jack Hosegood to issue his invitation. Money was undoubtedly one factor. The Exmoor had been navigating tricky financial waters for some time but had always baulked at asking someone to become a master just because they appeared to be rich. Ronnie's reputation as the most respected huntsman in England and his unequalled talent for organizing a country may have been another but if so, Hosegood's subsequent attempts to impose his will on affairs – remain 'top dog' in the words of one well-respected and established subscriber – were clearly destined to be at odds with what he knew would be Wallace's expectations. From the outset Jack, from his position of strength derived from a pre-eminent position among the older Exmoor followers, was irritatingly condescending to the new-comer. He attempted, for example, to demonstrate his superior knowledge of the country by producing a map showing all the coverts and earths complete with pithy comments on the farmers, a move which in normal circumstances would be extremely helpful but was hardly tactful treatment of a man who had hunted hounds on Exmoor during each of the previous thirty years. As the relationship grew more strained, minor disagreements were mag-nified into major rows; a quarrel over the exact location of a meet near Leworthy Bridge – a matter of 300 yards – went on for weeks.

The sour atmosphere generated by this struggle for supremacy was entirely foreign to Wallace. He had, over the whole of his hunting career, made a virtue out of getting on with everybody in his pursuit of the art of the possible. Now he found the constant undercurrent of criticism irksome and was both surprised and hurt by it. The farmers in the west of the country, in particular those based on Barnstaple market, were Hosegood supporters and lost few opportunities to point out that Ronnie's life-style and MFHA duties took him away from Exmoor far too often for their taste, especially in the summer. The hunt chairman Ted Stanbury, himself a farmer and admirer of Hosegood, was unflinching in his support of Wallace so that, despite the grumbling, most of the farmers came to respect him, both for his ability and for his obviously deep love of the country; the fact that there were no instances of withdrawal of hunting 'welcome' is in itself a testi-mony to their willingness to cooperate. Whether Ronnie, in those early days, ever quite got on to their wavelength must be open to doubt but his hard work in always being around and about in the time available to him, gradually won him acceptance and then their friendship and confidence.

Trying hard to sit on the fence during the frequent disputes was the third joint-master, Bobby Pollack. Pollack, who lived near Withypool, had been brought up and done most of his hunting with the Ledbury and had known Ronnie from Ludlow days. He was unfailingly cheerful, rich enough to be able to contribute handsomely to the Exmoor coffers and had been invited into the mastership by Wallace with (a rare occurrence this) Hosegood's complete approval – indeed Bobby had already been considered by Jack as a possible sleeping alternative to bringing Wallace in at all. Loyal to Ronnie as an old friend, he found himself, more often than he would wish, trying to pour oil on the troubled waters and found it increasingly difficult to maintain his natural good humour in the face of Hosegood's frequent insistence on button-holing him with complaints about Wallace's supposed iniquities.

In those first few years Ronnie hunted hounds three days a week. He had brought with him some 25 couple from Chipping Norton to supplement the considerable quantity of Heythrop blood already evident at the Exmoor kennels from drafts given to Hosegood over the years. He realized that the hounds in general needed some intensive work if they were to come to terms quickly with the differing techniques needed to hunt successfully as the dramatic Exmoor seasons changed. Scenting conditions in the spring, for instance, when the grass and moorland foliage were sparse, were at variance with those in the autumn and early winter when the ferns covered large tracts of the country. Exmoor hounds would need to be sharper and more adaptable than most to make the best of the fleeting chances which could turn an ordinary day into one to remember.

For three years Wallace hunted his hounds whilst Jack Hosegood hunted a separate pack on a fourth day, and this unusual division of responsibilities lasted until the auctioneer suffered a heart-attack and resigned the mastership in 1980. This unfortunate experience did little either to diminish his close interest in hunt affairs or loosen his grip on his supporters and he was later to attempt a comeback which led to further upheavals.

Ronnie's hound breeding programme produced quick results when Exmoor Fortescue '77 won the championship at Peter-borough in 1980, and that early success fired the interest of the Exmoor subscribers and puppy-walkers who had been unused to such high-flying. In all his endeavours he had an enthusiastic ally in Anthony Adams but the young man was rightly ambitious and by 1981 he had decided that, much as he enjoyed working with The Captain and loved the moorland hunting, it was time to move on. Thoroughly recommended by Ronnie who, as always, was keen to see talent recognized, he went to the Warwickshire, following in the illustrious footsteps of, among others, George Gillson and Clarence Webster who was retiring after 24 years. Adams was to remain there for six seasons before returning to the Heythrop – for him the wheel had turned full cycle. He was succeeded by Tony Wright whom Wallace had known since he had come to the Heythrop as a boy. His father had been either kennel-huntsman or huntsman to the Berkeley, Cotswold Vale and Albrighton and was anxious that his son should have a good start in his chosen profession. Wright showed that he was a natural horseman and, after some time as second-horseman at Chipping Norton, was sent to the Quorn as second whipper-in to Michael Farrin. There he was soon promoted but he was at heart a 'hound' man and came happily to Exmoor when offered the vacancy.

Away from the sometimes troubled but essentially local affairs of his mastership there was much to occupy the Chairman of the MFHA in the wider world of hunting politics. The League Against Cruel Sports had embarked on a programme of buying up land and denying access for hunting. Exmoor itself was a popular shopping place for the League largely because parcels of land were relatively cheap and because staghunting was perceived to be a softer target. By the early 1980s it had acquired 33 small areas in the district, totalling over 2000 acres. Although an irritant because of the potentially bad publicity which would inevitably arise over a case of trespass, this was hardly significant in hunting terms to either the fox or the staghounds. The League therefore turned its attention to a far more serious national campaign.

In 1979, Richard Course, the LACS's Director, persuaded sympathisers within the Cooperative Wholesale Society which, country wide, owned some 50,000 acres of farm land, to begin to bring pressure on the Cooperative movement to ban hunting on its holdings. He also turned his attention to Local Authorities in an attempt to encourage them to act similarly. In both cases he had powerful leverage to exert on Labour councillors and supporters since the League had donated £80,000 to the Labour Party during the run-up to the 1979 General Election in return for a pledge that the Party would introduce legislation against hunting if it formed the next government. The Conservative victory left Labour in an embarrassing position which the League was able to exploit in reminding the Party that it now owed, at the very least, a moral obligation to help promote anti-hunting measures in both local

Captain R.E.Wallace M.F.H. taking the salute at Paddington Station on his arrival in London for the Horse and Hound Ball.

Chairman of the MFHA; he had many important meetings in London.

government and in any other institutional body in which it had influence. A number of urban councils – notably Northampton – had always banned hunting on their land but because of the small acreage involved had never made a material impact. Many more were now forced to take a vote on the issue and it rapidly became clear that the political complexion of individual councils was crucial. In Labour-held Derbyshire, Humberside and Mid-Glamorgan, motions to abolish hunting on their land were passed; in Conservative Hampshire, Lincolnshire, Oxfordshire and Dorset such moves were defeated although, ominously for the sport, Tory East Sussex passed a motion of opposition to hunting without actually banning it.

The MFHA counter-attack was swift and was, naturally, led by Wallace who had realized that, although the parcels of land involved might do little to inconvenience the practicalities of hunting, the publicity being generated by the LACS in its campaign amounted to the biggest threat to the sport since the 1949 Bill and, most annoyingly, had succeeded in putting 'hunting on the agenda'. Quickly and efficiently he marshalled his resources. In March 1982 he chaired a meeting in London at which were represented not just the ruling bodies of the various Masters' Associations (Deerhounds, Beagles, Harriers) but also coursing and shooting interests. Public Relations matters were well to the fore with both Michael Clayton and Max Hastings (later Editor of the *Daily Telegraph*) contributing valuable advice. Task Forces were set up in each hunting country and there had already been an organized boycott of Coop establishments which was to culminate in the picketing of delegates to the Cooperative Conference in Brighton later that year by the Fernie (which had lost 5000 acres to the ban), complete with hounds. The packs in Leicestershire – which had a hung County Council with a handful of Independents and Liberals holding the balance – were particularly active under the local leadership of Brian Fanshawe of the Cottesmore. They arranged a huge protest meeting at Melton Mowbray which attracted considerable national publicity and also paraded all the county's foxhound and beagle packs past the council offices. A motion to ban hunting on county council owned land was later defeated by one vote – a vital result in the county with the greatest traditions of hunting and one in which rural communities accrued great economic benefit from the sport.

In the event only some 15 councils, with land totalling some 40,000 acres, passed anti-hunting legislation. Most of the banned areas were urban fringes and the restrictions had even less effect than the Coop action. Nevertheless the LACS had obtained some useful publicity in raising the profile of the arguments and had made some inroads into the general public's apathy. More important the League had pointed the way to other institutional landlords on whom, by a policy of entryism, it might in the future be able to exercise its influence. Particular targets were to be the National Trust and the Church.

More parochial matters were occupying the Wallace mind on Exmoor where he was faced with a financial crisis brought about by inflation. A new joint-master was required to replace Jack Hosegood and one of the imperatives was clearly an injection of cash. When Ronnie had agreed to take the hounds at the end of 1975 he had been offered, and accepted, a guarantee of £8,000. By the time he arrived, 18 months later, this was barely adequate and, by 1980, the then guarantee of £12,000 covered only half the costs. Exmoor subscribers and supporters have been traditionally generous and in a sparsely populated region in which there has always been keen competition for resources from the Staghounds, it has been remarkable how much money is raised year after year. But such a wide gap between expenditure and income was beyond even their open-handedness and ingenuity. Wallace's solution was to invite Anthony Edgar, a one-time master of the Hampshire (HH) Hunt, to join Bobby Pollack. Edgar was a member of the H. Samuel jewelry family, loved his hunting on the moor and had had a yen for some time to play a major role in the hunt's affairs. The initiative came from Edgar himself who had discussed the possibilities with Colonel Frank Mitchell, a master of the Hursley Hambledon, who had then recommended him to Ronnie. He bought Blackland Farm at Withypool and remained a master for ten successful years during which he showed a great enthusiasm for joining in the spirit of the sport. On one occasion he leapt off his horse into the river in an attempt to assist hounds catch their fox, later having to lie on his back on the bank, kicking his legs in the air to remove the water (and some say, fish), from his boots. Sadly, he too was eventually to leave in circumstances which were less than harmonious.

In 1982 Bobby Pollack resigned, still on the best of terms with Wallace and, indeed, everyone in the country. He had much valued the way in which he had been treated as an equal: his joint-master often dropping in at his home after hunting to discuss the day's sport and the plans for the future. He had provided Ronnie with stalwart support over the difficult years with Jack Hosegood although under no illusions about his lack of knowledge of the finer points of hunting and breeding. In later years he always claimed, with a characteristic twinkle, that in five seasons out in the field Ronnie only ever addressed one remark to him. He had been beckoned forward to hold Wallace's horse whilst the huntsman drew a field of kale on foot. When the operation was over Pollack attempted with great difficulty to manoeuvre the animal up against a bank so that Ronnie could more easily get back on. The horse seemed reluctant to cooperate and eventually Wallace led it away and clambered on unaided. 'This horse knows more about hunting than you ever will, Bobby,' he said.

A ready volunteer to fill his place in the mastership came forward in the shape of Tim Finch, a member of a Norfolk brewing family, who, like Anthony Edgar, was keen to hunt regularly on Exmoor where he had been much taken by the atmosphere. His first experience with Ronnie had been on a day with driving snow and degenerating visibility when, after 'a devil of a hunt', the whole field, led by the huntsman, had repaired to the Poltimore Arms to await the reappearance of both the hounds and their quarry. Finch had been master of the Dunston Harriers for eight years and a competent horseman who had ridden under rules. He bought Halsgrove Farm from Pollack and all seemed set fair for a tranquil and fruitful triumvirate.

Success there was in plenty. The tally of foxes was impressive and visitors came from far and wide, especially in the spring, to watch the maestro at work – and there are few better viewing countries in England. Hounds improved their performance steadily as Wallace introduced fresh breeding: stamina and wide drawing ability were provided by Fell foxhounds and low scenting conditions countered by American blood from Gorgeous '68 (sent to him by Bill Brainard of the Old Dominion Hunt in Virginia) and the rare West Country Harrier line from Taunton Vale Catlow '80. With an admixture of pure English provided by Brocklesby Ruler '79, he also began to produce hounds that won prizes all over England. In only three years in the decade did he fail to produce a Peterborough champion. In 1990, with Daresbury '87 and Ripple '89 he won both the doghound and bitch championships.

One popular and practical innovation illustrates the supreme importance that Wallace has always attached to the precept that, although success in the show-ring is a valuable part of the process of producing top class working hounds, it is the business of showing sport and killing foxes that hunting is all about. Exmoor farmers are troubled with foxes at lambing time more than most and Ronnie introduced a system whereby farmers were able to call on the hunt early in the morning to deal with a difficult customer. Either mounted or on foot, the huntsman, with a few couple of hounds, would then cope with it. The farmers much appreciated the effort involved in producing to order such a speedy service.

In 1984 Wallace's hips began to give him severe pain and he was forced to consider his hunting future. Wright began to share the burden by hunting hounds on one or more days a week and did so admirably in the Wallace mould. Michael Clayton, in company with Ronnie, recalls them watching the kennel-huntsman perform one morning. Things looked good and Wallace murmured over and over again: 'Watch him, he's awfully good, you know.' He was clearly enjoying seeing Tony at work even though his precious hounds were in someone else's hands. He would, of course, have been the first to criticize if things had not been going well.

In February 1985, he could bear the pain no longer and placed himself in the capable hands of the specialist, Professor Kevin Hardinge. Hardinge was intrigued; he had never operated on a huntsman and was keen to see what damage over forty years in a saddle had inflicted on his patient. Anthony Edgar had Wallace driven to hospital in Lancashire in his Rolls and, in what appeared to be a remarkably short space of time, he was hunting again with two new hips at the age of 66.

Despite his success in overcoming this serious disability and the fact that, due largely to his mastership, the reputation of the Exmoor Hunt and the performance of its hounds in the field and the show-ring had never stood higher, there was a renewed attempt in 1988 to remove him. The hunt's chairman, now Ted Gundry, wished to retire and hand over his responsibilities to Josh Brown the secretary. The anti-Wallace faction, still based in the west of the country, saw this as an opportunity to try and secure the appointment for one of their own men, Ken Walker, and at the same time, persuaded Tim Finch that they would support a move to make him the senior master. The plan envisaged that Finch would run the country, arrange the meets and so on with Wallace being relegated to the role of hound breeder. They consulted Brown, who farmed at Emmetts Grange near Simonsbath and was much respected by all in the country, who advised them that he would not be a party to any scheme aimed at supplanting the hunting world's acknowledged senior and most respected master. Any such action, he said, would make the Exmoor a laughing stock.

There is little doubt that Jack Hosegood, a close friend of Ken Walker, was involved and that he saw the elevation of Finch as a neat way of reimposing his authority. After a series of confused and acrimonious meetings of the hunt committee, it began to look as if Brown would fail to gain the number of votes necessary to make him chairman, but at that stage an added complication was introduced. The national press gossip columns printed a story that Finch's wife Annie was having an affair with Tony Wright. Finch went to Wallace and suggested that he sack the kennel-huntsman. Wallace refused, taking the view that Wright's private life was his own business and any moral misdemeanours that he may have been indulging in had not affected either his loyalty to the Exmoor or, in any way, impaired his performance as one of the best hunt servants in England. Ronnie reasoned that all that needed doing to sort the matter out had been done. The affair had ended; Annie Finch had been restored, as it were, to the bosom of her family; the status quo had been resumed. Tim Finch did not see it in quite that light and resigned, taking on the mastership of the Minehead Harriers in 1989. Walker having been elected chairman by one vote at a meeting which some of Brown's supporters were unable to attend, lost the stomach for infighting and also stood down. So ended a most turbulent and unhappy episode, but the final chapter had still to be written.

Finch and Anthony Edgar had also fallen out being at logger-heads over a seemingly trivial incident in the hunting field and the hunt's finance committee which had a pro-Finch majority recommended that Edgar should resign. This seemed to be grossly unfair and was discerned by most as another gambit to secure for Finch the undisputed senior mastership. Finch's resignation solved the matter but Edgar had formed the view that perhaps he, as the provider of a large proportion of the funds, should become the sole master. He made it clear that he would only continue if Wallace left. Not unnaturally, Ronnie refused to succumb to this threat and Anthony Edgar himself moved on. Charmian Green, daughter of Guy and Audrey Jackson, came to the mastership for a year in 1989 from the Warwickshire and in 1990 Wallace was joined by Lady Caroline Gosling, daughter of Lord Halifax and sister to Peter and Charles Wood. With Josh Brown as chairman and Tony Wood as secretary, Wallace was at last surrounded by friends.

So ended a period of strife such as Wallace had never before had to endure. Perhaps the geographical remoteness of the Exmoor had made it a more introspective organization than most – more resistant to change and prone to a tunnel vision which lacked a sense of proportion. As chairman of the MFHA and acknowledged doyen of his world, Wallace has often been consulted by hunts suffering similar problems. The three years of war on Exmoor, experienced at first hand, did much to give him a close, if unwelcome, insight on how they can be overcome. Great Hunt Rows are nearly always destructive and it is to the credit of the MFHA, and its chairman, that so many are resolved discreetly and without the publicity which could only give comfort to the abolitionists.

By 1990 the Exmoor was back on an even keel. Neither the sport nor the hounds had, it hardly needs saying, been allowed to deteriorate in quality during the troubles (the 1991–92 season was one of the best ever) but Wallace's hips had obliged him to share the hunting evenly with Tony Wright since the operation. Hunting the hounds himself for only two days each week (although almost invariably out during the other two) gave him a little more time to deal with the problems facing hunting as a whole and to contemplate both its future and his own place in it.

Three major issues continued to threaten the continued well-being of the sport and Wallace was determined that the MFHA should tackle them in a way which would minimize the potential damage. The first – and perhaps the most important – concerns the environment in which hunting has to operate – the changing face of the countryside. The bulk of the rural population is no longer steeped in the traditional activities which once dominated life in villages and market towns. Suburbia has been transplanted and with that population shift has come an escalating imperative to satisfy the needs of the migrants: more cars, more lorries to carry the consumer goods and faster, wider, roads to accommodate them. The incomers often arrive with high expectations of an idyllic rural lifestyle fuelled by the most modern of high-tech accoutrements – Finsbury Park with thatch and a village green. The dormitory dwellers and the weekend cottagers just do not have the time, possibly not even the inclination, to absorb country ways; a superficial appreciation is sufficient. Herds of slow-moving milking cows and flocks of sheep are barely to be tolerated as they meander along narrow lanes causing delays to Miranda's school run or unpunctuality at the office meeting. Foxhounds in the garden are an outrage ('Didn't I read somewhere that they actually tear the poor little fox to pieces?'). Hunting meets, or worse, a hundred strong mounted field, the cars of the foot-followers and horseboxes parked on narrow verges cause near apoplexy to those whose lives are geared to supermarket carparks and dual-carriageway school runs.

The net result of these alien attitudes is an alarming restriction on a hunt's freedom of action. Sprawling ribbon development and the different perception of so many new country dwellers (some of them with notable influence) have caused perceptible changes in the format of a day's hunting. Even at the Quorn, that mecca of hunting countries, the prospect from the covert at Gartree Hill is such that the field has to spread out on three sides to ensure that a fox is headed off in the desired direction so that the ladies and gentlemen can have the full benefit of crossing that splendid country without let or hindrance. If this is the case in parts of High Leicestershire, then how much worse it is in south-east England.

One, perhaps the only, answer is to amalgamate the smaller, more hemmed-in countries to give more scope. Wallace has been encouraging such moves for years but there is entrenched opposition. Farmers are not always willing to see an increase in the number of horses crossing their land even if the intervals between a hunt doing so are more widely spaced. There is also a natural reluctance to give up a long established identity; regiments of the army view similar mergers with equal misgiving but have to do as they are bid in the interests of the nation – or anyway the Treasury. Hunts, on the other hand, do not have to do what the MFHA perceives is best for the sport as a whole and jealously guard their independence. One master in Kent made it quite clear to Wallace that he and his subscribers actually enjoyed tearing round and round a small and ever-diminishing area. That may be so, but is it, argues the MFHA, foxhunting as laid down by the first rule of the Association handbook: 'Foxhunting as a sport is the hunting of the fox in his wild and natural state with a pack of hounds. No pack of hounds, of which the Master or Representative is a Member of this Association, shall be allowed to hunt a fox in any way that is inconsistent with this precept.' It may be that it is – but only just. Wallace continues to urge his members to move with the times and remember that, above all other considerations, hunts exist to control the fox population effectively.

The considerable independence enjoyed by individual hunts begs the whole question of MFHA authority. Many feel that it should have wider powers than those of the largely advisory service that it has become. Only in the event of gross mis-demeanour by a master is there a real threat of de-registration and, as we have seen, that sanction has been rarely exercised for fear of attracting unwelcome publicity. Wallace – ever the great con-ciliator – believes that these matters are better handled with a quiet word or the tactful exercise of diplomacy, but with a less authorita-tive and not so widely revered figure at its helm, the MFHA may have to revise its thinking.

A further environmental factor which has limited the activities of hunting and which has increasingly exercised the MFHA is the proliferation of commercial shooting under the control of landlords who, unlike the Rouse-Boughtons of Ludlow, do not always list the need to live in harmony with their fellow sportsmen as a priority. Wallace is concerned to see that both hunting and shooting interests are properly informed of each other's requirements and insists that the MFHA keeps in close contact with the Game Conservancy as well as seeing that his own members are properly briefed.

He also considers it of paramount importance to convey to politicians and the media (the opinion formers) the role of hunting in agriculture and conservation. Here he believes that the tide has turned. There is less pressure on farmers to produce food up to the absolute maximum and the set-aside scheme works heavily in hunting's favour. The use of the countryside for recreation, the maintenance of hedgerows, walls, coverts, gates, bridges and fieldways have always been part of hunting and all these factors are increasingly popular in the public perception.

The second major issue is one of politics and here Wallace and his Association planned for a number of contingencies, the most pressing at the turn of the decade being the possibility of a Labour Government in 1992. He viewed the promise of the Party to hold a free vote in the House of Commons on the whole question of 'hunting live animals with dogs' with some suspicion, believing that left-wingers, forced to keep their more radical social change policies under wraps to maximize the chances of a Labour victory, would insist on unanimity on this rather 'softer' issue and that, parliamentary time permitting, an official Bill along the lines of that muted in 1949 would be inevitable. Hunting, he believes therefore, must be prepared to assume a higher public profile with the aim of convincing the all-important opinion formers of its crucial importance to the diminishing countryside. The minimum objective would be to press any Labour government into holding a full and detailed enquiry into all aspects of hunting so that a comprehensive picture of all the arguments would be available to MPs and the public before any decisions were made.

He is also alive to the danger of the entryist tactics of those trying to persuade institutional landlords such as the Church of England and the National Trust that they should ban hunting over their properties. Ronnie sees the threat from the Trust as the more immediate and forecasts that the only effective counter is to ensure that its ruling body continues to take a benign, or anyway an apathetic view, of the sport. To this end, the MFHA and its allies, the BFSS and shooting and fishing bodies, actively encourage their members to join the National Trust and play a part in its elections. But again there can be no compulsion.

At least two campaigns fought by Wallace and his allies in parliament in 1990–91 produced notable victories. A bill to protect badgers was introduced (with general approbation) which would, as it was first drafted, have had a disastrous effect on hunting, making it illegal to stop badger setts under any circumstances.

Skillful lobbying in both Houses succeeded in obtaining a compromise which allowed hunts to stop setts with soft earth or with material which must be removed as early as practical after hunting. The Dangerous Dogs measure, born out of attacks by Pit-Bull Terriers and some other breeds, was also threatening in that in its original form it imposed conditions of control of animals which hunts would have found difficulty in meeting; patient negotiations between Wallace and the Home Office again produced an acceptable compromise.

Finally there are a number of financial problems: each is important in itself; together they are formidable. One aspect returns to the question of amalgamations and the fact that hunting people are now more mobile than ever before. Just as the advent of the railways opened up countries to itinerant visitors, so now do those who are dissatisfied by conditions in their own country, drive their horse-boxes and trailers elsewhere. This habit has two financial implications: one to the hunt that is thereby losing a valuable subscriber and the other to its more popular near (or not so near) neighbour which may find it difficult to justify to its farmers the significant influx of semi-permanent visitors who wish to gallop across their land.

There are no easy answers. The MFHA view is that only by a process of amalgamation and hard voluntary work in opening up unpopular countries can this trend be slowed up. Travelling to other hunting countries has always been a popular facet of the sport but a permanent transfer of loyalties has to be discouraged in the best interests of hunting as a whole.

Two rather more immediate cash-flow difficulties hit all hunts in the late eighties. The first resulted in an increase in expenditure and the second in a major drop of income. The introduction of the Community Charge resulted in kennels being given a business rating – a considerable inflation over the old rates – and to this had to be added the individual poll taxes levied on hunt servants and paid by the hunt on their behalf. Serious as these increases were to hunt treasurers, they paled into insignificance when compared to the fall in the value of animal waste – a situation made worse by the advent of Bovine Spongiform Encephalopathy. Traditionally farmers have disposed of animals that died or had to be destroyed, by telephoning the hunt which then collected the carcasses at no cost. The hunt staff fed the meat to the hounds and sold the hides, bones and offal to tanners, glue factories and knackermen to the benefit of everyone in the chain, including hunt servants who had a useful source of supplementary income. In 1989 the value of the waste products fell sharply and knackermen, instead of paying hunts, started to charge to pick up the product. Hunts had to devise a system to cover their costs (including making up their staffs' income) and did so either by asking the farmers to pay (a most unsatisfactory imposition on those on whom hunts are totally dependent for goodwill) or by seeking to make up the deficit from subscribers. BSE complicated the issue by giving birth to new regulations by which specified offal had to be disposed of separately, thus adding to the hunts' costs and causing a subsequent rise in the price of all materials manufactured from animal by-products.

The MFHA has counselled its members not to give up providing the traditional service to hard-pressed farmers but to ask those who can to contribute to the cost of the eventual disposal of the waste. This leaves the subscribers to balance the books by digging deeper into their pockets at a time when general economic recession is making hunting to some, an optional extra.

All these matters and countless others, Wallace at the age of 72 in 1991, continued to wrestle with and indeed in that year he was faced with one of the greatest challenges of his chairmanship.

Curiously it had echoes of that first major showdown between a hunt and the ruling body of the sport which had led to the demise of the Boodle's Committee: it concerned the Quorn.

In October 1991 a national newspaper, quickly followed by the whole panoply of the mass media, reported that video films of cubhunting showed foxes being removed from an earth; one being shot and thrown to the Quorn hounds whilst another was released under the very noses of the same waiting pack. There was an immediate furore and it became clear that the cameraman, posing as a supporter of hunting, had gained the trust of the Quorn management but was, in reality, an opponent whose sympathies lay with the League Against Cruel Sports. The timing, could hardly have been of greater moment. Not only had Labour MP, Kevin McNamara, made it clear that he proposed to introduce a Private Member's Bill which sought, under the guise of a wildlife protection measure, to ban all forms of hunting, but there was also to be the General Election in the first half of 1992 which posed the distinct threat of a Labour government whose declared policy was to sponsor abolitionist legislation.

Wallace and his committee had striven to avoid hunting becoming a party political matter but with the Labour Party seemingly united on this issue, the Conservatives not a hundred per cent in favour of the sport and the Liberal Democrats divided, the MFHA was busily engaged in putting together a Campaign for Hunting to combat both the Bill and possible official Labour legislation.

The Quorn video was a timely weapon in the hands of the LACS and the League was reported to be planning to circulate copies to all MPs. Wallace, therefore, was diverted from the main political battle to manage a damage limitation exercise on behalf of the Quorn conducted in the full blaze of publicity; hunting was now firmly 'on the agenda'.

In the event, the Second Reading of the McNamara Bill was defeated and the immediate danger receded. Nevertheless, hunting in general and the MFHA in particular had been thrown on to the defensive at a time when it sought to seize the initiative. An MFHA Committee of Enquiry, held on 14 November and chaired by Wallace, found that the mastership of the Quorn had breached the Association Rules and, in particular, Rule 1a which states that 'When a fox is run to ground, the master must decide what is to be done. If the decision is that the fox be killed it must be humanely destroyed before being given to hounds.' The four joint-masters, Barry Hercock, Joss Hanbury, Di Turner (formerly Aladren) and Alastair Macdonald-Buchanan had, together with the Hunt Chairman Lord Crawshaw, already resigned in the wake of the allegations and the MFHA ruled that they should cease to be members of the Association. It further announced that Hercock and Hanbury should not be considered for reinstatement for four years and Turner and Macdonald-Buchanan, as new and junior masters, were to be suspended for one year. The committee had decided that the era of dealing with breaches quietly behind the scenes was over; in the light of wide public interest it had, of course, little choice.

The Quorn Committee now asked Captain Fred Barker, a previous master for 13 years, and whose practice it had been rarely if ever to dig for and bolt foxes, to take over. This, to the general relief of the hunting world, he agreed to do.

The MFHA took two further – some would say belated – steps to put its house in order. For some years Wallace had been asking all his members to adopt a formal constitution for their hunts and the Quorn, which had not done so, was ordered to comply before 1 May 1992. The constitution was to be unequivocally acceptable to the MFHA if a new mastership after that date was to be approved. This stringent action also served as a clear and final warning to other hunts who had failed to act on his previous requests on the subject. The MFHA also set up a committee, chaired by Robin Simpson, a Queen's Counsel, to carry out a comprehensive review of the Association's rules and formulate a new code of conduct for foxhunting as a matter of urgency. Both these actions produced positive results: the Quorn duly produced its written constitution and Simpson proposed that a more exact procedure should be adopted when a fox went to ground. The MFHA agreed.

The Quorn's negligence, born perhaps in part out of its complacent view of itself as England's premier hunting country, quite capable of handling its own affairs without outside interference, severely damaged the image of the sport at a time when, because of the political situation and an unsuccessful but high profile campaign in 1991 within the National Trust to ban hunting over its land, it was very much in the public eye. But the hunt's capacity for shooting itself, and hunting, in the foot was not yet exhausted. In December its committee voted in a new mastership for the 1992/93 season which not only included two of its banned ex-masters (Turner and Macdonald-Buchanan), but excluded Fred Barker, its saviour only two months earlier and who, in the public perception, took office largely to clean up its activities in the field. There was an immediate row centred on the powerful and influential farmers among whom Barker enjoyed strong (but not unanimous) support. Barker, angry and hurt, threatened to resign forthwith and the press, egged on by a gleeful League, swooped eagerly; there was no shortage of people willing to express an opinion to hacks and cameras alike. Internal hunting politics were given exposure on a grand scale much to the delight of the antis who had hardly expected this bonus to their already successful efforts to gain damaging publicity for their opponents.

In what was now a farce, Wallace had to step in to help the participants reach a compromise. As a result and with the support of the new hunt chairman, David Samworth, Barker was invited after all to join the proposed mastership and, magnanimous as ever, he agreed to do so, whilst also withdrawing his threat to leave the Quorn high and dry half way through its current season. At the same time the MFHA made it clear that approval of the mastership list for the next season remained conditional on an acceptable constitution.

In the face of such problems and the need to deal firmly and publicly with them for day after long day it would be easy and understandable for Wallace to have neglected wider issues. There was no sign that he had done so as he grappled, for example, with the uncertainties of Europe and in particular how the European Commission might impose its collective will on hunting after 1992. France and Eire could be counted upon to support the status quo but there was much work to be done if MEPs were not to act out of ignorance, in a way contrary to the interests of the hunting community. The BFSS, whose hard-working director John Hopkinson had assumed the chairmanship of the Federation of Field Sports Associations of the EC, and Edmund Vestey, Wallace's right hand man at the MFHA had, by 1991, already begun the process of education in Brussels.

The Conservative victory in the 1992 election, by ensuring that a government sponsored anti-hunting Bill was unlikely to appear for at least four years, led to an outbreak of euphoria in field sports circles. This, Wallace and his committee felt, was dangerous and could lead to the sort of complacency which once again would mean that the hunting world would be unprepared for a further assault by a Private Member's Bill and this time one which could be expected to attract support from a more numerous abolitionist contingent.

In June 1992, he resigned the chairmanship of the MFHA to be replaced by Edmund Vestey, his chosen successor. A grateful Association presented him with a handsome silver fox and created for him the post of Honorary President. Few would quarrel with the choice of Vestey, a shipping magnate and influential in the City, as well as being a master of the Thurlow. Intelligent, popular and much respected well beyond the bounds of foxhunting, he was a natural selection but he faced a formidable task in following the man who, to all intents and purposes over two decades and more, had run the sport as a personal fiefdom.

Wallace's contribution had been remarkable. He had had the capacity, intellectual ability and energy to be an effective and unwavering bridge between hunting and the various ministries, statutory authorities and conservation bodies, to the sport's great advantage as well as leading the battle against the abolitionists. No matter of any substance inside individual hunts (and a number of trivialities besides) had been settled without his advice. He had striven by unmatched example to maintain the high standards on which he believed hunting must be based and often acted as a one man employment agency for hunt staff. As deputy governor of the Hunt Servants' Benefit Society he had been a driving force in looking after the welfare of those who had fallen on hard times.

These add up to a formidable workload. The shoes of the great persuader, the incomparable conciliator, would not be easy to fill, but Vestey above others had the full confidence of his peers as well as that of his predecessor.

History may judge that Ronnie Wallace's one weakness as chairman had been that to allow the MFHA to rely on him almost alone – that there had been too little delegation and that the structure of the Association did not allow for it. He would assert that the various sub-committees did in fact allow for de-centralization and that anyway it would be difficult for others to give up the necessary time to prowl effectively the corridors of power. He would not add (but it is arguably the case) that no-one else visible in the MFHA has had the essential negotiating skills, nor the single-minded application, to ensure success.

There are those, too, who believe that hunting has long needed a comprehensive body, incorporating not just the masters but representatives from all levels of hunting, in the same way as the other principal field-sports, and that Wallace had done little to bring such a nirvana about. In 1992 there were the first signs that this might be achieved through the embryonic National Hunting Club and the associated Campaign for Hunting but the wholehearted participation of the notoriously parochial hunting population was by no means assured and such moves, if they are to succeed to the extent of creating a truly national force, would require the Wallace personal seal of approval as well as that of the MFHA.

Beginning his seventy-fourth year in 1992, Ronnie Wallace was looking forward with some satisfaction to having more days to devote to his treasured Exmoor hounds. At the same time he was buoyantly convinced that his sport – his way of life – had a bright and continuing future on into the 21st century, not just as a traditional and colourful activity enjoyed (as it always has been) by men, women and children drawn from all strata of society but as a key factor in preserving the threatened rural communities. If this proves to be the case, then no man will have done more to bring it about. Foxhunting and countless numbers of its adherents owe a debt that can never be called in to this man with a magnificent obsession; the star not only of the West, but of the whole foxhunting firmament.

Index